Supreme Court Case Studies

New York, New York   Columbus, Ohio   Chicago, Illinois   Peoria, Illinois   Woodland Hills, California

To the Teacher

The *Supreme Court Case Studies* booklet contains 68 reproducible Supreme Court case studies. These cases include landmark decisions in American government that have helped and continue to shape this nation, as well as decisions dealing with current issues in American society. Every case includes background information, the constitutional issue under consideration, the court's decision, and where appropriate, dissenting opinions.

Each two-page study requires students to analyze the case and apply critical thinking skills. An answer key is provided in the back of the booklet.

Creating a Customized File

There are a variety of ways to organize Glencoe Social Studies teaching aids. Several alternatives in creating your own files are given below.

- Organize by category (all activities, all tests, etc.)
- Organize by category and chapter (all Chapter 1 activities, all Chapter 1 tests and quizzes, etc.)
- Organize sequentially by lesson (activities, quizzes, tests, for Chapter 1/Section 1, Chapter 1/Section 2, etc.)

No matter what organization you use, you can pull out individual worksheets from these booklets for your files, or you may photocopy directly from the booklet and file the photocopies. You will then be able to keep the original booklets intact and in a safe place.

Glencoe/McGraw-Hill

A Division of The **McGraw-Hill** Companies

Copyright © by The McGraw-Hill Companies, Inc. All rights reserved. Permission is granted to reproduce the material contained herein on the condition that such material be reproduced only for classroom use; be provided to students, teachers, and families, without charge; and be used solely in conjunction with Glencoe Social Studies products. Any other reproduction, for use or sale, is prohibited without written permission from the publisher.

Send all inquiries to:
Glencoe/McGraw-Hill
8787 Orion Place
Columbus, Ohio 43240

ISBN 0-07-825229-6

Printed in the United States of America

2 3 4 5 6 7 8 9 10 024 05 04

Table of Contents

To the Teacher ii

Supreme Court Case Studies

Case Study 1: *Marbury* v. *Madison*, 1803 1

Case Study 2: *McCulloch* v. *Maryland*, 1819 3

Case Study 3: *Dartmouth College* v. *Woodward*, 1819 5

Case Study 4: *Gibbons* v. *Ogden*, 1824 7

Case Study 5: *Dred Scott* v. *Sandford*, 1857 9

Case Study 6: *Ex Parte Milligan*, 1866 11

Case Study 7: *Slaughterhouse* Cases, 1873 13

Case Study 8: *Reynolds* v. *United States*, 1879 15

Case Study 9: *Plessy* v. *Ferguson*, 1896 17

Case Study 10: *Northern Securities Company* v. *United States*, 1904 19

Case Study 11: *Weeks* v. *United States*, 1914 21

Case Study 12: *Schenck* v. *United States*, 1919 23

Case Study 13: *Gitlow* v. *New York*, 1925 25

Case Study 14: *Whitney* v. *California*, 1927 27

Case Study 15: *Olmstead* v. *United States*, 1928 29

Case Study 16: *Near* v. *Minnesota*, 1931 31

Case Study 17: *Powell* v. *Alabama*, 1932 33

Case Study 18: *DeJonge* v. *Oregon*, 1937 35

Case Study 19: *West Coast Hotel* v. *Parrish*, 1937 37

Case Study 20: *Minersville School District* v. *Gobitis*, 1940 39

Case Study 21: *Betts* v. *Brady*, 1942 41

Case Study 22: *West Virginia State Board of Education* v. *Barnette*, 1943 43

Case Study 23: *Endo* v. *United States*, 1944 45

Case Study 24: *Korematsu* v. *United States*, 1944 47

Case Study 25: *Everson* v. *Board of Education*, 1947 49

Case Study 26: *McCollum* v. *Board of Education*, 1948 51

Case Study 27: *Dennis* v. *United States*, 1951 53

Case Study 28: *Feiner* v. *New York*, 1951 55

Case Study 29: *Brown* v. *Board of Education of Topeka, Kansas*, 1954 57

Case Study 30: *Yates* v. *United States*, 1957 59

Case Study 31: *Barenblatt* v. *United States*, 1959 61

Case Study 32: *Mapp* v. *Ohio*, 1961 63

Case Study 33: *Baker* v. *Carr*, 1962 65

Case Study 34: *Engel* v. *Vitale*, 1962 67

Case Study 35: *Abington School District* v. *Schempp*, 1963 69

Case Study 36: *Gideon* v. *Wainwright*, 1963 71

Case Study 37: *Escobedo* v. *Illinois*, 1964 73

Case Study 38: *Reynolds* v. *Sims*, 1964 75

Case Study 39: *Wesberry* v. *Sanders*, 1964 77

Case Study 40: *Heart of Atlanta Motel* v. *United States*, 1964 79

Case Study 41: *Miranda* v. *Arizona*, 1966 81

Case Study 42: *Sheppard* v. *Maxwell*, 1966 83

Case Study 43: *Katz* v. *United States*, 1967 85

Case Study 44: *Gregory* v. *Chicago*, 1969 87

Case Study 45: *New York Times* v. *United States*, 1971 89

Case Study 46: *Reed* v. *Reed*, 1971 91

Case Study 47: *Wisconsin* v. *Yoder*, 1972 93

Case Study 48: *Roe* v. *Wade*, 1973 95

Case Study 49: *United States* v. *Nixon*, 1974 97

Case Study 50: *Gregg* v. *Georgia*, 1976 99

Case Study 51: *Regents of the University of California* v. *Bakke*, 1978 101

Case Study 52: *Kaiser Aluminum and Chemical Corporation* v. *Weber*, 1979 103

Case Study 53: *New Jersey* v. *T.L.O.*, 1985 105

Case Study 54: *Wallace* v. *Jaffree*, 1985 107

Case Study 55: *Bethel School District* v. *Fraser*, 1986 109

Case Study 56: *Hazelwood School District* v. *Kuhlmeier*, 1988 111

Case Study 57: *Skinner* v. *Railway Labor Executives Association*, 1989 113

Case Study 58: *Cruzan* v. *Director, Missouri Department of Health*, 1990 115

Case Study 59: *California* v. *Acevedo*, 1991 117

Case Study 60: *International Union, UAW* v. *Johnson Controls, Inc.*, 1991 119

Case Study 61: *Payne* v. *Tennessee*, 1991 121

Case Study 62: *Arizona* v. *Fulminante*, 1991 123

Case Study 63: *Shaw* v. *Reno*, 1993 125

Case Study 64: *National Organization for Women (NOW)* v. *Scheidler*, 1994 127

Case Study 65: *Agostini* v. *Felton*, 1997 129

Case Study 66: *Illinois* v. *Wordlow*, 2000 131

Case Study 67: *Alexander* v. *Sandoval*, 2001 133

Case Study 68: *Whitman* v. *American Trucking Associations*, 2001 135

Answer Key 137

Name _____ Date _____ Class _____

Supreme Court Case Study 1

The Supreme Court's Power of Judicial Review
Marbury v. Madison, 1803

★★★★★★★★★★★★★★★ **Background of the Case** ★★★★★★★★★★★★★★★

The election of 1800 transferred power in the federal government from the Federalist Party to the Republican Party. In the closing days of President John Adams's administration, the Federalists created many new government offices, appointing Federalists to fill them. One of the last-minute or "midnight" appointments was that of William Marbury. Marbury was named a justice of the peace for the District of Columbia. President Adams had signed the papers, but his secretary of state, John Marshall, somehow neglected to deliver the papers necessary to finalize the appointment.

The new president, Thomas Jefferson, was angry at the defeated Federalists' attempt to "keep a dead clutch on the patronage" and ordered his new secretary of state, James Madison, not to deliver Marbury's commission papers. Marbury took his case to the Supreme Court, of which John Marshall was now the Chief Justice, for a *writ of mandamus*—an order from a court that some action be performed—commanding Madison to deliver the commission papers in accordance with the Judiciary Act of 1789.

Constitutional Issue ★★★★★★★★★★★★★★★★★★★★★★★★★★★★★★

Article III of the Constitution sets up the Supreme Court as the head of the federal judicial system. Historians believe that the Founders meant the Court to have the power of judicial review, that is, the power to review the constitutionality of acts of Congress and to invalidate those that it determines to be unconstitutional. The Constitution, however, does not specifically give the Court this right.

Chief Justice John Marshall, as a Federalist, believed strongly that the Supreme Court should have the power of judicial review. When the *Marbury* case presented the perfect opportunity to clearly establish that power, Marshall laid out several points which the court believed supported the right of judicial review. At the time, the decision was viewed as a curtailment of the power of the president, but people today recognize that the case established, once and for all, the importance of the Supreme Court in American government.

★★★★★★★★★★★★★★★ **The Supreme Court's Decision** ★★★★★★★★★★★★★★★

Justice Marshall reviewed the case on the basis of three questions: Did Marbury have a right to the commission? If so, was he entitled to some remedy under United States law? Was that remedy a writ from the Supreme Court?

Marshall decided the first question by holding that an appointment is effective once a commission has been signed and the U.S. seal affixed, as Marbury's commission had been. Therefore, Marbury had been legally appointed, and Madison's refusal to deliver the

(continued)

Supreme Court Case Study 1 (continued)

commission violated Marbury's right to the appointment. In response to the second question, Marshall held that Marbury was entitled to some remedy under United States law.

The final question examined whether the Court had the power to issue the writ. Marshall explained that the right to issue writs like the one Marbury was requesting had been granted the Court by the Judiciary Act of 1789. This law, however, was unconstitutional and void because the Constitution did not grant Congress the right to make such a law. In his written opinion, Marshall defended the right of the Court to declare a law unconstitutional: "It is emphatically the province and duty of the judicial department to say what the law is . . . . If two laws conflict with each other, the courts must decide on the operation of each." The Supreme Court thus became the final judge of constitutionality, thus establishing the principle of judicial review.

At the time, observers were much more interested in the practical result of the ruling—that the Court could not issue the writ, and could not, therefore, force the appointment of Marbury. Congress could not expand the Court's original jurisdiction, and the Constitution does not give the Court the authority to issue a writ. They paid much less attention to the long-term implications of the decision. Here is how a constitutional scholar evaluates the *Marbury* decision:

"Over the passage of time [the] *Marbury* [decision] came to stand for the monumental principle, so distinctive and dominant a feature of our constitutional system, that the Court may bind the coordinate branches of the national government to its rulings on what is the supreme law of the land. That principle stands out from *Marbury* like the grin on a Cheshire cat; all else, which preoccupied national attention in 1803, disappeared in our constitutional law."

Not until fifty years after rendering the *Marbury* decision did the Court again declare a law unconstitutional, but by then the idea of judicial review had become a time-honored principle.

DIRECTIONS: Answer the following questions on a separate sheet of paper.

1. Why is the *Marbury* case important in the history of the Supreme Court?

2. In what way did the *Marbury* decision enhance the system of checks and balances provided for in the Constitution?

3. Constitutional scholars have pointed out there is an inconsistency in Justice Marshall's opinion with respect to what the Constitution specifically provides. What is that inconsistency?

4. The United States is one of the few countries in which the highest court of the land has the power to declare a law unconstitutional. Do you believe that such a power is of benefit to a country? Explain your answer.

5. Justice John Marshall was a Federalist who believed in a strong national government and certainly moved in this direction with his *Marbury* ruling. Do you think it is proper for a Supreme Court Justice to allow his or her personal political opinions to influence the rulings of the Court? Explain.

Supreme Court Case Study 2

Power of the Federal Government v. Power of the State Government

McCulloch v. Maryland, 1819

★★★★★★★★★★★★★★★ Background of the Case ★★★★★★★★★★★★★★★

The Supreme Court first settled a dispute between a national and a state law in 1819. The Second Bank of the United States had been chartered by Congress in 1816. Large sections of the country, especially the West and South, bitterly opposed the Bank. The Bank's tight credit policies contributed to an economic depression, and many states reacted against what they saw as a "ruthless money trust" and "the monster monopoly." Two states even prohibited the bank from operating within their jurisdictions. Six other states taxed Bank operations. In 1818 the Maryland legislature placed a substantial tax on the operations of the Baltimore branch of the Bank of the United States. The cashier of the Baltimore branch, James McCulloch, issued bank notes without paying the tax. After Maryland state courts ruled against McCulloch for having broken the state law, he appealed to the United States Supreme Court.

Constitutional Issues ★★★★★★★★★★★★★★★★★★★★★★★★★★★★★★★

One of the issues that concerned the Founders at the Constitutional Convention was how to divide power between the federal government and state governments. Reconciling national and local interests proved difficult. In the *McCulloch* case, the Supreme Court ruled in favor of federal power.

The constitutional questions in the *McCulloch* v. *Maryland* case concern both the powers of Congress and the relationship between federal and state authorities.

★★★★★★★★★★★★★★ The Supreme Court's Decision ★★★★★★★★★★★★★★

Chief Justice John Marshall wrote the decision for a unanimous Court. He started with the question, "Has Congress the power to incorporate a bank?"

In first determining the extent of congressional power, Marshall held that the Constitution is a creation not of the states, but of the people, acting through statewide constitutional conventions. Therefore, the states are bound in obligation to the Constitution, which is "the supreme law of the land." Marshall summed up the decision based on the Supremacy Clause, saying, "If any one proposition could command the universal assent of mankind we might expect it to be this—that the government of the Union, though limited in its powers, is supreme within its sphere of action . . . . The states have no power to retard, impede, burden, or in any manner control, the operation of the constitutional laws enacted by Congress."

Although the specific powers of Congress do not include the power to charter a corporation, the section enumerating these powers includes a statement giving Congress the authority to make the laws "necessary and proper" for executing its specific tasks. In Marshall's analysis, the terms "necessary and proper" grant Congress implied powers to carry out granted, or enumerated, powers. "Let the end be legitimate, let it be within the scope of the Constitution,

(continued)

Supreme Court Case Study 2 (continued)

and all means which are appropriate, which are plainly adapted to that end, which are not prohibited, but consistent with the letter and spirit of the Constitution, are constitutional," the Chief Justice wrote. The choice of means is for Congress to decide. In the *McCulloch* case, the Court held that Congress had the power to incorporate a bank.

On the question of the validity of Maryland's bank tax, Marshall again noted the Constitution's supremacy, but he also recognized a state's constitutional right to impose taxes. Echoing his earlier argument, Marshall observed that a government may properly tax its subjects or their property. The federal government and its agencies, however, are not subjects of any state. A tax on a national institution by one state would be an indirect tax on citizens of other states, who would not benefit from such a tax.

Furthermore, the power to tax, if misused, is also the power to harm an institution. The power of Congress to establish an institution must imply the right to take all steps necessary for its preservation. In a conflict between the federal power to create and preserve a corporation and a state's power to levy a tax, the state must yield. Therefore, the Court denied Maryland's power to tax the Second Bank of the United States. In this way Marshall ensured the power of Congress to enact legislation "under a Constitution intended to endure for ages to come, and, consequently, to be adapted to the various crises of human affairs."

In conclusion, Marshall wrote, ". . . this is a tax on the operations of the bank, and is, consequently, a tax on the operation of an instrument employed by the government of the Union to carry its powers into execution. Such a tax must be unconstitutional . . . . "

The Court's decision in the *McCulloch* case brought a storm of abuse raining down on the Court. Virginia passed a resolution urging that the Supreme Court be divested of its power to pass on cases in which states were parties. Ohio, which like Maryland had a tax on the United States Bank, simply continued to collect the tax. The decision was particularly offensive to believers in the strict, literal interpretation of the Constitution because it sustained the doctrine of implied powers. Nevertheless, the *McCulloch* decision, in upholding the principle of implied powers, enlarged the power of the federal government considerably and laid the constitutional foundations for the New Deal in the 1930s and the welfare state of the 1960s.

DIRECTIONS: Answer the following questions on a separate sheet of paper.

1. What constitutional principle did the Supreme Court establish in the *McCulloch* case?
2. What is the objective of the "necessary and proper" clause?
3. What was the basis for the Court's ruling that Maryland could not tax the Second Bank of the United States?
4. How did the fact that Justice Marshall was a Federalist influence his ruling in the *McCulloch* case?
5. How did the *McCulloch* ruling contribute to the strength of the national government?

Supreme Court Case Study 3

The Meaning of a Contract

Dartmouth College v. Woodward, 1819

★★★★★★★★★★★★★★★ **Background of the Case** ★★★★★★★★★★★★★★★

Dartmouth College originally had been granted a charter by the British crown in 1769, prior to American independence from Great Britain, for the purpose of educating Native Americans and promoting learning generally. In the early 1800s, the college had become involved in state politics on the side of the Federalists. In 1815 the Dartmouth College trustees decided to remove the president of the college. The state legislature, now controlled by Republicans, sided with the college president against the Federalist trustees and sought to grasp control of the college away from them. In 1816, after independence, the legislature passed a series of statutes that had the effect of converting Dartmouth, a private college, into a state university under public control. The highest court of New Hampshire sustained the state statutes.

The trustees appealed the case to the United States Supreme Court, arguing that the New Hampshire statutes impaired their contractual rights in violation of the Constitution. They had as one of their attorneys the great statesman and orator, Daniel Webster.

Constitutional Issue ★★★★★★★★★★★★★★★★★★★★★★★★★★★★★★★★★

Under common law—the principles and rules established through court decisions over the years—a contract was an agreement between two or more parties to perform certain actions. Under Article I, Section 10, of the Constitution, states were prevented from impairing the obligation of a contract.

★★★★★★★★★★★★★★★ **The Supreme Court's Decision** ★★★★★★★★★★★★★★★

Chief Justice John Marshall wrote the Court's opinion, which held that the state acts placing Dartmouth under state control constituted an impairment of contract, and thus was unconstitutional. The state treasurer, Woodward, was required to return college records, the corporate seal, and other corporate property to the trustees.

The core of the decision was the Court's ruling that a charter for a private corporation, granted by the British crown before independence and the adoption of the Constitution, was protected by Article I, Section 10, of the Constitution. Marshall granted that this clause was not specifically designed to protect charters creating charitable, educational, or other nonprofit corporations of incorporation. "It is more than possible," he wrote, "that the preservation of rights of this description was not particularly in the view of the framers of the constitution when the clause under consideration was introduced into that instrument."

On the other hand, according to Marshall, the contract clause provided no exceptions with respect to private, nonprofit entities. "It is not enough to say that this particular case was not in the mind of the convention when the article was framed, nor of the American people when it was adopted," Marshall wrote. Therefore, he continued, since there was no proof that the language of the Constitution would have been changed if charters incorporating nonprofit entities had been considered, the case fell under the prohibition of state interference with

(continued)

Name _____ Date _____ Class _____

Supreme Court Case Study 3 (continued)

contracts. "There is no expression in the constitution, no sentiment delivered by its contemporaneous expounders, which would justify us in making it." If a charter of incorporation is lawfully bestowed, the charter has "every ingredient of a complete and legitimate contract and is protected from state infringement by the contracts clause."

The *Dartmouth College* decision made it clear that states were not permitted to take over private institutions, such as a private educational institution, and make them public. States, therefore, began to establish their own state universities. By protecting nonprofit entities, the Court was essentially protecting all corporations.

As the economy of the United States grew, the corporate form of business organization became more and more common. Corporate charters, granted by state governments, were increasingly used to establish manufacturing and commercial businesses. The *Dartmouth College* case provided a protection for owners and management interests and a climate of legal stability that promoted economic growth.

DIRECTIONS: Answer the following questions on a separate sheet of paper.

1. What effect did the Supreme Court's decision have on Dartmouth College?
2. The Constitution did not mention corporations in Article I, Section 10, so how did Justice Marshall justify ruling that Dartmouth's charter was a contract?
3. Why is the *Dartmouth* case considered to be important in the economic history of the United States?
4. Historians point out that the *Dartmouth* decision had an effect on the growth of state universities. Why do you think states established state universities after this decision?
5. Justice John Marshall believed in a strong central government. How did the *Dartmouth* decision relate to this belief?

Supreme Court Case Study 4

Regulation of Interstate Commerce

Gibbons v. *Ogden*, 1824

★★★★★★★★★★★★★★★ **Background of the Case** ★★★★★★★★★★★★★★★

In 1798 the New York legislature gave Robert Fulton a monopoly for steamboat navigation in New York. In 1811 Fulton's partner, Robert Livingston, assigned to Aaron Ogden an exclusive license to run a ferry service on the Hudson River between New York and New Jersey—a very profitable business. Seeking to take advantage of this flourishing trade, a competitor, Thomas Gibbons, secured a license from the federal government to operate a ferry between Elizabethtown, New Jersey, and New York City.

Claiming that his monopoly rights were being infringed, Ogden obtained an injunction in a New York state court forbidding Gibbons's boat from docking in New York. (An injunction is an order by a court prohibiting a person or a group from carrying out a specific action.) Gibbons appealed the state court's decision to the United States Supreme Court.

*C*onstitutional Issues ★★★★★★★★★★★★★★★★★★★★★★★★★★★★★

The Constitution did not make clear what was meant by interstate commerce or the extent to which it could be regulated. At the time of this case in 1824, New York had closed its ports to vessels not owned or licensed by a monopoly chartered by the state. In retaliation, other states passed similar laws that limited access to their ports. The United States attorney maintained that the country faced a commercial "civil war." In the absence of a clear statement of what is meant by interstate commerce, how did the federal government have the power to intervene?

The *Gibbons* v. *Ogden* case presented the Supreme Court with the first opportunity to consider the ramifications of the commerce clause contained in Article I, Section 8 of the Constitution. This clause gave Congress the power "to regulate commerce with foreign nations, and among the several States, and with the Indian tribes." Several constitutional questions were involved in the case, revolving around an interpretation of the commerce clause.

The first question was whether navigation should be considered to be a part of commerce. Then, if navigation should be so considered, to what extent might Congress regulate it? Another question was whether Congress had an exclusive right to regulate interstate commerce or if this was a "concurrent" power to be shared with the states.

★★★★★★★★★★★★★★★ **The Supreme Court's Decision** ★★★★★★★★★★★★★★★

The Court held in favor of Gibbons. Chief Justice John Marshall wrote that commerce "describes the commercial intercourse between nations, and parts of nations, in all its branches, and is regulated by prescribing rules for carrying on that intercourse. The mind can scarcely conceive a system for regulating commerce between nations which shall exclude navigation...."

(continued)

Name _____ Date _____ Class _____

Supreme Court Case Study 4 *(continued)*

Marshall applied the same reasoning to commerce between states. In fact, he noted, the United States government had always regulated navigation. "All America understands," he wrote, "and has uniformly understood the word 'commerce' to comprehend navigation . . . ." Thus the Court held that "a power to regulate navigation is expressly granted as if that term had been added to the word 'commerce.'"

Marshall now turned to the meaning of "among," as in "among the several states." He reasoned that since "among" means "intermingled with," "commerce among the states cannot stop at the external boundary line of each state but may be introduced into the interior." Congress had no power over commerce which was confined to one state alone, but that power was in full force as soon as a state's boundary line had been crossed. And the power to regulate must necessarily follow any commerce in question right across those boundaries."

Marshall concluded that, like other congressional powers, the power to regulate commerce is unlimited so long as it is applied to objects specified in the Constitution.

The case also raised the question as to whether Congress's power to regulate is exclusive. If it is, then a state would be prevented from making its own commerce regulations. Marshall chose not to resolve this question. Instead, he wrote that in the *Gibbons* case there was a conflict between the state's law and a federal statute. "In every such case, the act of Congress . . . is supreme; and the law of the state. . . must yield to it." Gibbons's right to operate ferry service in competition with Ogden was therefore upheld.

By broadening the meaning of interstate commerce, Marshall laid the groundwork for including not only such clearly interstate activities as railroads and pipelines, but also the minimum wage regulation and prohibition of child labor. Robert Jackson, a Supreme Court justice who served in the mid-1900s, was thus correct when he declared, "Chief Justice Marshall described the federal commerce power with a breadth never exceeded."

DIRECTIONS: Answer the following questions on a separate sheet of paper.

1. If you operated a trucking service between San Francisco, California, and Portland, Oregon, could you be subject to regulation by either or both of the states and the federal government? Explain.

2. Why was it necessary for Marshall to take the trouble to explain why navigation should be considered as part of commerce?

3. Explain in what way Justice Jackson's characterization of Marshall's *Gibbons* opinion was correct.

4. In what way is Marshall's ruling in the *Gibbons* case consistent with his other decisions, such as *McCulloch* v. *Maryland*, that related to federal versus state powers?

5. Do you agree with Marshall's ruling that Gibbons had a right to compete with Ogden's ferry line? Give reasons for your answer.

Supreme Court Case Study 5

The Right to Freedom of Enslaved Persons
Dred Scott v. *Sandford*, 1857

★★★★★★★★★★★★★★★ **Background of the Case** ★★★★★★★★★★★★★★★

John Emerson, a United States Army surgeon, took enslaved African Dred Scott to live at military posts in Illinois, a free state in 1834, and then to posts in the territory of Upper Louisiana (now Minnesota), where slavery had been forbidden by the Missouri Compromise of 1820. In 1838 Emerson and Scott returned to Missouri.

In 1846 Scott won a suit for his freedom against Emerson's widow in a Missouri court. Scott claimed that by having lived in free territory, he had earned his freedom. This ruling was overturned, however, by Missouri's Supreme Court. Aided by various antislavery interests, Scott then started a new suit in a federal district court against Mrs. Emerson's brother, John Sandford of New York, who had been acting as his sister's agent. Since the case was a dispute between people who live in two different states, it could be heard in a federal court. When the federal court ruled that Scott was still a slave, he appealed to the United States Supreme Court.

*C*onstitutional Issues ★★★★★★★★★★★★★★★★★★★★★★★★★★★★★★★

The Constitution left questions such as the legal rights of slaves for later lawmakers to solve. In 1850 Congress passed the Fugitive Slave Law, which stated that a slave was property and which required escaped slaves to be returned to their holders. Opponents of the law unsuccessfully challenged its legality before the Supreme Court.

The first major issue was whether Dred Scott—an African American—qualified as a citizen of the United States and was, therefore, entitled to sue in a federal court. The second issue concerned whether Scott had gained his freedom by moving to a free territory or state. The third issue focused on the Missouri Compromise of 1820, which banned slavery north of the southern boundary of Missouri (except for Missouri itself). Scott had lived in the non-slavery region. Did Congress have the power to prohibit slavery in the territories and to make the prohibition a condition of admission to the Union?

★★★★★★★★★★★★★ **The Supreme Court's Decision** ★★★★★★★★★★★★★★

The Court's decision was written by Chief Justice Roger B. Taney, although each justice wrote his own opinion, with only one justice concurring with Taney in every respect. Two justices dissented.

Taney's first ruling was that former Africans, "whether emancipated or not," did not qualify as United States citizens. Taney held that only those who were state citizens when the Union was formed became federal citizens. Even though a state may emancipate a slave, give him the right to vote, and admit him to state citizenship, Taney said, none of these actions gave a slave automatic federal citizenship. The right to grant federal citizenship belonged exclusively to Congress. Taney concluded that Scott was not, and never had become, a citizen of the United States, and was not, therefore, entitled to sue in a federal court.

(continued)

Supreme Court Case Study 5 (continued)

Taney next examined the question of whether Scott had gained his freedom when he entered the Upper Louisiana Territory. The Chief Justice attacked the Missouri Compromise as an unconstitutional exercise of congressional authority. Congress cannot forbid a state or a territory from making slavery legal. Taney explained that as long as slavery is authorized by the Constitution, Congress cannot alter the right of a person to own slaves or any other kind of property. In viewing the Missouri Compromise as unconstitutional, the Court determined that Scott's status did not change when he entered free territory. The Court held that Scott had been a slave in Illinois and had returned to Missouri as a slave. On his return to Missouri, he became subject to Missouri law alone. Taney ordered the suit dismissed for lack of jurisdiction.

★★★★★★★★★★★★★★★★★★★ **Dissenting Opinion** ★★★★★★★★★★★★★★★★★★★★

Justice Benjamin R. Curtis dissented. Curtis noted that free African Americans were among those who had voted to ratify the Constitution in a number of states. Nothing in the Constitution stripped these free African Americans of their citizenship. Curtis maintained that "under the Constitution of the United States, every free person born on the soil of a State, who is a citizen of that State, who is a citizen of that State by force of its Constitution or laws, is also a citizen of the United States . . . ."

The Court's decision is one example of judicial power being exercised in favor of racial segregation. It is also the first time that a major federal law was ruled unconstitutional.

DIRECTIONS: Answer the following questions on a separate sheet of paper.

1. What was the relationship between the Missouri Compromise and the Court's decision in the *Dred Scott* case?

2. What effect do you think the Court's decision in the *Dred Scott* case had on the efforts of many Americans to end slavery?

3. If you were a plantation owner in the South who held many slaves, how would you have reacted to the *Dred Scott* decision?

4. What did the Court say about enslaved African Americans' position in the United States?

5. Why is the *Dred Scott* decision regarded as one of the most important cases in the history of the Supreme Court?

Supreme Court Case Study 6

Rights of Citizens During Wartime

Ex Parte Milligan, 1866

★★★★★★★★★★★★★★ **Background of the Case** ★★★★★★★★★★★★★★★

In 1864 during the Civil War, Lambdin P. Milligan, a civilian resident of Indiana who was violently opposed to the war, was arrested by order of the commander of the military district of Indiana, General Hovey, for his part in a plot to free Confederate war prisoners and overthrow three state governments. He was tried in a military court even though state courts in Indiana were still functioning. The military court found Milligan guilty and sentenced him to death. This sentence was approved by President Andrew Johnson. Nine days before he was to be hanged, Milligan petitioned the United States Circuit Court for a writ of *habeas corpus*. *Habeas corpus* is an order requiring that a prisoner be brought before a court at a stated time and place to decide on the legality of his or her detention. Milligan claimed that the proceedings of his conviction were unconstitutional and that he was denied the right of a trial by jury. As a citizen of Indiana who was not in the military, Milligan claimed he should not have been tried by a military court. He appealed his case to the United States Supreme Court.

*C*onstitutional Issues ★★★★★★★★★★★★★★★★★★★★★★★★★★★★★

The Constitution gives Congress the power to declare war and raise armies to fight the war. In order to carry on a war, the federal government often assumes powers that would be illegal in times of peace. As Chief Justice Charles Evans Hughes stated in 1934, "the war power of the Federal government . . . is a power to wage war successfully." When the power assumed by the government in time of war is challenged, the Supreme Court most often does not declare the acts unconstitutional.

During the Civil War, for example, President Abraham Lincoln took many actions that would have been unconstitutional in peacetime.

Article I, Section 9, paragraph 2, of the Constitution provides that the "privilege of the writ of habeas corpus shall not be suspended, unless when in cases of rebellion or invasion the public safety may require it." The questions at issue in *Ex Parte Milligan* were whether Congress had the power to suspend the writ of habeas corpus and whether civilians may become subject to military law.

★★★★★★★★★★★★★★ **The Supreme Court's Decision** ★★★★★★★★★★★★★★

For the first time, the Court faced a decision involving the right of the president to suspend the writ of *habeas corpus* and to substitute the authority of a military court for that of a civilian court. Justice David Davis, writing for a 5 to 4 majority, declared the military had exceeded its power in trying and sentencing Milligan. He wrote, "No graver question was ever considered by this Court, nor one which more nearly concerns the rights of the whole people; for it is the birthright of every American citizen when charged with a crime to be punished according to law . . . ." Davis declared that Congress had not granted to the nation's military courts the power to try civilians, and indeed could not do so, especially so long as civilian courts were still operating. "One of the plainest constitutional privileges was, therefore, infringed when Milligan

(continued)

Supreme Court Case Studies 11

Supreme Court Case Study 6 (continued)

was tried by a court not ordained and established by Congress.... Such action," the Court ruled, "destroys every guarantee of the Constitution, and effectively renders the 'military independent of and superior to the civil power.'"

Davis agreed that "in a great crisis . . . there should be a power somewhere of suspending the writ of *habeas corpus*." However, in this case, such power was to be exercised by the judiciary. Davis declared that the writ itself may not be suspended, but rather the privilege the writ would grant. A court must decide whether the privilege is to be denied in a particular instance.

Davis recognized that there may be circumstances in which the courts might be closed and civil authority overthrown, thus making government by martial law necessary. Even then, military rule would "be strictly limited to the place where the crisis occurred and last only for the duration of that crisis." Military rule cannot be imposed while civil authority still operates.

With respect to martial law in this case, Davis wrote, "It is difficult to see how the safety of the country required martial law in Indiana. If any of the citizens were plotting treason, the power of [civil] arrest could secure them, until the government was prepared for their trial, when the courts were open and ready to try them. It was as easy to protect witnesses before a civil as well as a military tribunal; and as there could be no wish to convict, except on sufficient legal evidence, surely an ordained and established court were better able to judge of this than a military tribunal composed of gentlemen not trained to the profession of the law."

Milligan's death sentence had been commuted to life imprisonment by President Johnson in June 1865. After being released as a result of the Supreme Court decision, Milligan sued General Hovey for unlawful imprisonment and won, but the damages awarded him were nominal.

★★★★★★★★★★★★★★★★★ Dissenting Opinion ★★★★★★★★★★★★★★★★★

Chief Justice Salmon P. Chase, writing for the four members of the Court who dissented, held that Congress could extend military authority in Indiana under its war powers without diminishing Bill of Rights protections. It was up to Congress, not the courts, to make this decision.

Case Analysis Questions

DIRECTIONS: Answer the following questions on a separate sheet of paper.

1. What position did the Supreme Court take concerning the use of military or martial law?
2. If General Hovey's decision to try Milligan in a military court was so clearly unconstitutional, why do you think he did not bring Milligan before a civil court?
3. Describe a situation in which military rule would take precedence over civilian authority according to the Court's ruling.
4. Four Justices of the Supreme Court disagreed with the majority's decision in the *Milligan* case. Under their thinking, who was responsible for deciding whether military courts could try civilians?
5. Why do you think the privilege of writ of *habeas corpus* is an important part of the Constitution?

Name _____ Date _____ Class _____

Supreme Court Case Study 7

The Bill of Rights and State Rights

Slaughterhouse Cases, 1873

★★★★★★★★★★★★★★ Background of the Case ★★★★★★★★★★★★★★

In 1869 the Louisiana government granted the Crescent City Stock Landing and Slaughterhouse Company a monopoly on licensed butchering in New Orleans on the grounds that the action protected public health.

Local butchers, who were excluded from the monopoly, opposed it with legal action in the state courts. Losing there, they appealed to the federal courts and then to the United States Supreme Court. The butchers argued that they had been deprived of their livelihoods by the state's deliberate discrimination against them. Therefore, the law violated the Thirteenth Amendment's ban on involuntary servitude, as well as the 1866 Civil Rights Act, which had been passed to enforce that ban. In addition, they argued, the state law violated the Fourteenth Amendment's guarantees of equal protection under the law and of due process.

The state responded by claiming that no federal constitutional question was involved since both the Thirteenth and Fourteenth Amendments were irrelevant to the case. If, in fact, the Court did apply these amendments to the case, the federal system would be revolutionized by exempting individuals' claims from state regulation.

Constitutional Issue ★★★★★★★★★★★★★★★★★★★★★★★★★★★★★★

Before the Civil War, individuals who believed they had been deprived of their rights and liberties had only their state constitution to rely on for protection. According to an 1833 Supreme Court decision, the Bill of Rights of the United States Constitution applied only to the national government. In 1868, however, the Fourteenth Amendment was added to the United States Constitution. Although the amendment was intended to protect formerly enslaved people, who had been given their freedom by the Thirteenth Amendment, the Fourteenth Amendment contained a sentence that could be interpreted as applying to all persons in the United States: "No state shall make or enforce any law which shall abridge the privileges or immunities of citizens of the United States; nor shall any state deprive any person of life, liberty, or property, without due process of law; nor deny to any person within its jurisdiction the equal protection of the laws."

If the Supreme Court interpreted this sentence as applying to all persons, then the way was open to conveying to the national government the enforcement of rights that earlier had been limited to the states and denied to the national government.

The *Slaughterhouse* cases were the first involving the Fourteenth Amendment to be heard by the Court. The constitutional issues in the *Slaughterhouse* cases concerned the extent to which the Thirteenth and Fourteenth Amendments applied to all Americans, not only to formerly enslaved people.

(continued)

Supreme Court Case Study 7 (continued)

★★★★★★★★★★★★★ The Supreme Court's Decision ★★★★★★★★★★★★★

A majority of the Court held that the monopoly on butchering granted by Louisiana did not violate the rights of the other butchers. Justice Samuel F. Miller, writing the Court's opinion, dismissed the butchers' claim that the state law violated their rights under the Thirteenth Amendment. The monopoly created by the state law, he held, could not be interpreted as imposing servitude.

Miller now turned to the Fourteenth Amendment. This amendment, he wrote, "declares that persons may be citizens of the United States without regard to their citizenship of a particular state, and it overturns the *Dred Scott* decision by making all persons born within the United States and subject to its jurisdiction citizens of the United States. That its main purpose was to establish the citizenship of the negro can admit of no doubt."

Justice Miller assigned to the states, rather than the federal government, the protection of basic civil liberties. This meant that everyone, not just formerly enslaved people, who had assumed the federal government was their "guardian of democracy," had to look to the states to protect their rights. The Court agreed that there were certain "federal privileges and immunities," such as the right to petition for redress of grievances, which states were bound to respect, but otherwise, the Court concluded, a state determined the privileges and immunities of its citizens.

★★★★★★★★★★★★★★★★★ Dissenting Opinion ★★★★★★★★★★★★★★★★★

Four justices dissented from the Court's decision. Justice Joseph P. Bradley emphasized both the Privileges and Immunities Clause and the Due Process Clause. He insisted that both clauses protected an individual's right to choose a vocation or business. In denying that right or subordinating it to police powers, the states abridged the privileges and immunities of citizens, thus depriving the affected persons of both liberty and property, violating the Due Process Clause.

Also dissenting, Justice Stephen J. Field argued that the Thirteenth Amendment ban on involuntary servitude had been violated by creating the butchering monopoly. As for the Fourteenth Amendment, it embraced all the fundamental rights belonging to free men. "The amendment," he wrote, "does not attempt to confer any new privileges or immunities upon citizens or to enumerate or define those already existing. It assumes that there are such privileges and immunities which belong of right to citizens as such, and ordains that they shall not be abridged by state legislation."

DIRECTIONS: Answer the following questions on a separate sheet of paper.

1. How did the Court limit the protections of the Thirteenth and Fourteenth Amendments?
2. What effect did the Court's ruling in the *Slaughterhouse* cases have on the *Dred Scott* decision?
3. Suppose you had been a butcher in New Orleans. How would the Court's decision have affected you?
4. Who gained from the Court's decision, state governments or the federal government? Explain.
5. With whose opinions do you agree, those of the Court or the dissenting justices? Explain.

Name _____ Date _____ Class _____

Supreme Court Case Study 8

Protection of Religious Rights

Reynolds v. United States, 1879

★★★★★★★★★★★★★★ **Background of the Case** ★★★★★★★★★★★★★★

George Reynolds was a member of the Church of Jesus Christ of Latter-day Saints, also known as the Mormon Church. The Mormons believed in the religious duty of males, circumstances permitting, to practice polygamy, or to have more than one wife. Reynolds followed that teaching and was indicted for bigamy—the crime of having more than one spouse—under federal statutes governing the Utah Territory. That law, passed in 1862, had been directed specifically against the Mormons. Reynolds was sentenced to a term of imprisonment at hard labor. He appealed this decision to the United States Supreme Court.

Constitutional Issue ★★★★★★★★★★★★★★★★★★★★★★★★★★★★★

The federal law regarding bigamy read, "Every person having a husband or wife living, who marries another, whether married or single, in a Territory, or other place over which the United States have exclusive jurisdiction, is guilty of bigamy, and shall be punished by a fine of not more than $500, and by imprisonment for a term of not more than five years." *Reynolds* v. *United States* focused on whether this statute conflicted with the First Amendment clause guaranteeing free exercise of religion.

The First Amendment guarantees citizens the right to practice their chosen religion freely, without interference from the government. Many Supreme Court cases have reinforced this right; however, suppose a religion called for human sacrifice. Clearly that rite would not be protected by the First Amendment. Suppose a religious rite involved a practice not so obviously unlawful. Would the protections of the First Amendment apply here?

★★★★★★★★★★★★★★ **The Supreme Court's Decision** ★★★★★★★★★★★★★★

The Court ruled unanimously that Reynolds's conviction was legal under the Constitution. The Court subsequently ruled, however, that punishment under the law against bigamy could not include hard labor.

Chief Justice Morrison R. Waite wrote for the Court. Waite agreed that "Congress cannot pass a law for the government of the Territories which shall prohibit the free exercise of religion." The question in this case was whether the law against bigamy violated this prohibition. Waite asked, "The precise point is, What is the religious freedom which has been guaranteed?"

Waite undertook a historical analysis of religion and religious freedom from the late 1600s to 1780 and the ratification of the Constitution. He concluded that "Congress was deprived of all legislative power over mere opinion, but was left free to reach actions which were in violation of social duties or subversive of good order."

(continued)

Supreme Court Case Studies

Name _____ Date _____ Class _____

Supreme Court Case Study 8 *(continued)*

Waite reviewed the history of laws in England and elsewhere regarding polygamy. He found that "polygamy has always been odious among the Northern and Western Nations of Europe and, until the establishment of the Mormon Church, was almost exclusively a feature of the life of Asiatic and African people." He wrote, "We think it may safely be said there never has been a time in any State of the Union when polygamy has not been an offense against society, cognizable [recognized] by the civil courts and punishable with more or less severity. In the face of all this evidence, it is impossible to believe that the constitutional guarantee of religious freedom was intended to prohibit legislation in respect to this most important feature of social life."

Regarding marriage, Waite wrote, "Marriage, while from its very nature a sacred obligation, is, nevertheless, in most civilized nations, a civil contract, and usually regulated by law." Waite concluded, "In our opinion the statute immediately under consideration . . . is constitutional and valid . . . in all places over which the United States has control."

The Court thus found the law against bigamy valid. There remained the matter of determining whether the Mormons should be exempted from observing bigamy laws on grounds of religious beliefs. Waite asked, "Suppose one believed that human sacrifices were a necessary part of religious worship. Would it seriously be contended that the civil government could not interfere . . . ?"

Waite continued, "So here, as a law of the organization of society under the exclusive dominion of the United States, it is provided that plural marriages shall not be allowed. Can a man excuse his practices to the contrary because of his religious belief? To permit this would be to make the professed doctrines of religious belief superior to the law of the land, and in effect to permit every citizen to become a law unto himself. Government could exist only in name under such circumstances." In this way the Supreme Court determined that the freedom of religion, like other freedoms, has its constitutional limits. No freedom, based on the Constitution, is absolute.

DIRECTIONS: Answer the following questions on a separate sheet of paper.

1. According to Chief Justice Waite, what authority did Congress have to regulate religious practices in the territories?

2. Why could the religious freedom clause in the First Amendment not protect the practice of polygamy?

3. What did the Court mean when it ruled that "no freedom, based on the Constitution, is absolute"?

4. If marriage is, as the Court stated, a "sacred obligation," how could the Court justify regulating it?

5. If polygamy was a common practice among Mormons, do you think it was fair for one person, George Reynolds, to be singled out for punishment? Explain.

Name _____ Date _____ Class _____

Supreme Court Case Study 9

Legality of Segregation by Race

Plessy v. Ferguson, 1896

★★★★★★★★★★★★★★ **Background of the Case** ★★★★★★★★★★★★★★

In 1890 Louisiana passed a law ordering railroads in the state to "provide equal but separate accommodations for the white and colored races." Violations of the law carried a fine of $25 or 20 days in jail. Railway personnel were responsible for assigning seats according to race.

On June 7, 1892, Homer A. Plessy, who was one-eighth African American, decided to test the law's validity by sitting in the white section of a train going from New Orleans to Covington, Louisiana. When a conductor ordered Plessy to give up his seat, he refused. He was then arrested and imprisoned in a New Orleans jail. He was tried by a New Orleans court and found guilty of having violated the Louisiana law described above. He appealed to the Louisiana Supreme Court, which found the law valid. Plessy then appealed to the United States Supreme Court, claiming his conviction and the Louisiana railroad law were unconstitutional because they violated the Thirteenth and Fourteenth Amendments.

Constitutional Issue ★★★★★★★★★★★★★★★★★★★★★★★★★★★★★

In the Reconstruction period after the Civil War, although slavery had been abolished by the Thirteenth Amendment, African Americans lived in a segregated society, especially in the South. The Fourteenth Amendment banned the deprivation of life, liberty, or property without "due process of law." Yet laws were passed in southern states that required segregated schools, theaters, parks, buses, and railroad trains. The *Plessy* case challenged the constitutionality of these so-called Jim Crow practices.

Homer A. Plessy challenged the constitutionality of segregation laws in Louisiana. He based his appeal on the Thirteenth Amendment, which abolished slavery, and the Fourteenth Amendment, which prohibited the states from denying "the equal protection of the law" to any person.

★★★★★★★★★★★★★★ **The Supreme Court's Decision** ★★★★★★★★★★★★★★

A majority of the Court denied Plessy's appeal and upheld the practice of segregation as required by the Louisiana law. Justice Henry Brown wrote the majority opinion. First, the ruling brushed aside the relevance to the case of the Thirteenth Amendment. Brown wrote that "a legal distinction between white and colored races . . . has no tendency to destroy the legal equality of the two races."

The rest of the Court's opinion, however, dealt with the applicability of the Fourteenth Amendment. Brown concluded that this amendment aimed strictly "to enforce the absolute equality of the two races before the law," but that it "could not have been intended to abolish distinctions based on color, or to enforce social, as distinguished from political, equality . . . ."

(continued)

Supreme Court Case Studies

Name _____ Date _____ Class _____

Supreme Court Case Study 9 *(continued)*

Laws requiring segregation "do not necessarily imply the inferiority of either race to the other...." The majority noted that this was the "underlying fallacy" of Plessy's case. Just as valid under the Fourteenth Amendment would be a similar law enacted by an African American-controlled legislature with respect to whites or other races.

The Court ruled, then, that the matter ultimately depended on whether Louisiana's law was "reasonable." Segregation laws "have been generally, if not universally, recognized as within the competency of the state legislatures in the exercise of their police powers." In such matters, a legislature is free to take into account "established usages, customs, and traditions of the people," as well as "the preservation of public peace and good order."

Finally, the Court rejected the notion that "social prejudices may be overcome by legislation." Brown maintained, "If the civil and political rights of both races be equal, one cannot be inferior to the other civilly or politically. If one race be inferior to the other socially, the Constitution of the United States cannot put them on the same plane."

The Court, in effect, enunciated a doctrine that came to be called the separate-but-equal principle. If African Americans saw this as "a badge of inferiority," it was solely "because the colored race chooses to put that construction upon it."

★★★★★★★★★★★★★★★★★★ **Dissenting Opinion** ★★★★★★★★★★★★★★★★★★

Justice John Marshall Harlan entered a vigorous dissent from the majority's decision. He "regretted that this high tribunal . . . has reached the conclusion that it is competent for a state to regulate the enjoyment by citizens of their rights solely upon the basis of race." He saw segregation on racial lines as "a badge of servitude wholly inconsistent with the civil freedom and equality before the law established by the Constitution . . . . The thin disguise of 'equal' accommodations for passengers in railroad coaches will not mislead anyone, nor atone for the wrong this day done." Harlan saw the Constitution as "color-blind, and neither knows nor tolerates classes among citizens."

The separate-but-equal principle was finally overturned in a series of civil rights decisions of the Court in the 1950s, most notably in *Brown* v. *Board of Education*.

DIRECTIONS: Answer the following questions on a separate sheet of paper.

1. Explain how the Supreme Court justified the practice of segregating railroad passengers in Louisiana by race.
2. What is the meaning of the separate-but-equal principle?
3. On what grounds did Justice Harlan criticize the majority's ruling?
4. Why do you think Plessy based his appeal in part on the Thirteenth Amendment?
5. What do you think was the effect of the *Plessy* decision on the nation, especially on the southern states?

Name _____ Date _____ Class _____

Supreme Court Case Study 10

Extending the Meaning of the Commerce Clause

Northern Securities Company v. *United States*, 1904

★★★★★★★★★★★★★★ **Background of the Case** ★★★★★★★★★★★★★★

In 1890 Congress passed the Sherman Antitrust Act to curb the growing power of monopolies in the United States. The act made it illegal for businesses engaged in interstate commerce to combine for the purpose of reducing or restraining competition. The wording of the act was vague, however, because it did not make clear what the word *commerce* meant. In an 1895 case involving the E. C. Knight Company, the Supreme Court had ruled that the company had not violated the antitrust law, even though the purchase of four additional refineries gave the company almost complete control of the manufacturing of sugar in the United States. For the antitrust law to be effective, it was clear that the Supreme Court would have to interpret the meaning of *commerce* more broadly.

In 1901 the Northern Securities Company, a holding company, was formed by combining the ownership of two major railroads that served the Northwest, running parallel lines from the Great Lakes and the Mississippi River to the Pacific Ocean at Puget Sound. With this monopoly of ownership, consumers and businesses of the Northwest were at the mercy of one company that controlled the freight rates of goods brought into and out of the area.

In 1903 the federal government brought suit against the Northern Securities Company as part of its "trust-busting" campaign. The government charged that the company was a monopoly pursuing restraint of trade in violation of the Sherman Antitrust Act and demanded that the company be dissolved.

Constitutional Issue ★★★★★★★★★★★★★★★★★★★★★★★★★★★★★★★★

Did Congress exceed its constitutional authority to regulate interstate commerce when it enacted the Sherman Antitrust Act?

★★★★★★★★★★★★★★ **The Supreme Court's Decision** ★★★★★★★★★★★★★★

In a 5-to-4 ruling, the Court held that the Northern Securities Company should be dissolved because the arrangement was an illegal combination in restraint of interstate commerce and thus violated the Sherman Antitrust Act. Justice John Marshall Harlan wrote that a combination need not be directly involved in commerce in order to restrain it or to have the potential to restrain it. In this case Harlan found restraint of trade due to suppression of competition resulting from combining competing railroads: "... it is manifest that, if the Antitrust Act is held not to embrace a case such as is now before us, the plain intention of the legislative branch of the Government will be defeated. If Congress has not, by the words used in the act, described this and like cases, it would, we apprehend, be impossible to find words that would describe them." Harlan rejected the view that the state that charters a corporation should regulate that corporation, saying: "It means nothing less than that Congress, in regulating interstate commerce, must act in subordination to the will of the States when exerting their power to create corporations. No such view can be entertained for a moment."

(continued)

Name _____ Date _____ Class _____

Supreme Court Case Study 10 *(continued)*

Harlan also suggested that in this case, "The purpose of the combination was concealed under very general words that gave no clue whatever to the real purpose of those who brought about the organization of the Securities Company. If the certificate of the incorporation of the company had expressly stated the object of the company was to destroy competition between competing, parallel lines of interstate carriers, all would have seen, at the outset, that the scheme was in hostility to the national authority, and that there was a purpose to violate or evade the act of Congress."

Justice David Brewer agreed only with Harlan's conclusion. He wrote a concurring opinion in which he held that the Antitrust Act should apply only to unreasonable restraints of trade and that in this case such restraint was unreasonable.

★★★★★★★★★★★★★★★★★★★ **Dissenting Opinion** ★★★★★★★★★★★★★★★★★★★

The dissenting justices maintained that the holding company might have diminished competition in the railroad industry, but that did not make it a "restraint of trade." The dissenting justices thought the majority gave too broad a reading to the statute.

DIRECTIONS: Answer the following questions on a separate sheet of paper.

1. In what way did the Court broaden the meaning of the word *commerce* in the *Northern Securities* case?

2. On which issues did Justice Brewer agree and disagree with Justice Harlan?

3. The Northern Securities Company owned railroads that operated in several states. What role did this fact play in deciding whether the Sherman Antitrust Act applied to the company?

4. Why do you think there was disagreement among the justices who were in the majority?

5. How would you describe the importance of the decision in the *Northern Securities* case?

Name _____ Date _____ Class _____

Supreme Court Case Study 11

The Exclusionary Rule

Weeks v. United States, 1914

★★★★★★★★★★★★★★ **Background of the Case** ★★★★★★★★★★★★★★★

Weeks was arrested at his place of business on a charge of sending lottery tickets through the mail. The police had turned over to a United States marshal the various papers found there. The marshal in turn had searched Weeks's premises in the company of police officers and took still other papers. No warrant had ever been issued for any of the searches or for Weeks's arrest.

Prior to his trial, Weeks asked that his papers be returned to him. The request was denied. These documents were used in evidence against Weeks at his trial, and he was found guilty. The case then reached the United States Supreme Court on appeal.

Constitutional Issue ★★★★★★★★★★★★★★★★★★★★★★★★★★★★★

The Fourth Amendment protects people from unreasonable searches and seizures. Yet for the first hundred years after the Constitution was adopted, evidence unlawfully seized by the police was routinely admitted in trials. In considering *Weeks* v. *United States*, the Court had to weigh not only the rights of the defendant but also the possibility that a criminal could go unpunished.

The constitutional issue in *Weeks* v. *United States* concerned the Fourth Amendment's promise that "the right of the people to be secure in their persons, houses, papers, and effects against unreasonable searches and seizures, shall not be violated; and no warrants shall issue, but on probable cause . . . and particularly describing the place to be searched, and the persons or things to be seized."

★★★★★★★★★★★★★ **The Supreme Court's Decision** ★★★★★★★★★★★★★★

The Court decided that Weeks's Fourth Amendment rights had indeed been violated. Justice William R. Day wrote for a unanimous Court.

Common law had long held that illegally seized evidence could still be admitted as evidence at a trial. The source of the evidence was held to be of no direct concern to the court. If it had been taken illegally or stolen, the remedy was to be found in a subsequent civil suit for trespass or in criminal prosecution for theft. In an 1886 ruling in *Boyd* v. *United States*, the Court had implicitly reversed this common law principle, but it was not until the *Weeks* case that the exclusionary rule, as it came to be known, became a definite legal standard. This new rule means that if unconstitutional evidence is used at trial to establish guilt, the remedy is a retrial without use of the "tainted" evidence.

Justice Day wrote, "The tendency of those who execute the criminal laws of this country to obtain conviction by means of unlawful seizures and enforced confessions, the latter often obtained after subjecting accused persons to unwarranted practices destructive of rights secured by the federal Constitution, should find no sanction in the judgments of the courts,

(continued)

Supreme Court Case Study 11 (continued)

which are charged at all times with the support of the Constitution, and to which people of all conditions have a right to appeal for the maintenance of such fundamental rights...."

Day continued, "If letters and private documents can thus be seized and held and used as evidence against a citizen accused of an offense, the protection of the Fourth Amendment, declaring his right to be secure against such searches and seizures, is of no value, and, so far as those thus placed are concerned, might as well be stricken from the Constitution. The efforts of the courts and their officials to bring the guilty to punishment, praiseworthy as they are, are not to be aided by the sacrifice of those great principles established by years of endeavor and suffering which have resulted in their embodiment in the fundamental law of the land."

Day wrote further, "We therefore reach the conclusion that the letters in question were taken from the house of the accused by an official of the United States, acting under color of his office in direct violation of the constitutional rights of the defendant; that having made a reasonable application for their return, which was heard and passed upon by the court, there was involved in the order refusing the application a denial of the constitutional rights of the accused, and that the court should have restored these letters to the accused. In holding them and permitting their use upon the trial, we think prejudicial error was committed.

"As to the papers and property seized by the policemen, it does not appear that they acted under any claim of federal authority such as would make the amendment applicable to such unauthorized seizures. The record shows that what they did by way of arrest and search and seizure was done before the finding of the indictment in the Federal court; under what supposed right or authority does not appear. What remedies the defendant may have against them we need not inquire, as the Fourth Amendment is not directed to individual misconduct of such officials. Its limitations reach the Federal government and its agencies." Thus, this ruling was held to be applicable only in federal courts and/or against federal authorities. However, in the 1961 case *Mapp* v. *Ohio*, the exclusionary rule was made applicable to the states.

The *Weeks* decision held that if such evidence were to be admitted at trial, the courts would become as guilty as the police who seized the evidence, and the integrity of the entire judicial process would be threatened.

DIRECTIONS: Answer the following questions on a separate sheet of paper.

1. Why did the Supreme Court order that Weeks's papers be returned?

2. What is the meaning of the exclusionary rule?

3. What effect do you think the Court's ruling had on police officers?

4. How did the Court's decision in the *Weeks* case differ from what had become common law on illegally seized evidence?

5. If you had been a Supreme Court justice hearing this case, would you have joined the other justices in supporting the exclusionary rule? Explain.

Supreme Court Case Study 12

Wartime Freedom of Speech

Schenck v. *United States*, 1919

★★★★★★★★★★★★★ **Background of the Case** ★★★★★★★★★★★★★★★

The freedom of speech guarantee of the First Amendment was not tested in the Supreme Court for more than 100 years after the adoption of the Constitution, despite the number of federal and state laws that placed limits on free speech during that period. When the United States entered World War I in 1917, the federal government felt that it had to protect itself against efforts to influence people to oppose the war. Therefore, it passed the Espionage Act, which made it a crime to cause or attempt to cause insubordination in the armed forces, obstruct recruitment or enlistment, and otherwise urge, incite, or advocate obstruction or resistance to the war effort.

Charles Schenck, who was general secretary of the Socialist Party in the United States, carried on a campaign encouraging young men to resist the wartime draft. He mailed thousands of circulars to men who had passed exemption boards and to men who had been drafted. In the circulars he declared that the draft was unconstitutional despotism and urged the men to assert their rights to resist the draft. Further, he claimed that the Thirteenth Amendment, which banned involuntary servitude except as punishment for committing a crime, was violated by the conscription act and that a conscript was little better than a convict. The circular declared, "If you do not assert and support your rights, you are helping to deny or disparage rights which it is the solemn duty of all citizens and residents of the United States to retain." He described arguments in favor of the draft as coming from cunning politicians and a mercenary capitalist press. For these actions Schenck was convicted of conspiracy to violate the Espionage Act by attempting to obstruct the recruitment of men into the United States's armed forces. Schenck challenged his conviction on the grounds that his First Amendment rights had been violated.

Constitutional Issue ★★★★★★★★★★★★★★★★★★★★★★★★★★★★★

The Court had to decide whether Schenck had been properly convicted and whether the Espionage Act was constitutional in the light of the free speech guarantees of the First Amendment. Was such a broad limitation on the right of free speech as the Espionage Act allowed a violation of the First Amendment? Or was the fact that the Espionage Act was designed to protect the nation's war effort a sufficient enough reason for the Supreme Court to reject Schenck's First Amendment defense?

★★★★★★★★★★★★★ **The Supreme Court's Decision** ★★★★★★★★★★★★★★

The Court ruled unanimously that the Espionage Act was constitutional and affirmed that Schenck was guilty of having violated the act. Justice Oliver Wendell Holmes, Jr., wrote the Court's opinion. The opinion was based on the idea that the First Amendment guarantees are not absolute and must be considered in the light of the setting in which supposed violations occur. Holmes wrote, "We admit that in many places and in ordinary times the defendants in

(continued)

Supreme Court Case Study 12 *(continued)*

saying all that was said in the circular would have been within their constitutional rights. But the character of every act depends upon the circumstances in which it is done. . . . The most stringent protection of free speech would not protect a man in falsely shouting fire in a theater and causing a panic." Holmes then enunciated a principle that he felt defined the true scope of the First Amendment as it applied to political expression. "The question in every case," Holmes wrote, "is whether the words used are used in such circumstances and are of such a nature as to create a clear and present danger that they will bring about the substantive evils that Congress has a right to prevent. It is a question of proximity and degree. . . . When a nation is at war many things that might be said in time of peace are such a hindrance to its effort that their utterance will not be endured so long as men fight and that no Court could regard them as protected by any constitutional right."

The *Schenck* case clarified some limitations on free speech and supported the notion that the rights of the people are not absolute but must be balanced with national interests that are judged to be essential.

DIRECTIONS: Answer the following questions on a separate sheet of paper.

1. Why was the Espionage Act passed?

2. Explain the clear and present danger principle that Justice Holmes enunciated in the *Schenck* decision.

3. According to Holmes, what factor made Schenck's actions, which at other times would have been protected by the First Amendment, illegal at the time he performed them?

4. How far do you think the government should go in trying to protect itself against threats to its policies in times of war?

5. Eight months after the *Schenck* decision, the Court again applied the clear and present danger principle. Holmes dissented in that case, stating that unlike the *Schenck* case, actions of the convicted man in the second case had little or no effect on the nation's war effort. What do you think this reveals about Holmes's attitude toward free speech guarantees?

Supreme Court Case Study 13

The Right of Political Radicals to Free Speech
Gitlow v. New York, 1925

★★★★★★★★★★★★★★ **Background of the Case** ★★★★★★★★★★★★★★

Benjamin Gitlow was convicted of violating the 1902 New York Criminal Anarchy Act. The Act defined criminal anarchy as "the doctrine that organized government should be overthrown by force or violence, or by assassination of the executive head or any of the executive officials of government or by any unlawful means." The prohibition applied to speaking, teaching, advising, printing, publishing, circulating, selling, distributing, or publicly displaying such doctrine.

Gitlow had been charged with teaching the necessity and duty to overthrow the government in two publications based largely on Marx and Engels's *Communist Manifesto*. Gitlow's publications advocated "mass industrial revolts," which would develop into "mass political strikes and mass revolutionary action for the annihilation of the parliamentary state. . . ."

Constitutional Issue ★★★★★★★★★★★★★★★★★★★★★★★★★★★★★★★★

The First Amendment's free speech and press guarantee is one of the most cherished of all the provisions of the Bill of Rights. The right to freedom of speech and press is relative, however, not absolute, meaning that in certain circumstances, such as during a war, some limitations to these rights may be imposed. Free speech and press cases present courts with difficult problems to sort out, such as when freedom of speech and publication must be supported, and how to limit speech and publication when these could be dangerous or destructive to the country.

The Gitlow case examined whether the protection of press and speech accorded by the First Amendment was also included under the due process clause of the Fourteenth Amendment, thus making these protections applicable to the states.

Did the Fourteenth Amendment provide a citizen, in state court, the same First Amendment protections the citizen would have in federal court? The case also considered whether "subversive speech" was protected from government regulation, control, and punishment.

★★★★★★★★★★★★★★ **The Supreme Court's Decision** ★★★★★★★★★★★★★★

The Court voted 7 to 2 to uphold Gitlow's conviction. Justice Edward Sanford wrote for the Court.

The more general claim, that the states were bound by the First Amendment through the due process clause, was handled almost in passing. Sanford explained, "For present purposes we may and do assume that freedom of speech and of the press . . . are among the fundamental personal rights and liberties protected by the due process clause of the Fourteenth Amendment from impairment by the states. . . ."

In an earlier case, *Schenck v. United States* (1919), Justice Oliver Wendell Holmes, Jr., had

(continued)

Supreme Court Case Study 13 *(continued)*

formulated the "clear and present danger" test for unprotected speech. Holmes had maintained, "The question in every case is whether the words used are used in such circumstances and are of such a nature as to create a clear and present danger that they will bring about the substantive evils that Congress has a right to prevent."

Holmes went on to say that the "right" of Congress or the states to censor is their "primary and essential right of self-preservation." Therefore, "a state may punish utterances endangering the foundations of organized government and threatening its overthrow by unlawful means. These imperil its own existence as a constitutional state."

Following from Holmes's position, Sanford held that, as a legitimate exercise of its police power, a state may penalize "utterances advocating the overthrow of organized government by force, violence, and unlawful means," which are "inimical to the general welfare and involve ... danger of substantive evil."

The Court further ruled that the state was not required to prove in each case that there was any particular likelihood that a given utterance would in fact bring any result. The Court held that the entire class of subversive speech may be constitutionally controlled by a statute.

★★★★★★★★★★★★★★★★★★★ **Dissenting Opinion** ★★★★★★★★★★★★★★★★★★★

Justice Holmes dissented on the ground that "it is manifest that there was no present danger of an attempt to overthrow the government by force on the part of the admittedly small minority who shared the defendant's views."

Holmes concluded: "Every idea is an incitement. It offers itself for belief, and, if believed, it is acted on unless some other belief outweighs it.... The only difference between the expression of an opinion and an incitement in the narrower sense is the speaker's enthusiasm for the result.... If, in the long run, the beliefs expressed in proletarian dictatorships are destined to be accepted by the dominant forces of the community, the only meaning of free speech is that they should be given their chance and have their way."

DIRECTIONS: Answer the following questions on a separate sheet of paper.

1. How did the Court defend the application of the First Amendment to the states?

2. Did the Court require the state of New York to prove that Gitlow's publications constituted an actual danger? Explain.

3. Assume you are a political science teacher in a New York State college. You require your students to read and discuss Marx and Engels's *Communist Manifesto*. Do you think you could be found guilty of subversion on the basis of the *Gitlow* decision? Give reasons for your answer.

4. If you had participated in the *Gitlow* case as a justice of the Supreme Court, would you have agreed with the majority's position or with Justice Holmes's dissent? Give reasons for your answer.

5. Some constitutional experts maintain that there should be no limitations at all on the right to freedom of speech and the press. Do you agree or disagree with this position? Explain.

Supreme Court Case Study 14

Laws That Punish Speech

Whitney v. California, 1927

★★★★★★★★★★★★★★ **Background of the Case** ★★★★★★★★★★★★★★

In 1919 California passed the Criminal Syndicalism Act, which made membership illegal in an organization that advocates commission of crimes as a means of effecting political change. The term 'criminal syndicalism' is defined as "any doctrine or precept advocating, teaching or aiding and abetting the commission of crime, sabotage . . . or unlawful acts of force and violence or unlawful methods of terrorism as a means of accomplishing a change in industrial ownership or control, or effecting any political change."

Charlette Whitney, a member of the Communist Labor Party of California, was indicted for having violated the Criminal Syndicalism Act by having taken part in organizing the party and being a member of it. At her trial the Communist Labor Party was found to have been organized to advocate, teach, and abet criminal syndicalism. Whitney was convicted and sentenced to prison. Her conviction was upheld in the District Court of Appeals. Whitney then appealed her conviction to the Supreme Court on the grounds that she had been denied her Fourteenth Amendment rights of due process, including her right of free speech.

Constitutional Issue ★★★★★★★★★★★★★★★★★★★★★★★★★★★★★★★

In the case of *Schenck* v. *United States*, the Supreme Court adopted the clear and present danger principle as the basis for deciding whether, under certain circumstances, a law banning certain kinds of speech could be considered constitutional. The *Schenck* case, however, arose when the United States was involved in World War I. Would the same principle apply when the constitutionality of a law that banned certain kinds of speech in peacetime was challenged? The Court had decided that a federal law of this sort was valid in the case of *Gitlow* v. *United States* in 1925. In that case the Court had invoked not the clear and present danger principle, but a new one, called the bad tendency doctrine. Now, two years later, the Court had to decide whether the California Criminal Syndicalism Act could limit free speech as it did without violating a person's constitutional rights under the due process provision of the Fourteenth Amendment.

★★★★★★★★★★★★★★ **The Supreme Court's Decision** ★★★★★★★★★★★★★★

The Court upheld Whitney's conviction by declaring the California law constitutional. Justice Edward Sanford wrote the Court's opinion, finding that California's Syndicalism Act as applied in this case was not ". . . repugnant to the due process clause as a restraint of the rights of free speech, assembly, and association." He invoked the bad tendency test as the standard by which to evaluate speech cases. He held that ". . . the freedom of speech which is secured by the Constitution does not confer an absolute right to speak, without responsibility, whatever one may choose, or an unrestricted and unbridled license giving immunity for every possible use of language and preventing the punishment of those who abuse this freedom, and that a State in the exercise of its police power may punish those who abuse this freedom by utterances inimical

(continued)

Name _____ Date _____ Class _____

Supreme Court Case Study 14 *(continued)*

to the public welfare, tending to incite to crime, disturb the public peace, or endanger the foundations of organized government and threaten its overthrow by unlawful means. . . ." He added that "united and joint action involves even greater danger to the public peace and security than the isolated utterances and acts of individuals. . . ."

Justice Louis D. Brandeis, joined by Justice Holmes, issued a concurring opinion in which he agreed with the Court's decision for technical reasons, but forcefully invoked the clear and present danger principle. He pointed out, "Whenever the fundamental rights of free speech and assembly are alleged to have been invaded, it must remain open to a defendant to present the issue whether there actually did exist at the time a clear danger; whether the danger, if any, was imminent, and whether the evil apprehended was one so substantial as to justify the stringent restriction imposed by the legislature. . . ." In this case, however, he noted that Whitney had not claimed that there was no clear and present danger, and there was evidence from which a jury could find that such a danger existed. He wrote: "To courageous, self-reliant men, with confidence in the power of free and fearless reasoning applied through the processes of popular government, no danger flowing from speech can be deemed clear and present, unless the incidence of the evil apprehended is so imminent that it may befall before there is opportunity for full discussion. If there be time . . . to avert the evil by the process of education, the remedy to be applied is more speech, not enforced silence." He added, "The fact that speech is likely to result in some violence or in destruction of property is not enough to justify its suppression. There must be the probability of serious injury to the state."

The Court's decision in the *Whitney* case was overruled in 1969 in *Brandenburg* v. *Ohio*.

DIRECTIONS: Answer the following questions on a separate sheet of paper.

1. Of what crime was Whitney convicted?

2. What were the grounds for the Court's decision?

3. How did Justice Brandeis's concurring opinion conflict with Justice Sanford's opinion?

4. Do you agree or disagree with a law that is designed to punish people not for any action but for membership in a particular organization a state finds offensive?

5. The *Whitney* decision was overruled in 1969 in a subsequent case. What reasons might the justices have given for their decision in that case?

Supreme Court Case Study 15

Evidence from Tapped Phone Lines
Olmstead v. *United States*, 1928

★★★★★★★★★★★★★★ Background of the Case ★★★★★★★★★★★★★★★★

Roy Olmstead and his partners imported and supplied alcoholic beverages. They were prosecuted, tried, and convicted in federal court for conspiracy to violate the National Prohibition Act. Much of the evidence presented at their trials was gathered by wiretapping three telephone lines used by Olmstead's office. None of the taps had been placed as a result of physical trespass on any defendant's property.

The Eighteenth Amendment, or Prohibition Amendment, effective from 1919 to 1933, was widely violated by ordinary citizens and so-called bootleggers, who supplied illegal liquor, yet these people were rarely prosecuted. Violations of the liquor law were so extensive that the government was unable to prosecute more than a small percentage of the bootleggers; securing evidence that would hold up in court was extremely difficult. One way of obtaining evidence against bootleggers was by wiretapping their telephones.

*C*onstitutional Issue ★★★★★★★★★★★★★★★★★★★★★★★★★★★★★★★★★

> The Fourth Amendment provides that "the right of the people to be secure in their persons, houses, papers, and effects, against unreasonable searches and seizures, shall not be violated...." The Fifth Amendment protects a person charged with a criminal offense from being a witness against himself or herself. The question before the Court in *Olmstead* v. *United States* was whether either of these amendments prohibited evidence obtained from telephone wiretaps.

★★★★★★★★★★★★★ The Supreme Court's Decision ★★★★★★★★★★★★★★★

The Court ruled 6 to 3 against Olmstead. Chief Justice William Howard Taft delivered the opinion of the Court.

Olmstead had argued that because the prosecution's evidence came entirely from the wiretaps, it could not be used against him. He claimed he was protected by the Fourth Amendment against improper search and seizure, and by the Fifth Amendment against self-incrimination.

The Court confined its examination to Fourth Amendment questions. If the Fourth Amendment had not been violated, then neither had the Fifth Amendment since no one had compelled the defendants to speak over the telephone lines.

Justice Taft's decision turned on the issue of whether or not a wiretap was the constitutional equivalent of forcible entry. If so, the evidence obtained would be inadmissible in federal courts in accordance with previous decisions, such as in *Weeks* v. *United States*, 1914.

Taft held that the Fourth Amendment "shows that the search is to be of material things—the person, the house, his papers or his effects. The description of the warrant necessary to make the proceedings lawful is that it must specify the place to be searched and the person or *things* to be seized."

(continued)

Supreme Court Case Studies

Name _____ Date _____ Class _____

Supreme Court Case Study 15 (continued)

Taft rejected any analogy to sealed letters, which the Court had held to be protected by the Fourth Amendment. Taft explained, "The United States takes no such care of telegraph or telephone messages as of mailed, sealed letters. The Amendment does not forbid what was done here. There was no searching. There was no seizure. The evidence was secured by the use of the sense of hearing and that only. There was no entry of the houses or offices of the defendants." He insisted that it was an unwarranted expansion of the Fourth Amendment to apply it to hearing or sight.

The Court held further that telephone lines were not protected by the Fourth Amendment, since they "are not part of his house or office any more than are highways along which they are stretched. . . . The reasonable view is that one who installs . . . a telephone with connecting wires intends to project his voice to those outside, and that the wires beyond his house and messages while passing over them are not within the protection of the Fourth Amendment."

Finally, Taft ruled that this holding was in accord with the generally accepted common rule that "if the tendered evidence was pertinent, the method of obtaining it was unimportant." He concluded that "a standard which would forbid the reception of evidence if obtained by other than nice ethical conduct by government officials would make society suffer and give criminals greater immunity than has been known heretofore."

★★★★★★★★★★★★★★★★★★★ **Dissenting Opinion** ★★★★★★★★★★★★★★★★★★★

Justice Louis Brandeis disagreed with the Court's narrow view of the Fourth Amendment. He wrote, "Decency, security and liberty alike demand that government officials shall be subjected to the same rules of conduct that are commands to the citizen. In a government of laws, existence of the government will be imperiled if it fails to observe the laws scrupulously. Our Government is the potent, the omnipresent teacher. For good or for ill, it teaches the whole people by its example. . . . To declare that in the administration of the criminal law the end justifies the means . . . would bring terrible retribution. Against that pernicious doctrine this Court should resolutely set its face."

The decision of the Court was harshly criticized, but it stood until the 1967 *Katz* case when it was overruled on the grounds that a trespass was unnecessary for a violation of the Fourth Amendment and that the Amendment protected intangibles, including conversations.

DIRECTIONS: Answer the following questions on a separate sheet of paper.

1. Why did the Supreme Court hold that the Fourth Amendment did not apply to wiretaps?

2. What did the Court say about the means by which evidence is obtained?

3. Suppose you had broken a law, and the police found evidence of your crime by breaking into your home. Under the *Olmstead* ruling, would the evidence be admissible in a trial?

4. What did Justice Brandeis mean when he said that in the Court's decision, the end justified the means?

5. Do you agree with the decision of the Court? Explain your answer.

Supreme Court Case Study 16

Censorship of the Press Before Publication

Near v. *Minnesota*, 1931

★★★★★★★★★★★★★ **Background of the Case** ★★★★★★★★★★★★★

In 1925 Minnesota passed a law that sought to prevent newspapers, magazines, and other publications from printing obscene, malicious, scandalous and defamatory material. The law, called the "Minnesota gag law", allowed either public prosecutors or private citizens to request a court injunction to shut down such a publication as "a public nuisance." *The Saturday Press*, published by a journalist named Near, had printed articles charging that various criminal activities were controlled by gangsters, and that the local mayor, chief of police, and county attorneys were in league with the gangsters. Using the 1925 statute, the county attorney obtained an injunction "perpetually" prohibiting Near from publishing a "malicious, scandalous or defamatory newspaper." Near appealed to the Minnesota Supreme Court, and when that body ruled in the county's favor, he appealed to the United States Supreme Court.

Constitutional Issue ★★★★★★★★★★★★★★★★★★★★★★★★★★★★★★

One of the most treasured provisions of the Bill of Rights is the protection of freedom to publish as provided by the First Amendment. This protection applies to all kinds of publications, even those that print unpopular opinions. Most censorship cases have been attempts to suppress the written word after publication of a work. In the *Near* v. *Minnesota* case, however, censorship was attempted before publication by closing down the offending periodical. This attempt was made because Minnesota officials decided that the contents of Near's periodical would be offensive to the public. In *Near* v. *Minnesota* the Supreme Court had to decide whether Minnesota's statute violated the First Amendment's guarantee of freedom of the press, as applied to the states by the due process clause of the Fourteenth Amendment.

★★★★★★★★★★★★★ **The Supreme Court's Decision** ★★★★★★★★★★★★★

The Court voted 5 to 4 in Near's favor. Chief Justice Charles Evans Hughes presented the Court's opinion. He called the Minnesota statute "unusual, if not unique." It pitted the undoubted liberty of the press against the "necessarily admitted" authority of the state "to promote the health, safety, morals, and general welfare of its people." Both the state's attorney and the liberty of the press, Hughes observed, have claims and limits that must be delineated.

Hughes declared: "If we cut through mere details of procedure, the operation and effect of the statute in substance is that public authorities may bring the owner or publisher of a newspaper . . . before a judge upon a charge . . . of publishing scandalous and defamatory matter . . . and unless the owner or publisher is able and disposed to bring competent evidence to satisfy the judge that the charges are true and are published with good motives and for justifiable ends, his newspaper or periodical is suppressed and further publication is made punishable as a contempt. This is of the essence of censorship." This is not to say, however, that no forms of censorship are to be permitted, Hughes stressed. There are "exceptional cases," such as in times

(continued)

Supreme Court Case Study 16 (continued)

of war, when it may be permitted. Similarly, he wrote, "the primary requirements of decency may be enforced against obscene publications."

"In the present case," Hughes continued, "we have no occasion to inquire as to the permissible scope of subsequent punishment. For whatever wrong the appellant [Near] has committed or may commit, by his publications, the state appropriately affords both public and private redress by its libel laws." Here Hughes was making the point that if, in fact, the claims of the paper were to be proved libelous, another court case would be called for. The decision of the Court here was not in relation to whether the articles in question were true or false.

What was at issue, Hughes stressed, is prior or previous restraint upon the press in nonexceptional cases. On that score the "chief purpose" of the liberty of the press is "to prevent previous restraints upon publication." The court concluded that this in no way places the press beyond the reach of legal action. That is, the press is generally to be held accountable after, not before, publication. In summary, Hughes wrote, "For these reasons we hold the statute . . . to be an infringement of the liberty of the press guaranteed by the First Amendment."

The *Near* case represented a new level of Supreme Court concern for freedom of the press. Prior censorship of the press was condemned. *Near* was the first case in which a state law was held unconstitutional for violating the freedom of press protected by the due process clause of the Fourteenth Amendment.

★★★★★★★★★★★★★★★★★ **Dissenting Opinion** ★★★★★★★★★★★★★★★★★★

In one of the dissenting opinions, Justice Butler argued that "the distribution of scandalous matter is detrimental to public morals and to the general welfare. It tends to disturb the peace of the community. Being defamatory and malicious, it tends to provoke assaults and the commission of crime. It has no concern with the publication of the truth, with good motives and for justifiable ends. . . . In Minnesota no agency can hush the sincere and honest voice of the press; but our constitution was never intended to protect malice, scandal and defamation when untrue or published with bad motives or without justifiable ends. . . . It was never the intention of the constitution to afford protection to a publication devoted to scandal and defamation. . . ."

DIRECTIONS: Answer the following questions on a separate sheet of paper.

1. Does the Court's decision prohibit all censorship or prior restraint of the press? Explain.

2. How is the Fourteenth Amendment, which does not mention freedom of the press, related to the Court's decision?

3. Assume you own a newspaper that publishes articles claiming your city's mayor takes bribes. The mayor asks a court to shut down your paper. How should your lawyer respond to this attempt to limit freedom of the press?

4. If the mayor in Question 3 believes you have made false charges against him, what remedy does he have, according to the Supreme Court, other than trying to close down your paper?

5. What is the importance of the Court's decision in the *Near* case?

Supreme Court Case Study 17

Denial of Right to Counsel

Powell v. *Alabama*, 1932

★★★★★★★★★★★★★ Background of the Case ★★★★★★★★★★★★★★

On March 25, 1931, a fight took place between seven young African Americans and seven young white men. Ozie Powell and six friends—all African Americans—were on a freight train traveling through Alabama. Also on the train were seven white boys and two white women. In the fight all but one of the white boys were thrown off the train. A message was sent ahead reporting the fight, and the African Americans were asked to get off the train. The two women testified that each of them had been sexually assaulted by the African Americans.

A sheriff's posse seized the African Americans, and the women and the defendants were taken to the county seat in Scottsboro, Alabama.

Angry crowds had gathered in Scottsboro after hearing about the alleged assaults. The sheriff called in the militia to protect the defendants as they were escorted to Gadsden for safekeeping and back to Scottsboro for a trial a few days later. All of the defendants were described as "youthful, ignorant, and illiterate." They lived in other states and had no relatives or friends to help them in their situation.

Powell and his friends were indicted six days later on March 31 for the rape of the two white women. Their trials began on April 6, 1931, in this hostile southern community. There were three trials, each lasting one day. Between the times of the arrest and trials, no attorney was named to represent any of the defendants. Not until the very morning of the trials was a lawyer named to represent them, but they had no time to confer with counsel. All the young men were given the death penalty.

The Alabama Supreme Court upheld the convictions, but its chief justice wrote a dissent in which he maintained that the defendants had not received a fair trial. The United States Supreme Court agreed to hear the case.

There were widespread protests, especially in liberal northern circles, against the trial court's cursory handling of the cases. Many Americans viewed the trial as a sham aimed at finding the young men guilty as quickly as possible. Outraged people arranged for a northern attorney to become involved in the case, and some believe his participation was instrumental in having the decisions reversed.

*C*onstitutional Issue ★★★★★★★★★★★★★★★★★★★★★★★★★★★★

Although a number of issues were brought before the Supreme Court, the justices limited their examination to whether or not the defendants had been denied due process of the law because they had been denied the right to counsel. The question before the Court was whether the Fourteenth Amendment incorporates the Sixth Amendment right to counsel in a capital case, paid for if necessary, by the state.

(continued)

Supreme Court Case Studies   33

Name _____ Date _____ Class _____

Supreme Court Case Study 17 *(continued)*

★★★★★★★★★★★★★ **The Supreme Court's Decision** ★★★★★★★★★★★★★

Justice George Sutherland wrote the Court's decision for the majority in a 7 to 2 ruling in favor of Powell. The decision overturned the conviction of the defendants and ordered a new trial to be held in which the defendants were to have the benefit of legal counsel. Sutherland stated, "Defendants were immediately hurried to trial. . . . [A] defendant charged with a serious crime, must not be stripped of his right to have sufficient time to advise with counsel and prepare his defense." He stated that "in a capital case [one in which the death penalty is involved] where the defendant is unable to employ counsel, and is incapable adequately of making his own defense . . . it is the duty of the court, whether requested or not, to assign counsel for him as a necessary requisite of due process of law." This ruling covered not only the trial itself but provided for "effective counsel" for the defendant in preparation for the trial.

In making his decision, Justice Sutherland continued a process that had begun in previous cases that found certain rights mentioned in the Bill of Rights must be included in the Fourteenth Amendment's description of due process of law. The hurdle over which all such reasoning by the Supreme Court had to pass was that the Fourteenth Amendment does not specifically mention any of these Bill of Rights protections. Quoting an earlier case, Justice Sutherland found that the right to counsel "is of such character that it cannot be denied without violating those 'fundamental principles of liberty and justice which lie at the base of all our civil and political institutions'. . . ."

Sutherland acknowledged that the legal system too often delayed the enforcement of criminal law and people suffered as a result. The opposite had occurred in this case, however. Sutherland spoke for the defendants in this case as he wrote, ". . . a defendant, charged with a serious crime, must not be stripped of his right to have sufficient time to advise with counsel and prepare his defense. To do that is not to proceed promptly in the calm spirit of regulated justice but to go forward with the haste of the mob."

DIRECTIONS: Answer the following questions on a separate sheet of paper.

1. Why did the Supreme Court not address the question of whether or not Powell and his friends were guilty?

2. In what way was the Fourteenth Amendment an issue in the case?

3. Why do you think no counsel was appointed for the defendants until the morning of their trials?

4. In what way was time a factor in this case?

5. Why is the right to counsel so important that it is held to be a constitutional requirement?

Supreme Court Case Study 18

First Amendment Rights for Communists
DeJonge v. *Oregon*, 1937

★★★★★★★★★★★★★★★ Background of the Case ★★★★★★★★★★★★★★★

In July 1934 Dirk DeJonge spoke at a meeting in Portland, Oregon, organized by the local Communist Party to protest police raids on workers' halls and police shootings of striking dock workers. The meeting had been clearly advertised as under the auspices of the Communist Party and its speakers, including DeJonge, as party members. About 10 to 15 percent of the 150 to 300 people present were also Communist Party members.

In his speech DeJonge protested conditions in the county jail, police tactics relating to the dock workers' strike, and other matters pertaining to the strike. He also asked those present to help support the party and to purchase Communist literature. The meeting went on in an orderly fashion until police raided the hall, arrested DeJonge and others, and seized a large quantity of Communist literature.

DeJonge was tried under an Oregon law making it illegal to publish, print, distribute, or teach criminal syndicalism, defined as "the doctrine which advocates crime, physical violence, sabotage, or any unlawful acts or methods as a means of accomplishing or effecting industrial or political change or revolution." All these acts were felonies, punishable by up to 10 years in prison and/or a fine of up to $1,000.

DeJonge was charged with taking part in a meeting of the Communist Party, an organization that the state claimed advocated criminal syndicalism and sabotage. He was convicted and sentenced to seven years' imprisonment. The judgment was supported by the Oregon Supreme Court. DeJonge then appealed his case to the United States Supreme Court.

Constitutional Issue ★★★★★★★★★★★★★★★★★★★★★★★★★★★★★★★

In his defense, DeJonge claimed that Oregon's criminal syndicalism law violated the Fourteenth Amendment's due process clause. The Court examined whether or not the First Amendment's guarantee of the right of peaceful assembly was included under the Fourteenth Amendment.

★★★★★★★★★★★★★★ The Supreme Court's Decision ★★★★★★★★★★★★★★

The Court held unanimously for DeJonge. Chief Justice Charles Evans Hughes wrote for the Court.

Hughes summarized the charge against DeJonge as follows: "His sole offense as charged . . . was that he had assisted in the conduct of a public meeting, albeit otherwise lawful, which was held under the auspices of the Communist Party." As the Chief Justice pointed out, this meant that any meeting called by the Communist Party to discuss any subject should result in every speaker at that meeting being convicted and jailed like DeJonge. So, while the Court agreed that states may defend themselves against attempts to replace orderly political action by revolutionary

(continued)

Supreme Court Case Study 18 *(continued)*

force and violence, "none of our decisions go to the length of sustaining such a curtailment of the right to free speech and assembly as the Oregon statute demands. . . ."

Since the Court held that First Amendment rights of speech and press were binding on the states by the Fourteenth Amendment's due process clause, now it found that "the right of peaceable assembly is a right cognate to those of free speech and free press and is equally fundamental. . . . For the right is one that cannot be denied without violating those fundamental principles of liberty and justice which lie at the base of all civil and political institutions, principles which the Fourteenth Amendment embodies in its due process clause."

Based on these considerations, the Court concluded that it cannot be a crime to assemble peaceably for lawful discussion, to hold meetings for peaceable political action, or to assist at such meetings, no matter who sponsors them. Prosecutions are justified only for crimes committed elsewhere or for conspiracies against public peace and order. Hughes stated, however, "It is a different matter when the State, instead of prosecuting individuals for such offenses, seizes upon mere participation in a peaceable assembly and a lawful public discussion as the basis for a criminal charge."

This decision marked one of the early cases in which the Court incorporated the freedom of speech and freedom of assembly provisions of the First Amendment into the due process clause of the Fourteenth Amendment, thus making them binding on the states.

DIRECTIONS: Answer the following questions on a separate sheet of paper.

1. Why was the right to assemble called fundamental by the Court?

2. What made this decision particularly significant?

3. If you had been at DeJonge's meeting, would you have been surprised to learn that it was sponsored by the Communist Party?

4. Who stood to gain from the Court's decision in the *DeJonge* case?

5. Do you think that any limits should be set on the right to peaceful assembly? If so, explain what circumstances might call for such limits.

Supreme Court Case Study 19

Constitutionality of Minimum Wage Laws

West Coast Hotel v. Parrish, 1937

★★★★★★★★★★★★★★★ **Background of the Case** ★★★★★★★★★★★★★★★

In the latter years of the 1800s, many states began to enact laws limiting the number of work hours and setting minimum wages for workers. Business owners objected to such laws and appealed to the courts to have them set aside on constitutional grounds. For the most part the courts obliged, ruling the labor laws unconstitutional because they interfered with the "liberty of contract" or because they violated the due process provisions of the Fifth Amendment.

During the Great Depression of the 1930s, a number of states passed new minimum wage laws. This was also the period when President Franklin D. Roosevelt's New Deal launched a new program of social and economic laws. The Supreme Court was very conservative at the time and rejected many such laws. Infuriated by the Court's obstinacy, Roosevelt announced a plan to add additional justices to counterbalance the influence of the older and more conservative members. Although the country at large was thunderstruck by this attack on the Court, and it was never enacted, Roosevelt's plan did have an effect on Court rulings, and the Court began to change its attitude toward social and economic legislation.

Elsie Parrish was employed as a chambermaid at the West Coast Hotel in Seattle, Washington. She claimed that she was paid less than the state-mandated minimum wage of $14.50 for a 48-hour work week. She sued the hotel for the difference between what she had been paid and the minimum wage. In the trial court the hotel challenged the law on the grounds that it violated the due process clause of the Fourteenth Amendment. The trial court upheld this position, but the state supreme court reversed the trial court and sustained the minimum wage law, whereupon the hotel brought the case through the appeal process to the United States Supreme Court.

Constitutional Issue ★★★★★★★★★★★★★★★★★★★★★★★★★★★★★★

In light of the Court's previous decisions on minimum wage and related laws, would it now rule that such laws do not violate presumed constitutional rights of business, such as the freedom to enter into contracts?

★★★★★★★★★★★★★★ **The Supreme Court's Decision** ★★★★★★★★★★★★★★

In a majority opinion written by Chief Justice Charles Evans Hughes, the Court ruled in favor of the constitutionality of the state of Washington's minimum wage law. In doing so, the Court had to repudiate two earlier decisions. Hughes wrote that the Constitution does not enshrine freedom of contract and that "regulation which is reasonable in relation to its subject and is adopted in the interests of the community is due process." He declared, "What can be closer to the public interest than the health of women and their protection from unscrupulous and overreaching employers? And if the protection of women is a legitimate end of the exercise of state power, how can it be said that the requirement of the payment of a minimum wage

(continued)

Supreme Court Case Study 19 (continued)

fairly fixed in order to meet the very necessities of existence is not an admissible answer to that end?" A minimum wage law "cannot be regarded as arbitrary or capricious, and that is all we have to decide."

Hughes also pointed to "... an additional and compelling consideration which recent economic experience has brought into a strong light. The exploitation of a class of workers who are in an unequal position with respect to bargaining power and are thus relatively defenseless against the denial of a living wage is not only detrimental to their health and well being, but casts a direct burden for their support upon the community. What these workers lose in wages, the taxpayers are called upon to pay. The bare cost of living must be met. We may take judicial notice of the unparalleled demands for relief which arose during the recent period of depression and still continue to an alarming extent despite the degree of economic recovery which has been achieved. It is unnecessary to cite official statistics to establish what is of common knowledge through the length and breadth of the land."

★★★★★★★★★★★★★★★★★★ **Dissenting Opinion** ★★★★★★★★★★★★★★★★★★

Justice George Sutherland, joined by three other justices, entered a vigorous dissent in which he maintained that freedom of contract was still the rule. "The meaning of the Constitution," he wrote, "does not change with the ebb and flow of economic events."

DIRECTIONS: Answer the following questions on a separate sheet of paper.

1. What effect did the changing economic conditions of the 1930s have on the Supreme Court?
2. On what did the majority of the Court base its decision in the *West Coast Hotel* case?
3. How was the principle of precedent treated in this case?
4. A constitutional scholar has described Justice Sutherland's dissent as "an obituary for a judicial philosophy eclipsed by new realities." Explain what he meant by this statement.
5. How do you think the Supreme Court ruled the next time a case involving an economic regulation came before it?

Supreme Court Case Study 20

Flag Salute Requirement

Minersville School District v. *Gobitis*, 1940

★★★★★★★★★★★★★★★ **Background of the Case** ★★★★★★★★★★★★★★★

In 1898, after New York passed a law requiring school children to salute the American flag during opening exercises of the school day, other states began to pass similar laws. These early laws did not make the flag salute ceremony compulsory, but in later years many local school boards insisted that all students participate. Many patriotic organizations supported the flag salute requirement. Opposition came from civil libertarians and some religious groups, including the Jehovah's Witnesses.

The Jehovah's Witnesses is an evangelistic sect believing, among other things, that the biblical prohibition against worship of images forbids them to salute the flag. This religious group became the major opponent of the compulsory school flag salute.

Lillian and William Gobitis, aged 12 and 10 respectively, followed the Witnesses' teaching and refused to salute the flag in their Minersville, Pennsylvania, public schools. The board of education there, which required a daily flag salute, expelled the children.

Since school attendance in Pennsylvania was compulsory, the children's parents placed them in private schools. William Gobitis, their father, then sued the Minersville Board of Education for relief from this new financial burden. He sought an injunction that would prevent the Board of Education from requiring the flag salute as a condition of free public education.

Two lower courts held in favor of Gobitis, whereupon the Minersville School District filed an appeal with the United States Supreme Court. The *Minersville* case became the first flag salute case to reach the Supreme Court.

*C*onstitutional Issue ★★★★★★★★★★★★★★★★★★★★★★★★★★★★★★

The Court said the issue to be decided was "whether the requirement of participation in such a ceremony, exacted from a child who refuses upon sincere religious grounds, infringes without due process of law the liberty guaranteed by the Fourteenth Amendment."

★★★★★★★★★★★★★★ **The Supreme Court's Decision** ★★★★★★★★★★★★★★

The Court decided against Gobitis by an 8 to 1 majority. Justice Felix Frankfurter wrote for the Court.

Although individuals are protected by the Constitution in their religious beliefs or disbeliefs, Frankfurter explained that sometimes the "manifold character of man's relations may bring his conception of religious duty into conflict with the secular interests of his fellow men." As viewed by the Court, its task was "to reconcile two rights in order to prevent either from destroying the other."

Historically, Frankfurter wrote, "the religious liberty which the Constitution protects has never excluded legislation of a general scope not directed against doctrinal loyalties of particular

(continued)

Supreme Court Case Study 20 (continued)

sects." Like freedom of speech, religious freedom may sometimes necessarily be limited in order to "maintain that orderly, tranquil and free society without which religious toleration itself is unattainable."

The Court realized that this case did not deal with societal needs or interests such as defense, taxation, health, or family protection. However, stated Frankfurter, "all these specific activities of government presuppose the existence of an organized political society. The ultimate foundation of a free society is the binding tie of cohesive sentiment." He went on, "The precise issue, then, for us to decide is whether the legislatures of the various states . . . are barred from determining the appropriateness of various means to evoke that unifying sentiment. . . ." On that consideration, the Court declared its lack of competence to overrule the wisdom of the legislatures. "Even were we convinced of the folly of such a measure (i.e., a required flag salute), such belief would be no proof of its unconstitutionality." Furthermore, "the court room is not the arena for debating issues of educational policy. . . . So to hold would in effect make us the school board of the country."

The Court also declined to rule that the law was unconstitutional for not making any exception to its requirement. Frankfurter concluded, "But for us to insist that, though the ceremony may be required, exceptional immunity must be given to dissidents, is to maintain that there is no basis for legislative judgment that such an exemption might introduce elements of difficulty into the school discipline. . . ."

★★★★★★★★★★★★★★★★★★ **Dissenting Opinion** ★★★★★★★★★★★★★★★★★★

Justice Harlan Stone wrote a powerful dissenting opinion in the case. Likewise, the Court's decision was widely criticized and some members began to have second thoughts. Later, when a case similar to *Gobitis* came before the Court, the *Gobitis* ruling was overruled. However, more important was the fact that the *Gobitis* decision was followed by a wave of prosecutions of Jehovah's Witnesses throughout the country.

DIRECTIONS: Answer the following questions on a separate sheet of paper.

1. What function, according to the Supreme Court, did the flag salute serve?

2. What were the basic reasons the Court overruled the lower courts?

3. If a flag salute case came before the Court today, what do you think the ruling would be?

4. If you had been a member of a group that did not believe in compulsory flag salutes, would you have protested, like the Gobitises, or accepted the board of education's requirement? Explain your answer.

5. On what grounds do you think civil libertarians were disappointed in the Court's *Gobitis* decision?

Supreme Court Case Study 21

Denial of Counsel to Defendants

Betts v. Brady, 1942

★★★★★★★★★★★★★★★ **Background of the Case** ★★★★★★★★★★★★★★★

In Carroll County, Maryland, an unemployed farm hand named Betts had been charged with robbery. At his trial Betts asked the judge to appoint counsel to represent him because he could not afford an attorney. Since local practice required free counsel to be appointed only in murder and rape cases, Betts's request was denied.

Without withdrawing his claim to court-appointed counsel, Betts conducted his own defense. He pleaded not guilty and chose to be tried without a jury. He examined his own witnesses and cross-examined those of the prosecution. Betts was found guilty and sentenced to eight years in prison. After he was unsuccessful in his appeal to the Maryland court for a writ of habeas corpus, he appealed to the United States Supreme Court.

Constitutional Issue ★★★★★★★★★★★★★★★★★★★★★★★★★★★★★★

In his appeal to the United States Supreme Court, Betts claimed that he had been denied the "due process of law" guaranteed by the Fourteenth Amendment. Specifically, Betts argued that the Sixth Amendment's guarantee of the "assistance of counsel" in all criminal prosecutions should be applicable to state trials through the matching due process clause in the Fifth and Fourteenth Amendments.

Betts's claim was based in part on an earlier ruling in the case of *Powell* v. *Alabama* (1932). Because the defendants in that case had been denied the right of counsel, the Court had overturned the rape convictions and resulting death sentences.

★★★★★★★★★★★★ **The Supreme Court's Decision** ★★★★★★★★★★★★★★

The Court denied Betts's claim for counsel in a 6 to 3 decision. Justice Owen Roberts wrote for the Court.

Justice Roberts carefully avoided making a rule that "in every case, whatever the circumstances, one charged with a crime, who is unable to obtain counsel, must be furnished counsel by the state." Each case, he stated, must be examined separately and the "totality of the facts" considered. To deny counsel might be shocking to the universal sense of justice in one case but not in another, the justice wrote.

Roberts reaffirmed the *Powell* decision. He noted that the trial in that case had violated "every principle of fairness," and a capital crime had been involved. Now the Court had to consider whether to enlarge that decision to include all state criminal cases.

Roberts reviewed common, colonial, and early state laws. He found that these laws could be reasonably interpreted to allow or permit a defendant to obtain counsel. However, he concluded they could not serve as a precedent "to compel the state to provide counsel for a defendant."

(continued)

Name _____ Date _____ Class _____

Supreme Court Case Study 21 *(continued)*

States had dealt previously with this matter "by statute rather than by constitutional provision," Roberts observed. The Court, then, declined to interfere with the "considered judgment of the people, their representatives, and their courts that appointment of counsel is not a fundamental right, essential to a fair trial." Nevertheless, "Every court has power . . . to appoint counsel where that course seems to be required in the interest of fairness," Roberts emphasized.

The Court concluded that "the Fourteenth Amendment prohibits the conviction and incarceration of one whose trial is offensive to the common and fundamental ideas of fairness and right." Roberts noted, however, that this interpretation does not include the notion that the amendment requires a defendant always to be represented by counsel.

★★★★★★★★★★★★★★★★★★ **Dissenting Opinion** ★★★★★★★★★★★★★★★★★★

Three justices dissented vigorously. Justice Hugo L. Black wrote the dissent, in which he was joined by Justices William O. Douglas and Frank Murphy.

Justice Black felt strongly that Betts had been denied his constitutional rights. He made the point that the right to counsel in a criminal proceeding is fundamental. He based this on the Court's ruling in the *Powell* case. Further, he wrote, the right to counsel "is guarded from invasion by the Sixth Amendment, adopted to raise an effective barrier against arbitrary or unjust deprivation of liberty by the federal government." He conceded that the Sixth Amendment lays down no rule for conduct of the states, but this protection is "so fundamental to a fair trial . . . that it is made obligatory upon the states by the Fourteenth Amendment."

Referring to the fact that Betts was a poor unemployed farm hand, Black said, "Denial to the poor of the request for counsel in proceedings based on charges of serious crime has long been regarded as shocking to the 'universal sense of justice' throughout this country."

DIRECTIONS: Answer the following questions on a separate sheet of paper.

1. What did Justice Roberts find in his examination of earlier American law?

2. Why is the Sixth Amendment not directly applicable to the states?

3. What is the basis of Justice Black's dissent?

4. How does Justice Roberts distinguish the *Betts* decision from the *Powell* decision?

5. In Justice Roberts's opinion, what serves as the ultimate guarantee of a fair trial? Do you agree or disagree? Give reasons for your answer.

Name _____ Date _____ Class _____

Supreme Court Case Study 22

Flag Salute Requirement

West Virginia State Board of Education v. Barnette, 1943

★★★★★★★★★★★★★★★ **Background of the Case** ★★★★★★★★★★★★★★★

Barnette was a member of the Jehovah's Witnesses, a religious group whose members refuse to participate in government, bear arms, serve in the military, or salute the flag. The flag salute is forbidden on grounds that it constitutes idol worship, which is forbidden in the Bible.

After the *Gobitis* decision of 1940, West Virginia instituted a compulsory flag salute in public schools. Disobedience was punishable by a child's expulsion from the state's schools, and the child's parents were liable to a jail term not exceeding 30 days and a fine not to exceed $50.

For refusing to give the required salute, Barnette's children and the children of other parents who were Jehovah's Witnesses were expelled from their schools. State officials also threatened to have the children sent to reformatories for criminally inclined juveniles.

Barnette sued in federal district court for an injunction against the enforcement of the flag salute law. The district court held in Barnette's favor, after which the state Board of Education appealed to the United States Supreme Court.

Constitutional Issue ★★★★★★★★★★★★★★★★★★★★★★★★★★★★★★

The Court had to decide whether the West Virginia law violated the Fourteenth Amendment's due process clause, insofar as that clause is held to include the First Amendment's protections of free exercise of religion and free speech. In the *Gobitis* case presented earlier, the Supreme Court had ruled that a compulsory flag salute in schools did not violate an individual's First Amendment rights. Three years after that case, the Court was presented with essentially the same issue.

★★★★★★★★★★★★★ **The Supreme Court's Decision** ★★★★★★★★★★★★★★

The Court ruled 6 to 3 in Barnette's favor on the grounds that the West Virginia statute violated the First and Fourteenth Amendments. Justice Robert H. Jackson wrote the Court's opinion.

The Court ruled that the flag salute is a form of utterance. "It requires the individual to communicate by word and sign his acceptance of the political ideas it thus bespeaks. Objection to this form of communication when coerced is an old one, well known to the Framers of the Bill of Rights. . . . To sustain the compulsory flag salute, we are required to say that a Bill of Rights, which guards the individual's right to speak his own mind, left it open to public authorities to compel him to utter what is not in his mind."

Against this stood the *Gobitis* decision, which had "assumed" the state's power to impose the flag salute requirement on school children in general. The Court in the West Virginia case undertook to reexamine the existence of that power. In each instance it favored the individual citizen, stressing the limited nature of government under the Constitution.

(continued)

Supreme Court Case Study 22 (continued)

Regarding citizen versus state, the Court wrote that "the Fourteenth Amendment, as now applied to the States, protects the citizen against the State itself and all of its creatures—Boards of Education not excepted." In fact, Jackson explained, the "very purpose of a Bill of Rights was to withdraw certain subjects from the vicissitudes of political controversy, to place them beyond the reach of majorities and officials and to establish them as legal principles to be applied by the courts."

The state's power to regulate is properly applied to public utilities, where the legislature can impose any rational restrictions without fear of violating the due process clause. However, wrote Jackson, "freedoms of speech and of press, of assembly, and of worship may not be infringed on such slender grounds. They are susceptible of restriction only to prevent grave and immediate danger.... It is important to note that while it is the Fourteenth Amendment which bears directly upon the State it is the more specific limiting principles of the First Amendment that finally govern this case."

In conclusion, the Court dealt with what it called "the very heart of the *Gobitis* opinion"— "It reasons that 'national unity is the basis of national security,' that the authorities have 'the right to select appropriate means for its attainment,' and hence reaches the conclusion that such compulsory measures toward 'national unity' are constitutional." The Court, however, rejected that reasoning, holding instead that "to believe that patriotism will not flourish if patriotic ceremonies are voluntary and spontaneous instead of a compulsory routine is to make an unflattering estimate of the appeal of our institutions to free minds.... We think the action of the local authorities in compelling the flag salute and pledge transcends constitutional limitations on their power and invades the sphere of intellect and spirit which it is the purpose of the First Amendment to our Constitution to reserve from all official control."

DIRECTIONS: Answer the following questions on a separate sheet of paper.

1. According to the Court's decision in this case, what is the relationship of the principle of free speech to the flag salute?
2. Compare the Court's decision in this case to that of the *Gobitis* case.
3. Why does the Court believe that making a flag salute compulsory is not necessary to foster national unity?
4. The Court's decision mentions that freedom of speech and press may be restricted under certain circumstances. Give an example of such circumstances.
5. Why might a person who objects to the religious ideas of the Jehovah's Witnesses still support their rights under the First Amendment?

Supreme Court Case Study 23

Japanese Internment in World War II
Endo v. *United States*, 1944

★★★★★★★★★★★★★★★ **Background of the Case** ★★★★★★★★★★★★★★★

Early in 1942, a few months after the United States had been attacked at Pearl Harbor by Japanese airplanes, President Franklin D. Roosevelt issued an executive order, on the grounds of national security, authorizing the evacuation of Japanese Americans and other persons of Japanese descent from the Pacific Coast region. Thousands of people were then sent to relocation centers farther inland.

Mitsuye Endo, a United States citizen, was one of the thousands of persons of Japanese ancestry who were rounded up and transported to relocation camps. In July 1942 she filed a petition for a writ of habeas corpus in a federal district court "asking that she be discharged and restored to her liberty." She pointed out that "she was a loyal and law-abiding citizen of the United States, that no charge had been made against her, that she was being unlawfully detained, and that she was confined in the Relocation Center under armed guard and held there against her will." The district court denied her application for a writ of habeas corpus. Endo then appealed to a United States Court of Appeals; but before the appeal was heard, the United States Supreme Court took the case.

Constitutional Issue ★★★★★★★★★★★★★★★★★★★★★★★★★★★★★★★

The constitutionality of the government's relocation of United States citizens of Japanese ancestry was challenged and upheld by the Supreme Court in the *Korematsu* case. What the Court had not ruled on at that time was whether a loyal citizen of Japanese ancestry had the right to be released from a relocation center in order to return to his or her home in the evacuated region.

The Department of Justice conceded that Mitsuye Endo was a loyal and law-abiding citizen, and they made no claim that she was detained on any charge or that she was suspected of disloyalty, but they maintained that detention for an additional period after leave clearance was granted was essential to the evacuation program. Would the Supreme Court allow the continued detention of a Japanese American citizen and, if so, upon what grounds?

★★★★★★★★★★★★★★ **The Supreme Court's Decision** ★★★★★★★★★★★★★★

Without dissent the Court ruled that Endo, like all persons of Japanese ancestry whose loyalty to the United States had been established, could not be held in a relocation center and must be unconditionally released. The Court did not rule on the constitutional issues raised; instead, it held that the War Relocation Authority had exceeded its authority in detaining loyal Americans indefinitely.

Justice William O. Douglas wrote the opinion of the Court. In the opinion, Douglas took great pains to justify Endo's release without overruling the Court's recent approval of the general evacuation plan. Douglas wrote that "whatever power the War Relocation Authority may

(continued)

Supreme Court Case Study 23 (continued)

have to detain other classes of citizens, it has no authority to subject citizens who are concededly loyal...."

Douglas acknowledged that the Constitution gives the president and Congress broad discretion in times of war. But, Douglas said, "the Constitution is as specific in its enumeration of many of the civil rights of the individual as it is in its enumeration of the powers of ... government. Thus it has prescribed procedural safeguards surrounding the arrest, detention and conviction of individuals."

He continued, "We mention these constitutional provisions not to stir the constitutional issues which have been argued at the bar but to indicate the approach which we think should be made to an Act of Congress or an order of the Chief Executive that touches the sensitive area of rights specifically guaranteed by the Constitution."

Douglas maintained that, "In interpreting a war-time measure we must assume that their purpose was to allow for the greatest possible accommodation between those liberties and the exigencies of war. We must assume, when asked to find implied powers in a grant of legislative or executive authority, that the law makers intended to place no greater restraint on the citizen than was clearly and unmistakably indicated by the language they used.... A citizen who is concededly loyal presents no problem of espionage or sabotage. Loyalty is a matter of the heart and mind not of race, creed, or color. He who is loyal is by definition not a spy or a saboteur. When the power to detain is derived from the power to protect the war effort against espionage and sabotage, detention which has no relationship to that objective is unauthorized.... The authority to detain a citizen or grant him a conditional release as protection against espionage or sabotage is exhausted at least when his loyalty is conceded."

Justice Frank Murphy concurred in the Court's decision but strongly disagreed with its reasoning. He claimed the Court should have ruled earlier the entire evacuation program unconstitutional, in which case there would have been no question about releasing Endo.

Case Analysis Questions

DIRECTIONS: Answer the following questions on a separate sheet of paper.

1. What elements in Endo's background did the Court find most important in ordering her release?
2. Based on the Court's decision in the *Endo* case, on what grounds might other Japanese Americans have successfully sued for their release from the evacuation centers?
3. How did Justice Murphy's view of the case differ from that of Justice Douglas?
4. If you had been a member of the Supreme Court in the *Endo* case, would you have agreed with Justice Douglas's reasoning or with Justice Murphy's?
5. How do you think it was possible for Endo, interned in an evacuation center, to afford the costs of appealing first to the United States Court of Appeals and then to the Supreme Court?

Supreme Court Case Study 24

The Rights of People of Suspect Ethnic Backgrounds
Korematsu v. United States, 1944

★★★★★★★★★★★★★★ **Background of the Case** ★★★★★★★★★★★★★★

After the bombing of Pearl Harbor in December 1941 by Japanese planes, anti-Japanese sentiment on the West Coast rose to almost hysterical proportions. All people of Japanese ancestry, even citizens of the United States, were suspected of being pro-Japan, or worse—saboteurs and spies for Japan. Yielding to such sentiments, President Franklin D. Roosevelt issued an executive order that authorized the military to evacuate and relocate "all or any persons" in order to provide "protection against espionage and against sabotage to national defense. . . ." The military first set curfews on the West Coast for persons of Japanese ancestry. Later the military removed all persons of Japanese ancestry to war relocation centers. The order affected approximately 112,000 persons of Japanese ancestry, of whom about 70,000 were native-born American citizens. An act of Congress later reinforced the president's order by providing penalties for violations.

Korematsu, a Japanese American citizen, refused to leave his home in California for a relocation camp. He was convicted in a federal court. His appeal to a United States circuit court failed, and he then brought the case before the United States Supreme Court.

*C*onstitutional Issue ★★★★★★★★★★★★★★★★★★★★★★★★★★★★★

Since the president is commander in chief of the armed forces and Congress is given the power to declare war, was the executive order and its Congressional counterpart a constitutional exercise of the war power?

★★★★★★★★★★★★★ **The Supreme Court's Decision** ★★★★★★★★★★★★★★

The Court decided against Korematsu by a vote of 6 to 3. Justice Hugo Black wrote for the Court.

In 1943 the Court had upheld the government's position in a similar case, *Hirabayashi* v. *United States*. That case concerned the legality of the West Coast curfew order. In *Hirabayashi*, as well as in *Korematsu*, the Court's language pointed toward the necessity of giving the military the benefit of the doubt on the grounds of wartime necessity.

In the earlier case, the Court had held that "we cannot reject as unfounded the judgment of the military authorities and of Congress. . . ." Likewise, in the *Korematsu* case, the Court declared, "We are unable to conclude that it was beyond the war power of Congress and the Executive to exclude those of Japanese ancestry from the West Coast area at the time they did."

Justice Black cited evidence that, following internment, "approximately five thousand citizens of Japanese ancestry refused to swear unqualified allegiance to the United States and to renounce allegiance to the Japanese Emperor, and several thousand evacuees requested repatriation to Japan." Although the Court admitted awareness of the hardships internment imposed on American citizens, it stated "hardships are part of war. . . . Citizenship has its responsibilities as well as its privileges, and in time of war the burden is always heavier."

(continued)

Supreme Court Case Studies

Name _____ Date _____ Class _____

Supreme Court Case Study 24 (continued)

The question of racial prejudice "merely confuses the issue," said the Court. The true issues are related to determining "military dangers" and "military urgency." These issues demanded that citizens of Japanese ancestry be relocated by the military authorities. Black observed, "Congress, reposing its confidence in this time of war in our military leaders..., determined that they should have the power to do just this.... The need for action was great, and the time was short. We cannot—by availing ourselves of the calm perspective of hindsight—now say that at that time these actions were unjustified."

★★★★★★★★★★★★★★★★★★★ **Dissenting Opinions** ★★★★★★★★★★★★★★★★★★★

Justices Frank Murphy and Robert H. Jackson wrote separate dissents. Murphy called the Court's decision "legalization of racism." He objected particularly on the grounds that the Japanese Americans affected had been deprived of equal protection of the law as guaranteed by the Fifth Amendment. Further, Murphy wrote, as no provision had been made for hearings "this order also deprives them of all their constitutional rights to procedural due process." He saw no reason why the United States could not have done as Great Britain had done earlier in hearings during which about 74,000 German and Austrians residing in Britain were examined. Of these, only 2,000 had been interned.

In his dissent, Justice Jackson conceded that there might have been reasonable grounds for the internment orders. But, he wrote, "Even if they were permissible military procedures, I deny that it follows that they are constitutional.... A military commander may overstep the bounds of constitutionality, and it is an incident. But if we review and approve, that passing incident becomes the doctrine of the Constitution."

After the war, many people realized the injustice of the Court's decision. Finally, in 1988, Congress issued a formal apology to all internees and voted to give every survivor of the camps $20,000 in reparation.

DIRECTIONS: Answer the following questions on a separate sheet of paper.

1. On what constitutional basis did the Supreme Court deny Korematsu's appeal?

2. If you had been a native-born Japanese American in 1942, what do you think would have been your reaction to the internment order?

3. Justice Black became known as one of the staunchest defenders of the rights provided in the first ten amendments. Is his decision in the *Korematsu* case in keeping with his reputation?

4. What was the constitutional basis of Justice Murphy's dissent?

5. The Court's decision in the *Korematsu* case has been described as involving "the most alarming use of military authority in our nation's history." Do you think this description of the case is justified?

Supreme Court Case Study 25

Public Support for Non-Public Schools

Everson v. Board of Education, 1947

★★★★★★★★★★★★★★★ **Background of the Case** ★★★★★★★★★★★★★★★

A 1941 New Jersey law gave school districts the authority to provide transportation for children to and from private and parochial, as well as public, schools. The board of education for the township of Ewing, New Jersey, established a plan to reimburse parents for the cost of public transportation to and from these schools.

A local taxpayer, Everson, objected to having his tax money used to pay for transporting children to religious schools. A New Jersey district court ruled in Everson's favor, noting that the 1941 law was unconstitutional under the state constitution. However, New Jersey's highest court reversed the lower court's decision. Everson then appealed to the United States Supreme Court and the Court took the case to consider the First Amendment issues involved.

Constitutional Issue ★★★★★★★★★★★★★★★★★★★★★★★★★★★★★★★★

The First Amendment states that "Congress shall make no law respecting an establishment of religion, or prohibiting the free exercise thereof. . . ." The Court had previously ruled that the religion clauses apply to the states through the due process clause of the Fourteenth Amendment. Everson claimed that the New Jersey statute amounted to unlawful taxation in support of religion. Such action, he maintained, violated the establishment clause of the First Amendment.

★★★★★★★★★★★★★★ **The Supreme Court's Decision** ★★★★★★★★★★★★★★

The Court held by a 5 to 4 majority that the New Jersey law was constitutional. Justice Hugo Black wrote the majority decision. He interpreted the religious clause of the First Amendment to mean: "Neither a state nor the federal government can set up a church. Neither can pass laws which aid one religion over another. . . . No tax in any amount, large or small, can be levied to support any religious activities or institutions, whatever they may be called, or whatever form they may adopt to teach and practice religion." In the words of Jefferson, the clause against the establishment of religion by law was intended to erect 'a wall of separation between Church and State.'" However, said Justice Black, the wall had not been breached here.

Black then examined whether the New Jersey statute constituted unlawful taxation in support of religion. He also noted that the First Amendment prevents a state from hampering the free exercise of religion. He reasoned that if the statute provided only for "public welfare legislation" benefiting all citizens equally, then withholding those benefits would result in discrimination against religion. Tax subsidized bus fares, he concluded, fell into the same category as police and fire protection. Such benefits are available to the public as a whole. He went on, "The state contributes no money to the schools. It does not support them. Its legislation . . . does no more than provide a general program to help parents get their children, regardless of their religion, safely and expeditiously to and from accredited schools."

(continued)

Supreme Court Case Study 25 (continued)

Therefore, the New Jersey law was valid, since the First Amendment only "requires the state to be neutral in its relations with groups of religious believers and nonbelievers; it does not require the state to be their adversary. State power is no more to be used so as to handicap religions than it is to favor them."

★★★★★★★★★★★★★★★★★★★ **Dissenting Opinion** ★★★★★★★★★★★★★★★★★★★

Justice Wiley Rutledge disagreed with the Court's verdict. In his dissent, Rutledge wrote that the cost of transportation is no less a part of the cost of education or religious instruction than teachers or textbooks. He continued, "The very purpose of the state's contribution is to defray the cost of conveying the pupil to the place where he will receive not simply secular, but also and primarily religious teaching. . . ." On this ground the reimbursement for transportation costs is not allowable.

Justice Rutledge continued, quoting the writings of Presidents Madison and Jefferson often to support his argument that the New Jersey program could not be justified as a public safety expenditure. He considered the transportation to be aid to church-related schools.

In the view of Justice Rutledge, "It does not make the state unneutral to withhold what the Constitution forbids it to give. On the contrary, it is only by observing the prohibition rigidly that the state can maintain its neutrality and avoid partisanship. . . ."

DIRECTIONS: Answer the following questions on a separate sheet of paper.

1. What reasons did Justice Black give for supporting the constitutionality of the New Jersey law?
2. Do you think the Court's ruling allowed the state to pay for transportation to private, nonreligious schools?
3. On what principle did Justice Rutledge base his dissent?
4. Do you think Justice Black would have reached the same decision if the New Jersey law had provided for the state to pay part of the salaries of teachers in parochial schools? Explain your answer.
5. Do you agree with Justice Black's ruling or Justice Rutledge's dissent in this case? Give reasons for your answer.

Supreme Court Case Study 26

Released Time Religious Education in Public Schools
McCollum v. *Board of Education*, 1948

Background of the Case

The Board of Education in Champaign County, Illinois, permitted teachers of religion into the public schools to provide 30 to 45 minutes of weekly religious instruction for grades four through nine in public schools. Parents signed printed cards authorizing their children to attend these classes, and absences were reported to school authorities. Children who did not attend the religious instruction were not excused from their regular classes. The religion teachers were employed by the Champaign Council on Religious Education at no cost to the schools. Classes had originally been offered for Protestant, Catholic, and Jewish students. Similar programs were popular around the country in the 1940s. They were known as "released time programs."

Vashti McCollum, mother of a child in the Champaign school system, objected to the use of tax-supported school time and buildings for this purpose. She challenged the practice on the grounds that it violated the establishment clause of the First Amendment. A county court refused her petition to have these classes halted, and that decision was upheld by the Illinois Supreme Court. McCollum then appealed to the United States Supreme Court.

Only a year after its ruling in the *Everson* case, the Supreme Court was faced with another case involving religious education. The circumstances of these cases, however, were different. The same justice, Hugo L. Black, wrote both decisions.

Constitutional Issue

Did the Champaign program violate the First Amendment prohibition against any law regarding the establishment of religion as applied to the states through the Fourteenth Amendment?

The Supreme Court's Decision

The Court voted 8 to 1 in McCollum's favor. Justice Hugo L. Black wrote the majority opinion for the Court.

Justice Black went directly to the heart of the issue. He stated that the facts of the case "show the use of the tax-supported property for religious instruction and the close cooperation between the school authorities and the religious council in promoting religious education. . . . This is beyond all question a utilization of the tax-established and tax-supported public school system to aid religious groups to spread their faith. And it falls squarely under the ban of the First Amendment (made applicable to the States by the Fourteenth). . . ."

The Court denied that ruling for McCollum's claim would "manifest a governmental hostility to religion or religious teachings. . . . The First Amendment rests upon the premise that both religion and government can best work to achieve their lofty aims if each is left free from the other within its respective sphere."

(continued)

Supreme Court Case Studies

Supreme Court Case Study 26 (continued)

In a concurring opinion, Justice Felix Frankfurter wrote, "Religious education so conducted on school time and property is patently woven into the working scheme of the school. The Champaign arrangement thus presents powerful elements of inherent pressure by the school system in the interest of religious sects. The fact that this power has not been used to discriminate is beside the point. Separation is a requirement to abstain from fusing functions of Government and of religious sects, not merely to treat them all equally. That a child is offered an alternative may reduce the constraint. . . . [However,] the result is an obvious pressure upon children to attend."

Frankfurter continued, "Separation means separation, not something less. Jefferson's metaphor in describing the relation between Church and State speaks of a 'wall of separation,' not of a fine line easily overstepped. The public school is at once the symbol of our democracy and the most pervasive means for promoting our common destiny. In no activity of the State is it more vital to keep out divisive forces than in its schools, to avoid confusing, not to say fusing, what the Constitution sought to keep strictly apart."

Quoting the decision in the *Everson* case, Justice Frankfurter stated, "We renew our conviction that 'we have staked the very existence of our country on the faith that complete separation between the state and religion is best for the state and best for religion.'"

In another concurring opinion, Justice Robert Jackson pointed out that there was little real cost to the taxpayers in Champaign. He also agreed that the "formal and explicit instruction" of the Champaign schools should be ended. However, he cautioned that the Court might be flooded with petitions to rid public schools of materials that any group might regard as religious.

★★★★★★★★★★★★★★★★★★★ **Dissenting Opinion** ★★★★★★★★★★★★★★★★★★★

Justice Stanley Reed, the lone dissenter, had concurred in the *Everson* decision. Here he argued that the Court's interpretation of the First and Fourteenth Amendments was too strict. He agreed that the nation and the states were not to make law regarding establishment of religion, but he felt, "A state is entitled to have great leeway in its legislation when dealing with the important social problems of its populations. . . . Devotion to the great principle of religious liberty should not lead us into a rigid interpretation of the constitutional guarantee that conflicts with accepted habits of our people."

DIRECTIONS: Answer the following questions on a separate sheet of paper.

1. On what grounds did the Court declare the Champaign religious program unconstitutional?
2. What did Justice Frankfurter mean when he wrote that Thomas Jefferson's description of the relation between Church and State was a "wall of separation," not a fine line easily overstepped?
3. In Justice Reed's view, what should the Court take into account in ruling on religion cases?
4. If the Court voted so heavily to rule the Champaign practice unconstitutional, why do you think four of the nine justices concurred?
5. Do you agree with the Court's decision in this case? Explain.

Supreme Court Case Study 27

Rights of a Leader of the Communist Party

Dennis v. *United States*, 1951

★★★★★★★★★★★★★★ Background of the Case ★★★★★★★★★★★★★★★

Many Americans have had mixed feelings about whether political radicals such as Communists should have the free speech protection provided by the First Amendment, since their presumed purpose is to overthrow the United States government. This feeling was particularly prevalent in the 1940s and during the Cold War with the Soviet Union. American Communists were suspected of being agents of the Soviet Union, and in 1940 Congress enacted the Smith Act, which made it illegal to teach or advocate the violent overthrow of the United States government.

When the government convicted Communists under the Smith Act, the Supreme Court faced the challenge of deciding whether this law was constitutional. In 1949 Eugene Dennis and 10 co-defendants, all leaders of the United States Communist Party, were convicted of violating the Smith Act during a stormy, nine-month New York District Court trial.

In his instructions to the jury, the trial judge said that it would not be enough to convict the defendants if they had only taught or conspired to teach subversion. He instructed the jury that it must be satisfied that the defendants had an intent to cause the overthrow or destruction of the government of the United States by force and violence, and as speedily as circumstances would permit. The jury convicted the defendants of having violated the Smith Act. The defendants appealed their convictions to the United States Supreme Court, maintaining that their rights to freedom of speech had been compromised.

*C*onstitutional Issue ★★★★★★★★★★★★★★★★★★★★★★★★★★★★★★★★

The central questions in this case were these: Did the Smith Act unconstitutionally limit the rights of free press and speech under the First Amendment? Did the act conflict with the Fifth Amendment's guarantee of due process of law?

★★★★★★★★★★★★★★ The Supreme Court's Decision ★★★★★★★★★★★★★★★

The Court held 6 to 2 (one justice did not participate in deciding the case) that the Smith Act was constitutional. The majority opinion was written by Chief Justice Fred Vinson, although there were also two concurring opinions. The Court first supported the power of Congress to protect itself against rebellion, especially since "the existing structure of the government provides for peaceful and orderly change." The true question, however, "is not whether Congress has such *power*, but whether the *means* conflict with the First and Fifth Amendments to the Constitution."

The defendants had claimed that the Smith Act amounted to a prohibition even of academic discussion of Marxist or Communist thought. The Court rejected this contention, stating that the act "is directed at advocacy, not discussion."

At this point the Court's examination shifted to the circumstances under which free speech may be limited. The primary precedent case had been *Schenk* v. *United States* (1919), in which

(continued)

Supreme Court Case Study 27 (continued)

Justice Oliver Wendell Holmes had devised the "clear and present danger" test. Holmes had explained, the "question in every case is whether the words used are used in such circumstances and are of such a nature as to create a clear and present danger that they will bring about the substantive evils that Congress has a right to prevent."

Vinson now attempted to develop a more precise determination of the meaning of the clear and present danger principle. He cited the opinion of the first appeals of Judge Learned Hand, who wrote the majority opinion in this case when it was in the intermediate appellate court. Hand had interpreted the principle this way: "In each case [courts] must ask whether the gravity of the 'evil' discounted by its improbability, justifies such invasion of free speech as is necessary to avoid the danger." Hand adapted Holmes's principle to a test of "clear and probable danger." This principle made it easy for the Court to deal with the issues of conspiracy and advocacy. The Communist Party of the United States was characterized as a highly organized conspiracy, with rigidly disciplined members subject to call when the leaders felt that the time had come for action. In other words, the danger or threat of rebellion already existed, although no overt action had been taken yet. Vinson concluded that "this analysis disposes of the contention that a conspiracy to advocate, as distinguished from the advocacy itself, cannot be constitutionally restrained, because it compromises only presentation. It is the existence of the conspiracy which creates the danger. . . ."

★★★★★★★★★★★★★★★★★★★ **Dissenting Opinion** ★★★★★★★★★★★★★★★★★★★

Justices Hugo Black and William O. Douglas felt that the clear and present danger test had been destroyed by the majority decision. Douglas emphasized that the defendants had been charged with no overt acts. Rather, they had been charged only for their speeches and publications. He also felt that the matter of clear and present danger should have been decided by the trial court's jury and not by the Supreme Court.

DIRECTIONS: Answer the following questions on a separate sheet of paper.

1. What test did the Smith Act have to meet in order to be declared constitutional?
2. What was the main difference between Justice Vinson's opinion and the opinions of Justices Black and Douglas?
3. Suppose you had written an essay during the same time period as the *Dennis* case, in which you stated that you believed that the government of the United States should be overthrown. You did not show the essay to anyone, but someone found it among your papers. Do you think you would have been found guilty of violating the Smith Act? Explain.
4. Do you believe that people who belong to an organization whose objectives are clearly opposed to democratic principles are entitled to protection under the Constitution? Give reasons for your answer.
5. Ten years after the Court's *Dennis* decision, the Supreme Court unanimously set aside a conviction under the Smith Act of a member of the Communist Party. What reasons might the Court have given for its 1961 decision?

Supreme Court Case Study 28

Right of Free Speech

Feiner v. *New York*, 1951

★★★★★★★★★★★★★★★ **Background of the Case** ★★★★★★★★★★★★★★★

One evening in March 1949, Irving Feiner, a student at Syracuse University, was addressing an open-air meeting on a street corner in Syracuse, New York. Feiner spoke to a mixed race crowd of about 75 people. He denounced various national and local officials and reportedly sought "to arouse the Negro people against the whites, urging that they rise up in arms and fight for equal rights."

Two policemen, who had been watching from across the street, stepped in to urge people out of the path of traffic and back onto the sidewalk. After a while, the crowd became restless and unruly, and the officers believed that a fight was imminent. Some people in the crowd made comments to the officers about their inability to handle the crowd.

At least one person threatened violence if the police did not act. Several times over the next few minutes the police demanded that Feiner cease speaking. Feiner ignored them. Finally, the police arrested Feiner, charging him with disorderly conduct. He was later convicted by a local court. Two New York courts later upheld Feiner's conviction, after which Feiner took his case to the United States Supreme Court.

Constitutional Issue ★★★★★★★★★★★★★★★★★★★★★★★★★★★★★★

The First Amendment guarantees the right of free speech and is applicable to the states through the due process clause of the Fourteenth Amendment. The question for the Court to decide was whether the protection of these amendments prevents the police from interfering when they believe free speech threatens to incite listeners to violate public order.

★★★★★★★★★★★★★★ **The Supreme Court's Decision** ★★★★★★★★★★★★★★

Chief Justice Fred Vinson wrote for the 6 to 3 vote upholding Feiner's conviction as constitutional. The Court found the lower court records persuasive as to the threat of impending crowd disorder. The principle they applied was from a 1940 case in which the Court declared: "When clear and present danger of riot, disorder, interference with traffic upon the public streets, or other immediate threat to public safety, peace, or order appears, the power of the state to prevent or punish is obvious."

In agreeing with the lower courts' finding, Vinson wrote, "It is one thing to say that the police cannot be used as an instrument for the suppression of unpopular views, and another to say that, when as here the speaker passes the bounds of argument or persuasion and undertakes incitement to riot, they are powerless to prevent a breach of the peace. Nor in this case can we condemn the considered judgment of two New York courts approving the means which the police, faced with crisis, used in the exercise of their power and duty to preserve peace and order. The findings of the state courts as to the existing situation and the imminence

(continued)

Name _____ Date _____ Class _____

Supreme Court Case Study 28 *(continued)*

of greater disorder coupled with the petitioner's deliberate defiance of the police officers convince us that we should not reverse this conviction in the name of free speech."

The Court said it was well aware of the dangers of allowing a hostile audience to prevent someone from speaking and is "also mindful of the possible danger of giving overzealous police officials complete discretion to break up otherwise lawful public meetings." Nevertheless, Vinson wrote, the Court was unwilling to rule that the police had not properly used their power to preserve order in this instance.

★★★★★★★★★★★★★★★★★★ **Dissenting Opinions** ★★★★★★★★★★★★★★★★★★★

Justices Hugo Black and William O. Douglas (joined by Justice Sherman Minton) wrote dissenting opinions on largely identical grounds. Both thought, in Black's words, that "if, in the name of preserving order, [the police] ever can interfere with a lawful public speaker, they first must make all reasonable efforts to protect him. . . . Their duty was to protect the petitioner's right to talk. . . . Instead, they shirked that duty and acted only to suppress the right to speak." In a strong statement against the Court's ruling, Black wrote, "I think this conviction makes a mockery of the free speech guarantees of the First and Fourteenth Amendments. The end result . . . is to approve a simple and readily available technique by which cities and states can with impunity subject all speeches, political or otherwise, on streets or elsewhere, to the supervision and censorship of the local police. I will have no part or parcel in this holding which I view as a long step toward totalitarian authority."

Justice Douglas argued in his dissent that, "A speaker may not, of course, incite a riot. . . . It is against that kind of threat that speakers need police protection (i.e., against an unsympathetic audience.) If they do not receive it and instead the police throw their weight on the side of those who would break up the meetings, the police become the new censors of speech. But this record shows no such extremes. It shows an unsympathetic audience and the threat of one man to haul the speaker from the stage."

DIRECTIONS: Answer the following questions on a separate sheet of paper.

1. How did Justice Vinson justify the action of the police?

2. What danger did Justice Black see in the Court's decision?

3. Do you agree with Justice Vinson's ruling or the dissents of Justice Douglas and Justice Black? Give reasons for your opinion.

4. If you had been one of the police officers who was present while Feiner was speaking, what should you have done, according to Justice Black?

5. How might the Court's decision affect how speakers at street meetings conduct themselves?

Supreme Court Case Study 29

Nullifying the Separate but Equal Principle

Brown v. Board of Education of Topeka, Kansas, 1954

★★★★★★★★★★★★★★★ **Background of the Case** ★★★★★★★★★★★★★★★

Linda Brown, an African American teenager, applied for admission to an all-white public school in Topeka, Kansas. The board of education of Topeka refused to admit her. In a 1950 case, *Sweatt* v. *Painter*, the Supreme Court had for the first time questioned the constitutionality of the *Plessy* decision. The Court had held in that case that African Americans must be admitted to the previously segregated University of Texas Law School because no separate but equal facilities existed in Texas. The National Association for the Advancement of Colored People (NAACP) now saw denying admission to Linda Brown and other young African Americans as an opportunity to challenge segregation in the public schools, even though the facilities in other segregated schools for African Americans were equal to those for white students.

Brown represents a collection of four cases, all decided at one time. The cases had one common feature: African American children had been denied admission to segregated, all-white public schools. The cases reached the United States Supreme Court by way of appeals through lower courts, all of which had ruled in accordance with the 1896 *Plessy* decision.

Constitutional Issue ★★★★★★★★★★★★★★★★★★★★★★★★★★★★

The *Brown* case called for an explicit reappraisal of the *Plessy* decision. Did separate but equal public facilities violate the equal protection clause of the Fourteenth Amendment? In the case of *Plessy* v. *Ferguson*, the Supreme Court had established the separate but equal principle, which allowed the continuation of segregated schools and public facilities. During the 56 years since the *Plessy* decision, however, Americans' views on segregation had changed. To many people, the very idea of segregated schools as well as other segregated public facilities seemed to be out of step with the times. In the years after World War II, the NAACP and other civil rights groups began pressing for nullification of the separate but equal idea. The justices were not immune to the changing social forces in the United States. Still, if in fact they wished to overturn *Plessy* in the *Brown* case, they faced the challenge of finding a constitutional basis for their decision.

★★★★★★★★★★★★★★★ **The Supreme Court's Decision** ★★★★★★★★★★★★★★★

The Court ruled unanimously to overrule the separate but equal principle. Chief Justice Earl Warren, who wrote the decision, was keenly aware that in overruling *Plessy*, an act of enormous social and political consequences, it was important for the entire Court to be in agreement. The *Brown* ruling was thus issued by a unanimous Court.

In his decision, Warren explained that since the relation of the Fourteenth Amendment to public schools was difficult to determine, the Court would "look instead to the effect of segregation itself on public education." The chief justice explained, "We must consider public education in the light of its full development and its present place in American life

(continued)

Supreme Court Case Study 29 (continued)

throughout the Nation. Only in this way can it be determined if segregation in public schools deprives these plaintiffs of the equal protection of the law."

The Court concluded that segregation of African American schoolchildren "generates a feeling of inferiority as to their status in the community that may affect their hearts and minds in a way unlikely ever to be undone." To bolster his claim about the huge psychological impact of segregation, Warren quoted the finding of a lower court, even though the lower court ruled against the African American children. That court had stated: "Segregation of white and colored children in public schools has a detrimental effect upon the colored children. The impact is greater when it has the sanction of the law; for the policy of separating the races is usually interpreted as denoting the inferiority of the Negro group. A sense of inferiority affects the motivation of a child to learn. Segregation with the sanction of law, therefore, has the tendency to [retard] the education and mental development of Negro children and to deprive them of some of the benefits they would receive in a racially integrated school system."

Agreeing with this statement, Warren concluded, "Whatever may have been the extent of psychological knowledge at the time of *Plessy* v. *Ferguson*, this finding is amply supported by modern authority. Any language in *Plessy* v. *Ferguson* contrary to this finding is rejected."

On this basis the Court concluded "that in the field of public education the doctrine of 'separate but equal' has no place. Separate educational facilities are inherently unequal. Therefore we hold that the plaintiffs and others similarly situated for whom the actions have been brought are, by reason of the segregation complained of, deprived of the equal protection of the law guaranteed by the Fourteenth Amendment. This disposition makes unnecessary any discussion whether such segregation also violates the due process clause of the Fourteenth Amendment."

In a follow-up to the *Brown* case, in 1955 the Court ordered that the integration of the public schools was to go forward "with all deliberate speed."

DIRECTIONS: Answer the following questions on a separate sheet of paper.

1. Why do you think the Court recognized the huge psychological impact that segregated schools had on children who attended them?
2. A constitutional scholar has called the Court's ruling in the *Brown* case "the Supreme Court's most important decision of the twentieth century." Why do you think he would make this claim?
3. Do you agree or disagree with the Court's ruling in the *Brown* case? Give reasons for your answer.
4. How do you think the Court's *Brown* ruling was received in the South?
5. Initially all the justices may not have agreed that separate but equal schools were unconstitutional. Why then do you think they ultimately agreed with the chief justice?

Supreme Court Case Study 30

Rights of Communists

Yates v. *United States*, 1957

★★★★★★★★★★★★★★ **Background of the Case** ★★★★★★★★★★★★★★

The rights of Communists to the freedoms of the Bill of Rights was a persistent question that troubled the public in the 1950s. In *Dennis* v. *United States* (1951), the Supreme Court had ruled that Dennis and other Communists had been guilty of conspiracy under the Smith Act. Between 1951 and 1956, convictions were obtained in every Communist case brought to trial. With the *Yates* case, the Supreme Court took the opportunity to reexamine its policy on Communists.

Oleta O'Connor Yates was one of 14 leaders of the Communist Party in California. All were charged under the Smith Act of 1940 with conspiracy to teach and advocate the violent overthrow of the United States government and with organizing the Communist Party for that purpose. All were found guilty, fined $10,000, and sentenced to five years in prison. They appealed their convictions to the federal courts, which upheld the trial court's judgment. However, the United States Supreme Court agreed to review their convictions (grouped under Yates's name) in order to reexamine and refine its decision in the 1951 *Dennis* case.

Constitutional Issue ★★★★★★★★★★★★★★★★★★★★★★★★★★★★★★★★

The *Dennis* case had focused on a substantially identical question of Communist Party violations of the Smith Act. The Court had held that the Smith Act did not violate First Amendment protections of speech and press. Furthermore, the Court had concluded in *Dennis* that the defendants' purpose had been the ultimate overthrow of the United States government by force. The mere fact that they had not yet put their plans into action was not considered a defense.

The *Dennis* decision had been generally understood to be a modification of the 1919 *Schenk* v. *United States* case, which had held that First Amendment protection needed to be weighed against "clear and present danger" to the government. The *Dennis* case had modified this to consider whether or not some danger was not only present but also probable.

The precise question at issue, then, was whether or not advocating violent overthrow of the government was prohibited. Did advocacy have to be accompanied by actual incitement to action in order to override the First Amendment protections?

★★★★★★★★★★★★★★ **The Supreme Court's Decision** ★★★★★★★★★★★★★★

The Court reversed all the original convictions in the *Yates* case on constitutional grounds. However, based on the Court's review of the original trial record, five defendants were cleared and new trials were ordered for the other nine. Justice John Marshall Harlan wrote for the majority.

(continued)

Name _____ Date _____ Class _____

Supreme Court Case Study 30 *(continued)*

Harlan's opinion centered on the trial judge's instructions to the jury. The judge had not informed the jury of the necessity to prove that any advocacy to overthrow the government had also intended to incite people to take such action. Both the prosecution and defense had suggested such instructions, but the trial judge had rejected the suggestions on the grounds that the decision made in the *Dennis* case made this unnecessary. In other words, the trial judge had interpreted the *Dennis* decision as requiring only that intent to forcibly overthrow the government needed to be shown and that it was unnecessary to prove actual incitement to action. Justice Harlan wrote, "we are thus faced with the question whether the Smith Act prohibits advocacy and teaching of forcible overthrow as an abstract principle, divorced from any effort to instigate action to that end, so long as such advocacy or teaching is engaged in with evil intent. We hold that it does not."

The Court found that "the legislative history of the Smith Act and related bills shows beyond all question that Congress was aware of the distinction between the advocacy or teaching of abstract doctrine and the advocacy or teaching of action, and that it did not intend to disregard it. The statute was aimed at the advocacy and teaching of concrete action . . . and not of principles divorced from action."

The Court defined the distinction between *Dennis* and *Yates*. In *Dennis* "advocacy was aimed at building up a seditious group and maintaining it in readiness for action at a propitious time." The district judge in the *Yates* case had been under the impression that "mere doctrinal justification of forcible overthrow, if engaged in with the intent to accomplish overthrow, is punishable per se under the Smith Act." Harlan called the latter "too remote from concrete action" to fall under the standard announced in *Dennis*. "The essential distinction is that those to whom the advocacy is addressed must be urged to *do* something, now or in the future, rather than merely to *believe* in something." The Court recognized that these distinctions "are often subtle and difficult to grasp." For that very reason, the trial judge ought to have given more adequate instructions to the jury.

It should be noted that the *Yates* decision, although it claims not to overturn the *Dennis* decision, was effectively understood as having signaled a return to the pre-*Dennis* standard that "clear and present danger" must always be proved before First Amendment rights can be limited. By virtue of the *Yates* decision, the Court, in the words of a constitutional scholar, "erected a stern new standard for evaluating convictions under the Smith Act, making conviction under the measure difficult."

DIRECTIONS: Answer the following questions on a separate sheet of paper.

1. What is the difference between advocacy of a cause and incitement to action?
2. Why did the Court hold that the trial judge had erred in his instructions to the jury?
3. How did the Court's decision in the *Yates* case differ from its decision in the *Dennis* case?
4. What was the outcome of the Court's *Yates* decision?
5. Do you think the Court made the right decision in the *Yates* case? Give reasons for your answer.

Supreme Court Case Study 31

Congress's Power to Punish

Barenblatt v. United States, 1959

★★★★★★★★★★★★★★ **Background of the Case** ★★★★★★★★★★★★★★

In 1938 Congress set up a House committee to investigate un-American activities. The committee directed most of its efforts at unmasking left-wing groups and individuals. In 1946 the Senate authorized a competing committee, the Senate Judiciary Committee. It quickly overshadowed the House committee, but the actions of both committees alarmed civil libertarians. Witnesses were browbeaten, denied the opportunity to examine charges of so-called subversive conduct, and denied the right of cross-examination.

Many witnesses felt that any statement they made might incriminate them; they refused to testify against themselves. The committees assumed that persons pleading Fifth Amendment protection were guilty, labeling them "Fifth Amendment Communists." Ten prominent Hollywood figures refused to testify and were jailed for contempt of Congress.

Neither the House nor the Senate committees made any effort to introduce legislation related to their investigations. When this issue arose in the case of *Watkins* v. *United States* (1957), the Court held that "there is no congressional power to expose for the sake of exposure."

As part of the House Un-American Activities Committee's investigation into education, the committee called Lloyd Barenblatt, a professor of psychology at Vassar College from 1950 until shortly before his appearance before the committee in 1954. A friend had identified Barenblatt as a Communist. Barenblatt appeared but refused to answer questions about his Communist affiliation. He contended that the committee's charge, as set forth by the House, was vague. He argued further that the questions posed to him by the committee violated his First Amendment right of free speech.

Barenblatt was found guilty of refusing to answer pertinent questions and sentenced to six months in a federal penitentiary and fined $250. The Supreme Court reviewed his conviction.

𝒞onstitutional Issue ★★★★★★★★★★★★★★★★★★★★★★★★★★★★★★

The case involved several issues. First, did the committee have the right to compel testimony and punish those who refused to testify? Second, was the witness's First Amendment right of free speech breached? Third, did the House committee have the right to investigate for the sake of investigation rather than for the purpose of drafting legislation?

★★★★★★★★★★★★★ **The Supreme Court's Decision** ★★★★★★★★★★★★★★

The Court ruled 5 to 4 against Barenblatt. Justice John Marshall Harlan wrote the majority opinion. The Court followed the *Watkins* approach of denouncing Congress's power "to expose for the sake of exposure" and the requirement that a committee of Congress have a legislative purpose in its investigations. However, it assumed that the committee, as a branch of Congress, did have such a purpose. Justice Harlan held that the Court could not agree with Barenblatt's contention that the vagueness of the rule setting up the committee deprived it of the right to

(continued)

Supreme Court Case Study 31 (continued)

compel testimony. He said the House "has steadily continued the life of the Committee ... and has continuingly supported the Committee's activities with substantial appropriations" and noted that the "Committee was raised to the level of a standing committee of the House in 1945."

As to Barenblatt's First Amendment rights, Harlan wrote that "the protections of the First Amendment, unlike a proper claim of the privilege against self-incrimination under the Fifth Amendment, do not afford a witness the right to resist inquiry in all circumstances. Where First Amendment rights are asserted to bar governmental interrogation, resolution of the issue always involves a balancing by the courts of the competing private and public interests at stake in the particular circumstances shown.... We conclude that the balance between the individual and the governmental interests here at stake must be struck in favor of the latter, and that therefore the provisions of the First Amendment have not been offended."

★★★★★★★★★★★★★★★★★★★ **Dissenting Opinions** ★★★★★★★★★★★★★★★★★★★★

Two dissenting opinions were presented. Justice Hugo L. Black's dissent was concurred with by Chief Justice Earl Warren and Justice William O. Douglas. Black dissented on these grounds: First, that the term "un-American" in the committee's mission was so vague as to make the committee's mandate void under the due process clause of the Fourteenth Amendment. Second, the Court's "balancing test" as to the applicability of First Amendment rights was not the way to determine the scope of freedom of speech, and if it were, the Court should have balanced the interest of society in "being able to join organizations, advocate causes and make political 'mistakes' " against the government's limited interest in making laws in the area of free speech...." Third, "the chief aim, purpose, and practice of the House Un-American Activities Committee ... is to try witnesses and punish them because they are or have been Communists or because they refuse or admit or deny Communist affiliations."

Justice William J. Brennan, also dissenting, wrote, "... no purpose for the investigation of Barenblatt is revealed by the record except exposure purely for the sake of exposure. This is not the purpose to which Barenblatt's rights under the First Amendment can validly be subordinated. An investigation in which the processes of law-making and law-evaluating are submerged entirely in exposure of individual behavior—in adjudication, of a sort, through the exposure process—is outside the constitutional pale of congressional inquiry."

DIRECTIONS: Answer the following questions on a separate sheet of paper.

1. On what grounds did the Court reject Barenblatt's claim that he had been deprived of his First Amendment rights?

2. How did the Court defend the House committee's purpose against Barenblatt's charge of vagueness?

3. On what issue did all the dissenting justices agree?

4. After the Court's decision, would the House committee have to modify its procedures? Explain.

5. Do you agree with the Court's decision or with the dissenting justices' criticisms? Explain.

Supreme Court Case Study 32

The Legality of Evidence Seized by the Police
Mapp v. *Ohio*, 1961

★★★★★★★★★★★★★★ Background of the Case ★★★★★★★★★★★★★★★

In May 1957, three police officers arrived at Dollree Mapp's home after having received a tip that a fugitive had hidden there. Mapp, who had phoned her attorney, refused to admit the police officers. They notified their headquarters, and the officers began their surveillance of the house.

Three hours later four more police officers arrived. They knocked on the door, and when Mapp did not immediately answer, they forced the door and entered. Mapp demanded to see a search warrant. One of the officers held up a piece of paper, claiming it was the warrant. Mapp snatched the paper and stuffed it into her blouse. After a scuffle, the officers recovered the paper and handcuffed Mapp.

While this was transpiring, Mapp's attorney arrived, but the police refused to let him enter the house or have access to his client. The police then began to search the house. They did not find a fugitive in the house; however, in the course of their search which covered the entire residence, they turned up some material they deemed obscene. Mapp was charged and eventually convicted of having lewd and lascivious books and pictures in her possession, a violation of an Ohio statute.

At her trial, the state produced no search warrant, but the failure to produce one went unexplained. Mapp was convicted of having violated the Ohio law. On appeal, the Ohio Supreme Court upheld the conviction even though the evidence against her had been illegally seized. Mapp appealed her case to the United States Supreme Court.

*C*onstitutional Issue ★★★★★★★★★★★★★★★★★★★★★★★★★★★★★★★★★

Suppose the police arrive at your house in response to a call reporting an intruder. While looking for the reported intruder, the police undertake, without a warrant, a search of dresser drawers in various bedrooms where they find a supply of illegal drugs. Can this evidence be introduced at your trial on charges of drug possession? This question involves what has been called the "exclusionary rule"—that is, a rule that evidence seized in violation of a person's constitutional rights may not be used against that person in a trial.

In *Wolf* v. *Colorado* (1949), a case similar to the *Mapp* case, the Supreme Court had recognized that the Fourth Amendment embodies the right of an individual to privacy but declined to forbid illegally seized evidence from being used at trial. Since the 1914 decision in *Weeks* v. *United States*, illegally seized evidence could not be used in federal courts. The issue in the *Mapp* case was whether or not the exclusionary rule of *Weeks*, applied to the states through the Fourteenth Amendment, also prohibited illegally seized evidence in state courts.

(continued)

Supreme Court Case Study 32 (continued)

★★★★★★★★★★★★★ The Supreme Court's Decision ★★★★★★★★★★★★★★

The Court voted 6 to 3 to reverse the Ohio Supreme Court's decision. Justice Tom C. Clark wrote for the majority:

"In extending the substantive protection of due process to all constitutionally unreasonable searches—state or federal—it was logically and constitutionally necessary that the exclusion doctrine—an essential part of the right to privacy—be also insisted upon. . . . In other words, privacy without the exclusionary rule would be a hollow right. . . ." The Court held that this right could not continue to tolerate the admission of unlawfully seized evidence.

The *Mapp* decision was seen by the Court as the end of a double standard by which "a federal prosecutor may make no use of evidence illegally seized, but a State's attorney across the street may. . . ." Justice Clark wrote that this decision also ended an unfortunate situation in which "the State, by admitting evidence unlawfully seized, serves to encourage disobedience to the Federal Constitution which it is bound to uphold."

Clark was aware that the Court's ruling would sometimes result in criminals going free because of an error on the part of the police. To this possibility he responded, "The criminal goes free, if he must, but it is the law that sets him free. Nothing can destroy a government more quickly than its failure to observe its own laws, or worse, its disregard of the charter of its own existence."

★★★★★★★★★★★★★★★★★★★ Dissenting Opinions ★★★★★★★★★★★★★★★★★★★★

Justice John Marshall Harlan dissented. He doubted the federal exclusionary rule was constitutional and suggested that, under federalism, court remedies for illegally seized evidence should be left to the states.

DIRECTIONS: Answer the following questions on a separate sheet of paper.

1. According to the Court's decision, why may illegally seized evidence not be used in a trial?
2. Why, according to Justice Clark, is it better for a criminal to go free than to convict the criminal with illegally seized evidence?
3. What was the illegally seized evidence in the *Mapp* case?
4. What was the "double standard" referred to in the Court's decision?
5. Do you agree with the Court's decision in the *Mapp* case? Give reasons for your answer.

Supreme Court Case Study 33

The Court's Role in State Apportionment
Baker v. *Carr*, 1962

★★★★★★★★★★★★★★ Background of the Case ★★★★★★★★★★★★★★

One issue throughout the history of the Supreme Court is that of how far the federal government may infringe on state matters. Early on, the Court was reluctant to allow federal authorities to "intrude" in state matters. However, for a considerable period of time in the 1900s, the issue was decided in favor of the federal government.

The constitution of the state of Tennessee provided for reapportionment of state legislative districts every ten years based on the United States census. Many people of Tennessee had moved from rural to urban and suburban districts since 1901, but no redistricting had been done. Voters in city districts felt they were second-class citizens whose needs were being neglected by the state legislature.

In 1959 Baker brought suit on his own behalf and that of other Tennessee voters to force reapportionment. He sued various Tennessee state officials in federal court for relief from denial of equal protection of the law under the Fourteenth Amendment. The court dismissed the case because it presented a political question beyond the competence of the judiciary.

*C*onstitutional Issue ★★★★★★★★★★★★★★★★★★★★★★★★★★★★★

The central issue in the *Baker* case concerned the applicability of Article III, Section 2, of the Constitution, which deals with the power of the federal courts. The question the Supreme Court had to resolve was whether federal courts had jurisdiction to consider cases of state reapportionment.

★★★★★★★★★★★★★★ The Supreme Court's Decision ★★★★★★★★★★★★★★

The Court voted 6 to 2 (one justice did not participate in the decision) in favor of the federal district's jurisdiction. Justice William Brennan wrote the decision of the Court. He dealt simply with the question of jurisdiction. The federal district court had claimed it had no jurisdiction because the case would involve impermissible political questions. Since no political questions were present, the matter therefore had to be subject to judicial inquiry—it qualified as a case or controversy arising under the Constitution in accord with Article III, Section 2.

In addition, Brennan explained, the matter under consideration was justiciable—that is, the subject of the case was something that could be decided by a court. "The mere fact that the suit seeks protection of a political right," Brennan noted, "does not mean it presents a political question."

Brennan gave as examples of nonjusticiable political questions matters concerning Native American nations, foreign relations, and, in general, matters that are properly the concern of the executive or legislative branches under the separation of powers.

(continued)

Supreme Court Case Study 33 *(continued)*

"The question here," Brennan went on to state, "is the consistency of state action with the Federal Constitution. We have no question decided, or to be decided, by a political branch of government co-equal with this Court. . . . Nor need the appellants, in order to succeed in this action, ask the Court to enter upon policy determinations for which the judicially manageable standards are lacking. Judicial standards under the equal protection clause are well-developed and familiar. . . ."

★★★★★★★★★★★★★★★★★★ Dissenting Opinion ★★★★★★★★★★★★★★★★★★

Justice Felix Frankfurter wrote a vigorous dissenting opinion. He wrote, "In effect, today's decision empowers the courts of the country to devise what should constitute the proper composition of the legislatures of the fifty states." He said that if the state courts could not solve this question, the ruling in this case now made the Supreme Court ultimately the decision-maker in such cases.

He went on, "The Framers carefully and with deliberate forethought refused to so enthrone the judiciary. In this situation . . . appeal for relief does not belong here. Appeal must be to an informed, civically militant electorate." In summary, Frankfurter felt that the Supreme Court should not be the source of decisions about state legislative reapportionment. He felt that there was no constitutional justification for the Court's decision in this case and that the ruling would send the lower courts into a "mathematical quagmire."

Chief Justice Warren called the *Baker* case the most important of the Warren court. The decision was the first to hold that federal courts could hear suits challenging voting district apportionment, and in a short time thirty-nine states started legal action to challenge local apportionment practices.

DIRECTIONS: Answer the following questions on a separate sheet of paper.

1. On what grounds did the Supreme Court claim it had a right to rule in the *Baker* case?

2. What practice did the *Baker* decision address?

3. If you felt that the legislature in your state did not reflect the population distribution of the state, what did the *Baker* decision say you could successfully do?

4. Do you agree with Justice Brennan's majority opinion or Justice Frankfurter's dissent? Give reasons for your answer.

5. Why do you think Chief Justice Warren called the *Baker* decision the most important of his court?

Name _____ Date _____ Class _____

Supreme Court Case Study 34

Constitutionality of Prayer in Public Schools

Engel v. *Vitale*, 1962

★★★★★★★★★★★★★★ **Background of the Case** ★★★★★★★★★★★★★★

In the early years of the country, prayers in schools had been considered a legitimate, even essential, part of education. Since most of the students were of the same religion, there was no question about the appropriateness of prayer in the schools. However, as the population became more diversified, questions began to be raised as to the legality of this practice. Civil libertarians were prominent in the move to abolish prayer in the schools.

In 1951 the New York State Board of Regents, which supervises the state's public school system, approved a brief prayer at the start of each day. The prayer read: "Almighty God, we acknowledge our dependence upon Thee, and we beg Thy blessings upon us, our parents, our teachers, and our Country." School districts were not required to use the prayer, and students were not required to recite it. In 1958 the New Hyde Park school board adopted the prayer and directed that it be recited each day in every class, although students could be excused from reciting it.

Steven Engel, the parent of two children in the New Hyde Park schools, objected to this practice and asked a state court to order the prayer dropped. Engel directed his suit against the head of the school board, William J. Vitale, Jr. The state court and the New York Court of Appeals refused to enjoin—prohibit—recitation of the prayer. Engel then appealed to the United States Supreme Court. The question before the Court was whether the daily prayer, although noncompulsory, violated the First Amendment.

Constitutional Issue ★★★★★★★★★★★★★★★★★★★★★★★★★★★★★★★

The First Amendment, applied to the states through the due process clause of the Fourteenth Amendment, prohibits laws respecting the establishment of religion. Did the daily prayer of New York State schools, although noncompulsory, violate the establishment clause?

★★★★★★★★★★★★★★ **The Supreme Court's Decision** ★★★★★★★★★★★★★★

The Court ruled in Engel's favor 6 to 1. (Two justices did not participate in the decision.) Justice Hugo Black wrote the majority opinion.

No one had contested the fact that the prayer was essentially religious. The school board had argued, however, that it was permissible because it was "nondenominational"—that is, that it did not relate to any particular religious group. Furthermore, Vitale had noted that no student was compelled either to say the prayer or to remain in the classroom while it was being recited.

The Court disagreed, calling the practice "wholly inconsistent with the establishment clause." It held that a prayer "composed by government officials as part of a governmental program to further religious beliefs . . . breaches the constitutional wall of separation between Church and State." Neither the nondenominational nature of the prayer nor the fact that it was not compulsory could save it from unconstitutionality under the establishment clause.

(continued)

Supreme Court Case Study 34 (continued)

Black pointed out, "It is a matter of history that this very practice of establishing governmentally composed prayers for religious services was one of the reasons which caused many of our early colonists to leave England and seek religious freedom in America." He went on, "Under that [First] Amendment's prohibition . . . government in this country . . . is without power to prescribe any particular form of prayer which is to be used as an official prayer in carrying on any program of governmentally sponsored religious activity."

Black specified several purposes of the establishment clause. Among them, the clause sought (a) to prevent the "union of government and religion [which] tends to destroy government and to degrade religion"; (b) to express the principle "that religion is too personal, too sacred, too holy, to permit its 'unhallowed perversion' by a civil magistrate"; and (c) to prevent religious persecutions which have historically arisen from governmentally established religions.

The nation, the Constitution, and the Bill of Rights were all established in order to avoid these sorts of problems, Black concluded. Therefore, "the New York laws officially prescribing the Regents' prayer are inconsistent both with the purposes of the establishment clause and with the establishment clause itself."

★★★★★★★★★★★★★★★★★★★ **Dissenting Opinion** ★★★★★★★★★★★★★★★★★★★

Justice Potter Stewart challenged the Court's reasoning in the case. He wrote, "The Court does not hold, nor could it, that New York has interfered with the free exercise of anybody's religion. For the state courts have made it clear that those who object to reciting the prayer may be entirely free of any compulsion to do so, including any 'embarrassments and pressures.' . . . But the Court says that in permitting schoolchildren to say this simple prayer, the New York authorities have established 'an official religion.' With all respect, I think the Court has misapplied a great constitutional principle. I cannot see how an official religion is established by letting those who want to say a prayer say it." He went on, "On the contrary, I think that to deny the wish of these schoolchildren to join in reciting this prayer is to deny them the opportunity of sharing in the spiritual heritage of our Nation."

The Court's decision provoked widespread controversy. Civil libertarians hailed it as a victory. Conservatives attacked it vigorously. One member of Congress from Alabama asserted, "They put the Negroes in the schools [in the *Brown* case]. Now they have driven God out."

Case Analysis Questions

DIRECTIONS: Answer the following questions on a separate sheet of paper.

1. On what basis did the majority of court justices find school prayer unconstitutional?
2. Do you agree with Justice Black's opinion or with Justice Stewart's? Give reasons for your answer.
3. What was the New Hyde Park school district required to do after the Court's decision?
4. United States coins and paper money carry the phrase "In God We Trust." Does this inscription violate the principle of separation of Church and State? Explain your answer.
5. Almost all public schools are closed during certain religious holidays, such as Christmas and Easter. Do you think the *Engel* decision should apply to this custom?

Name _____ Date _____ Class _____

Supreme Court Case Study 35

Constitutionality of Bible Reading in the Public School

Abington School District v. *Schempp*, 1963

★★★★★★★★★★★★★★★ **Background of the Case** ★★★★★★★★★★★★★★★

Two cases were decided in one opinion: *Abington School District* v. *Schempp* and *Murray* v. *Curlett*. In the *Abington* case, Pennsylvania law required that "at least ten verses from the Holy Bible shall be read, without comment, at the opening of each school day. Any child shall be excused from such Bible reading . . . upon written request of his parent or guardian."

Two children of the Schempp family, who were Unitarians, were enrolled in Abington public schools. The Schempps objected to the readings because Unitarians do not believe that the Bible is always intelligible when read literally. Further, they objected to having their children sent out into the hallway during readings. They claimed that Bible reading violated their rights under the free exercise clause of the First Amendment and brought suit to have the practice abandoned. A federal district court sided with the Schempps and found Pennsylvania's law unconstitutional.

In the *Murray* case, Madalyn Murray and her son William Murray III objected to a Baltimore, Maryland, school board ruling that allowed daily readings of a Bible chapter or the Lord's Prayer in the classroom. The local statute was in accord with a state law at the time. The Murrays objected, as atheists, to the doctrine of God as the "source of all moral and spiritual values," and to the Bible itself, which they characterized as "nauseating, historically inaccurate, replete with the ravings of madmen." They also contended that the practice of religious reading violated their liberty of conscience by placing a premium on belief as opposed to non-belief.

A Maryland appeals court supported the school board. The state's highest court supported this ruling, whereupon the Murrays asked the United States Supreme Court to review their case.

*C*onstitutional Issue ★★★★★★★★★★★★★★★★★★★★★★★★★★★★★

During the *Engel* case the Court had decided that a religious prayer had no place in public schools. However, reading the Bible in schools had been a common practice for many years. Now the Court had to decide on the constitutionality of Bible reading in public schools.

The issue in both cases was whether the First Amendment's prohibition of governmental support of the establishment of religion, made binding on the states by the due process clause of the Fourteenth Amendment, was violated by Bible recitation in public schools. (Note that the Court viewed these as establishment clause cases, not free exercise cases despite the complaints of Schempp and Murray.)

★★★★★★★★★★★★★★ **The Supreme Court's Decision** ★★★★★★★★★★★★★★

The Court ruled in an 8 to 1 decision that "the practices at issue and the laws requiring them are unconstitutional under the establishment clause." Justice Tom C. Clark wrote the Court's ruling.

(continued)

Supreme Court Case Studies

Supreme Court Case Study 35 (continued)

The Court pointed to the American tradition of both religious belief and religious freedom. It reaffirmed earlier rulings that civil authority and religious activity must remain separate, and that no support of religion could be given from public sources. The Court set up a test as to whether a law violated either the establishment clause or the free exercise clause. A state program touching upon religion or religious institutions must have a valid secular purpose and must not have the primary effect of advancing or inhibiting religion.

The state in both cases insisted that its Bible reading served "secular purposes . . . the promotion of moral values, the contradiction to the materialistic trends of our times, the perpetuation of our institutions and the teachings of literature." The Court, however, found that the school districts used the Bible for religious purposes. The Bible when used for these purposes constituted a religious ceremony. The Bible may properly be used for historical or literary studies, "but the exercises here do not fall into those categories. They are religious exercises, required by the States in violation of the command of the First Amendment that the Government maintain strict neutrality, neither aiding nor opposing religion."

In his concluding statement, Clark echoed the sentiments of the majority of the Court as he wrote, "The place of religion in our society is an exalted one, achieved through a long tradition of reliance on the home, the church, and the inviolable citadel of heart and mind. We have come to recognize through bitter experience that it is not within the power of government to invade that citadel, whether its purpose or effect be to aid or oppose, to advance or retard. In the relationship between man and religion, the State is firmly committed to a position of neutrality. Though the application of that rule requires interpretation of a delicate sort, the rule itself is clearly and concisely stated in the words of the First Amendment."

★★★★★★★★★★★★★★★★★★★ **Dissenting Opinion** ★★★★★★★★★★★★★★★★★★★

Justice Potter Stewart was the sole dissent to the *Abington* decision. His concerns were mainly that the rights of parents who wish to have their children take part in a religious prayer exercise, and the rights of the children themselves, were being denied. He made the point that the prayers in question were not being forced upon any children who did not wish to participate, and he expressed the fear that "school boards all might eventually find it impossible to administer a system of religious exercises during school hours in such a way to meet this constitutional standard. . . ."

DIRECTIONS: Answer the following questions on a separate sheet of paper.

1. How might schools familiarize pupils with the Bible without violating the Court's ruling?
2. What test must laws concerning religion meet to be acceptable under the First Amendment?
3. How did the states defend the practice of Bible reading in public schools?
4. Do you agree with the Court's ruling or with Justice Potter's dissent? Give reasons for your answer.
5. Suppose a school board in a largely Muslim neighborhood required a portion of the Koran to be read in classes each day. Would this be allowed under the Court's *Abington* decision? Explain.

Supreme Court Case Study 36

A Poor Defendant's Right to a Lawyer

Gideon v. *Wainwright*, 1963

★★★★★★★★★★★★★★★ **Background of the Case** ★★★★★★★★★★★★★★★

"From time to time in constitutional history an obscure individual becomes the symbol of a great movement in legal doctrine. Character and circumstances illuminate a new understanding of the Constitution. So it was in the case of Clarence Earl Gideon," according to Anthony Lewis, a noted civil libertarian.

In 1961 Clarence Earl Gideon, a petty thief who had served four prison terms, was arrested for breaking into a poolroom in Panama City, Florida, and stealing a pint of wine and some change from a cigarette machine.

At his trial Gideon asked the judge to appoint a lawyer for him since he could not afford to hire one himself. The judge refused because under Florida law a lawyer could be provided only if the defendant was charged with a capital offense—one in which death was a possible penalty.

Gideon then pleaded not guilty; he conducted his own defense, but was found guilty and sentenced to five years in prison. From prison Gideon submitted a handwritten petition to the United States Supreme Court to accept his case as a pauper. In such cases the Court may accept petitions from indigent individuals and then appoint counsel to represent them before the Court. In this case, the Court appointed Abe Fortas, who later was to become a Supreme Court justice, as Gideon's attorney.

Constitutional Issue ★★★★★★★★★★★★★★★★★★★★★★★★★★★★★★

The Court accepted Gideon's case in order to reconsider its decision in the case of *Betts* v. *Brady* (1942). In that case, the Court had ruled that, outside of special circumstances, the due process clause of the Fourteenth Amendment did not require the application of the Sixth Amendment's guarantee of counsel in criminal cases to state trials. In a still earlier case, *Powell* v. *Alabama*, the Court had ensured that state courts would provide counsel in capital cases. The issue in the *Gideon* case deals with whether a defendant in a criminal case who cannot afford a lawyer is deprived of his or her Sixth Amendment right to counsel if he is not supplied with one.

★★★★★★★★★★★★★★★ **The Supreme Court's Decision** ★★★★★★★★★★★★★★★

The Court ruled in Gideon's favor, overturning its decision in the *Betts* case. Justice Hugo Black wrote for the opinion for the Court.

Black's opinion stated that the decision in *Betts* represented an abrupt break from precedents such as those found in *Powell*. These precedents, he observed, as well as "reason and reflection," convinced the Court that "in our adversary system of criminal justice, any person haled [brought] into court, who is too poor to hire a lawyer, cannot be assured a fair trial unless counsel is provided for him."

(continued)

Supreme Court Case Study 36 (continued)

Black went on to stress that poor and rich alike are entitled to counsel. "Lawyers to prosecute are everywhere deemed essential to protect the public's interest in an orderly society. Similarly, there are few defendants charged with crime, few indeed, who fail to hire the best lawyers they can get to prepare and present their defenses. That government hires lawyers to prosecute, and defendants who have money hire lawyers to defend are the strongest indications of the widespread belief that lawyers in criminal courts are necessities, not luxuries. The right of counsel of one charged with a crime may not be deemed fundamental and essential for fair trials in some countries, but it is in ours."

Black continued, "From the very beginning, our state and national constitutions and laws have laid great emphasis on procedural and substantive safeguards designed to assure fair trials before impartial tribunals in which every defendant stands equal before the law. This noble ideal cannot be realized if the poor man charged with crime has to face his accusers without a lawyer to assist him."

In making the point that Gideon, like most people, did not have the expertise to defend himself, Black quoted the words of the Court in the *Powell* case: "The right to be heard would be, in many cases, of little avail if it did not comprehend the right to be heard by counsel. Even the intelligent and educated layman has small and sometimes no skill in the science of law. If charged with crime, he is incapable, generally, of determining for himself whether the indictment is good or bad. Left without the aid of counsel he may be put on trial without a proper charge, and convicted upon incompetent evidence, or evidence irrelevant to the issue or otherwise inadmissible. He lacks both the skill and knowledge to prepare his defense adequately, even though he may have a perfect one. He requires the guiding hand of counsel at every step of the proceedings against him. Without it, though he be not guilty, he faces the danger of conviction because he does not know how to establish his innocence."

Gideon was tried again in the court that had convicted him, this time with a court-appointed lawyer. Before the same judge and in the same courtroom, Gideon was acquitted.

DIRECTIONS: Answer the following questions on a separate sheet of paper.

1. Why did the Court believe that Gideon could not defend himself?

2. Did the Court rule that a defendant could never act as his or her own lawyer? Explain.

3. In overturning its *Betts* ruling, what did the Court in effect say about its judgment in that case?

4. Under the *Gideon* ruling, why is a trial judge required to appoint a lawyer for defendants who claim they are too poor to pay for one?

5. Why is the *Gideon* decision regarded as a historic civil liberties victory?

Name _____ Date _____ Class _____

Supreme Court Case Study 37

The Right to Counsel

Escobedo v. *Illinois*, 1964

★★★★★★★★★★★★★★ **Background of the Case** ★★★★★★★★★★★★★★

Danny Escobedo was arrested in Chicago for the murder of his brother-in-law. The arrest took place at 2:30 A.M. on the morning of January 19, 1960, after the fatal shooting. Escobedo made no statement and was released. On January 30, 1960, Escobedo was taken into custody after an informant implicated him in the shooting. He declined to make any statement and asked to see his lawyer. Even though his lawyer was present in the police station, the police denied Escobedo the right to talk with him, and in fact, told Escobedo that his lawyer did not want to see him. Despite repeated attempts, Escobedo's lawyer was not permitted to see his client until the police had completed their interrogation.

Police testimony later revealed that Escobedo had been handcuffed in a standing position during the interrogation and that he was agitated and upset. During the police interrogation, Escobedo made incriminating statements that led to his indictment for the murder of his brother-in-law. He spoke in Spanish to an officer who spoke his language, and during that conversation Escobedo revealed that he was aware of the shooting. Motions made before and during the trial to have these statements suppressed (not used) as evidence were denied. After Escobedo's murder conviction, the United States Supreme Court took the case for review.

Constitutional Issue ★★★★★★★★★★★★★★★★★★★★★★★★★★★★

By 1964 the Court had generally settled the question that the defendant in a state criminal trial has the Fifth Amendment right not to speak and the Sixth Amendment right to counsel. But it remained unclear exactly when a defendant needed a lawyer to protect his or her right not to speak. For example, it was not uncommon for police officers to deny a suspect the right to counsel in the early stages of an investigation, when the suspect might yield to police pressure and provide incriminating information or even confess to a crime. If the suspect had not had his or her counsel present at that time, did this violate the right-to-counsel principle? The Court had to consider whether the Sixth Amendment's provision of the right to counsel also applied to the interrogation of a suspect of a crime.

★★★★★★★★★★★★★★ **The Supreme Court's Decision** ★★★★★★★★★★★★★★

The Court voted 5 to 4 to reverse Escobedo's conviction. Justice Arthur Goldberg wrote the Court's opinion.

Goldberg determined that although the questioning of Escobedo had preceded formal indictment, this fact "should make no difference" as to a person's right to counsel. At the point of interrogation, he stated, the investigation was no longer a "general investigation" of an unsolved crime. Escobedo "had become the accused, and the purpose of the investigation was to 'get him' to confess his guilt despite his constitutional right not to do so." It was at this point, Goldberg noted, that many confessions are obtained and this fact "points up its critical

(continued)

Supreme Court Case Studies 73

Name _____ Date _____ Class _____

Supreme Court Case Study 37 *(continued)*

nature as a stage when legal aid and advice are surely needed. . . . Our Constitution, unlike some others, strikes a balance in favor of the right of the accused to be advised by his lawyers of his privilege against self-incrimination . . . . A system of criminal law enforcement which comes to depend on the 'confession,' will, in the long run, be less reliable and more subject to abuses than a system which depends on extrinsic evidence independently secured through skillful investigation. . . . If the exercise of constitutional rights will thwart the effectiveness of a system of law enforcement, then there is something very wrong with that system."

Goldberg replied to objections that the police would henceforth get fewer confessions because lawyers would automatically advise their clients to say nothing. Goldberg countered that this argument "cuts two ways" since it points out the critical importance to the accused of having an attorney at this stage in the investigation. Goldberg continued, "There is necessarily a direct relationship between the importance of a stage to the police in their quest for a confession and the criticalness of that stage to the accused in his need for legal advice."

In summarizing the Court's opinion, Goldberg noted that "when the process shifts from investigatory to accusatory—when its focus is on the accused and its purpose is to elicit a confession—our adversary system begins to operate, and . . . the accused must be permitted to consult with his lawyer."

★★★★★★★★★★★★★★★★★★★ **Dissenting Opinion** ★★★★★★★★★★★★★★★★★★★

Four justices dissented. One, Justice John Marshall Harlan, stated, "I think the rule announced today is most ill-conceived and that it seriously and unjustifiably fetters [restricts] perfectly legitimate methods of criminal law enforcement."

Justice Potter Stewart also dissented, agreeing with Justice Harlan that the ruling gave advantages to the criminal and took away too much authority from law enforcers. He stated that this decision ". . . perverts those precious constitutional guarantees, and frustrates the vital interests of society in preserving the legitimate and proper function of honest and purposeful police investigation."

DIRECTIONS: Answer the following questions on a separate sheet of paper.

1. At which point, according to the Court's decision, must a lawyer be provided to a suspect of a crime?

2. Which right of the accused does Justice Goldberg refer to as coming under the protection of the Constitution?

3. How do you think a police officer would react to the Court's decision? Give reasons for your answer.

4. What criticism do both Justice Harlan and Justice Stewart make of the Court's decision?

5. Do you agree with the Court's ruling in this case or with those justices who dissented? Explain.

Supreme Court Case Study 38

One Person, One Vote

Reynolds v. *Sims*, 1964

★★★★★★★★★★★★★★ **Background of the Case** ★★★★★★★★★★★★★★

Alabama was divided into voting districts for the election of 35 senators and 106 representatives to the state legislature. Each voting district consisted of a county in the state. The Alabama constitution of 1901 established district boundaries and allocated senators and representatives, with each senatorial and house district being as nearly equal as possible. As no reapportionment of voting districts had been made for sixty years, there was a vast discrepancy in the size of the population in the voting districts. The proportion of population of largest to smallest districts was about 41 to 1.

Two different reapportionment plans had passed the legislature in 1962 for the 1966 election. Neither one, however, would result in a majority of the state's population being able to elect a majority of the legislators in either house.

A group of citizens and taxpayers sued to have the reapportionment plans declared unsatisfactory. After a district court had approved temporary use of portions of both plans, the citizens appealed to the United States Supreme Court.

Constitutional Issue ★★★★★★★★★★★★★★★★★★★★★★★★★★★★★

The question before the Court was whether or not the apportionment plans for the Alabama legislature violated the equal protection clause of the Fourteenth Amendment. In 1962 the Court had held in *Baker* v. *Carr* that voting districts must be substantially equal in numbers of voters. Once the Supreme Court had established its right to rule on the validity of state legislative districting, over thirty cases challenging existing state apportionments were filed in federal court. What the *Baker* case left unanswered was the question of the proper remedy in malapportionment cases. The Court now had to decide whether the equal protection clause implied that both houses of a state legislature must reflect equal numbers of people in voting districts.

★★★★★★★★★★★★★★ **The Supreme Court's Decision** ★★★★★★★★★★★★★★

The Court ruled 8 to 1 that the equal protection clause had been violated. Chief Justice Earl Warren wrote for the Court.

Warren wrote that "legislators are elected by voters, not farms or cities or economic interests." If voters in one area have votes whose numbers would have a disproportionately large impact in the election of representatives, then the votes of people in other areas become that much less effective. Warren held that "full and effective participation by all citizens in state government requires, therefore, that each citizen have an equally effective voice in the election of members of his state legislature." Otherwise his vote is debased, and he is that much less a full citizen, explained Warren. The weight of a vote cannot depend on whether the voter resides in a sparsely populated rural district or a thickly populated urban area.

(continued)

Supreme Court Case Study 38 *(continued)*

Lawyers for Alabama had defended the state's plan by using the United States Senate as an example of voting districts of unequal populations. The Court rejected this analogy to the Senate. In the first place, the arrangement whereby each state gets an equal number of senators was "conceived out of compromise and concession indispensable to the founding of our federal republic." Warren explained that whereas the United States is a collection of independent and sovereign entities—states—the counties were never independent governments. Warren noted that the national government was created by the states; the states, however, were not created by the counties. Counties were and remain subordinate governments with no independent rights.

Following this reasoning, the Court said, "We hold that, as a basic constitutional standard, the equal protection clause requires that seats in both houses of a bicameral state legislature must be apportioned on a population basis."

The precise arrangements for this requirement could vary, Warren explained. The two houses could represent different constituencies. The two houses could be of different sizes; the two houses could be elected on different timetables for different lengths of terms. All, however, must be worked out in lower courts, which would make adjustments according to local complexities.

This decision by the Court is often described in abbreviated fashion as the "one person, one vote" principle.

★★★★★★★★★★★★★★★★★★★★ **Dissenting Opinion** ★★★★★★★★★★★★★★★★★★★★

In his dissent, Justice John Marshall Harlan based his objection on his view that state legislative apportionments are wholly free of constitutional limitations. He expressed the view that the Constitution guarantees only that each state have a republican form of government and that the judiciary should not decide issues of individual state legislative apportionments.

Although the public in general welcomed the Court's decision in the *Reynolds* case, many politicians were dismayed by the ruling. They anticipated losing their seats, and many foresaw that representatives from rural districts would lose their power. One United States Senator, Everett Dirksen of Illinois, proposed a constitutional amendment that would withdraw federal courts' jurisdiction over reapportionment cases. The proposal did not pass either house of Congress.

DIRECTIONS: Answer the following questions on a separate sheet of paper.

1. What decision did the Supreme Court have to make in *Reynolds* v. *Sims*?
2. Why did the Court reject Alabama's comparison of its system to that of the United States Senate?
3. Under the Court's ruling in this case, what changes would the states have to make?
4. If you lived in an Alabama city, how would you have reacted to the Court's decision?
5. In what way is the "one person, one vote" principle a victory for democracy?

Supreme Court Case Study 39

Legislative Districting

Wesberry v. *Sanders*, 1964

★★★★★★★★★★★★★★★ **Background of the Case** ★★★★★★★★★★★★★★★

Like other congressional districts in Georgia, the Fifth District elected one representative to Congress. The Fifth District, however, had two to three times the population of other Georgia districts. Contending that this situation made his vote worth much less than the votes of some other Georgia citizens, Wesberry, a Georgia citizen, brought suit against Sanders, the governor of Georgia. The suit asked that Sanders be prevented from holding elections under Georgia's statutes governing congressional district apportionment.

The federal district court which heard the case denied Wesberry's claim. It ruled that Wesberry's claim presented a nonjusticiable political question—one that is for the political branches rather than the courts to decide. The case reached the United States Supreme Court for decision.

Constitutional Issue ★★★★★★★★★★★★★★★★★★★★★★★★★★★★★★★

Wesberry's suit raised questions under various sections of the Fourteenth Amendment and Article I, Section 2, of the Constitution. This article provides that "the House of Representatives shall be composed of members chosen . . . by the people of several states." The Court's decision was confined to a consideration of Article I and of *Baker* v. *Carr* (1962), in which the Court had ruled that voter district apportionment could be subject to judicial review.

In the case of *Baker* v. *Carr* the Supreme Court held that legislative districting by the states was a controversy in which the Court could get involved. The case assigned the federal district courts the task of policing the time and speed with which the redistricting was to take place. But the case left unanswered the question of the basis on which legislative districts were to be judged as meeting constitutional standards. Without such guidelines, many federal district courts had to turn to the Supreme Court for answers.

★★★★★★★★★★★★★★★ **The Supreme Court's Decision** ★★★★★★★★★★★★★★★

Justice Hugo L. Black wrote for a 6 to 3 majority. The Court held that Georgia's districting statute did violate Article I, Section 2, of the Constitution. Since the federal district court had refused to intervene in what it held to be a political question, Black's first task was to address that view. The Court rejected that position because of the *Baker* decision, which had stated that "the right to vote is too important in our free society to be stripped of judicial protection . . . on the ground of 'nonjusticiability.'"

Next, the Court announced that "in its historical context, the command of Article I, Section 2, . . . means that as nearly as is practicable one man's vote in a congressional election is to be worth as much as another's." The remainder of the decision spells out the historical context.

Reviewing the debates of the Constitutional Convention, Black wrote that "it would defeat the principle solemnly embodied in the Great Compromise—equal representation in the House

(continued)

Supreme Court Case Study 39 *(continued)*

of equal numbers of people—for us to hold that, within the States, legislatures may draw the lines of congressional districts in such a way as to give some voters a greater voice in choosing a Congressman than others."

Black's review continued. He quoted James Madison, Charles Cotesworth Pinckney, and James Wilson, all of whom had attended the Constitutional Convention, to the effect that the Founders intended equally-sized congressional voting districts. So, in Wilson's words, "in this manner, the proportion of the representatives and of the constituents will remain invariably the same."

The Court's final conclusion was that "while it may not be possible to draw congressional districts with mathematical precision, that is no excuse for ignoring our Constitution's plain objective of making equal representation for equal numbers of people the fundamental goal for the House of Representatives. That is the high standard of justice and common sense which the Founders set for us."

★★★★★★★★★★★★★★★★★★ **Dissenting Opinion** ★★★★★★★★★★★★★★★★★★

Justice John Marshall Harlan argued in his dissent that, first, "congressional Representatives are to be apportioned among the several States largely, but not entirely, according to population"; second, that the states have the power to choose "any method of popular election they please, subject only to the supervisory power of Congress"; and third, "the supervisory power of Congress is exclusive."

Above all, Harlan could find no justification for interpreting the phrase "by the people" in Article I, Section 2, as a requirement for equally proportioned voting districts. In support of his view, Harlan noted that all states, no matter how sparsely settled, are granted one representative in Congress, and that the three-fifths clause of Article I originally provided precisely for weighing some votes by three-fifths of the enslaved population. Harlan concluded: "The unstated premise of the Court's conclusion quite obviously is that the Congress has not dealt, and the Court believes it will not deal, with the problem of congressional apportionment in accordance with what the Court believes to be sound political principles. . . . The Court is not simply undertaking to exercise a power which the Constitution reserves to the Congress; it is also overruling a congressional judgment."

DIRECTIONS: Answer the following questions on a separate sheet of paper.

1. Suppose in your state one congressional district had 250,000 residents, while another had 500,000 people. What effect would the Court's *Wesberry* decision have on this situation?
2. What did Justice Black say is the meaning of Article I, Section 2, of the Constitution?
3. According to Justice Black, what did some of the Founders say about equal representation?
4. What would Justice Harlan say about the population distribution mentioned in question 1 above?
5. Do you agree with the Court's decision? Why or why not?

Supreme Court Case Study 40

Racial Discrimination in Privately Owned Facilities

Heart of Atlanta Motel v. *United States*, 1964

★★★★★★★★★★★★★★ **Background of the Case** ★★★★★★★★★★★★★★★

The ground-breaking *Brown* decision of 1954 banned racial discrimination in public schools and was gradually extended to other public facilities. The ruling did not apply to privately owned places such as hotels and restaurants. As a result, many of these places continued to refuse to accommodate African Americans. Professional baseball teams, for example, which had become racially integrated in 1947, could do nothing when their black players were not allowed to register at the same hotels as the white players.

Civil liberties lawyers tried to find some constitutional way to make these discriminatory practices illegal. The lawyers first had to prove that the federal courts had jurisdiction over these places, and second that they violated the Civil Rights Act of 1964. This act forbade racial discrimination by hotels, restaurants, theaters, and other public accommodations.

The Heart of Atlanta Motel was located in downtown Atlanta, but had ready access to two interstate highways. The motel solicited guests from outside Georgia by advertising in various national media. It also accepted reservations for conventions from organizations outside of Georgia. About 75 percent of its business came from outside the state.

Before the passage of the Civil Rights Act, the motel refused to rent its rooms to African Americans and stated that it planned to continue to do so. In order to do so legally, the motel sued the United States government, which had the responsibility of enforcing the Civil Rights Act. Through the appeal process, the case reached the United States Supreme Court.

Constitutional Issue ★★★★★★★★★★★★★★★★★★★★★★★★★★★★★★

The motel based its appeal on three claims. First, it claimed that the Civil Rights Act was unconstitutional because it exceeded Congress's power to regulate commerce under the commerce clause of the Constitution. Second, the motel asserted that the Civil Rights Act violated the Fifth Amendment because, in being deprived of the right to choose its customers and operate its business as it wished, its liberty and property were being taken from it without due process of law and its property was taken without just compensation. Third, it claimed that requiring the motel to rent rooms to African Americans against its will subjected it to involuntary servitude in violation of the Thirteenth Amendment.

The Court had to decide whether the Civil Rights Act deprived the motel owners of their constitutional rights.

★★★★★★★★★★★★★★ **The Supreme Court's Decision** ★★★★★★★★★★★★★★

The Court ruled against the motel in a decision written by Justice Tom C. Clark. The Court chose to deal only with the question of whether the Civil Rights Act was constitutional because it was based on the power of Congress to regulate interstate commerce. Justice Clark cited earlier cases which dealt with the meaning of interstate commerce and Congress's power to regulate

(continued)

Supreme Court Case Study 40 *(continued)*

it. As to the constitutionality of the Civil Rights Act of 1964, the Court held that the commerce clause of the Constitution permitted Congress to ban discrimination in places like the motel. Clark cited the *Gibbons* v. *Ogden* case and other cases that defined the meaning of "interstate commerce" in such a way as to include the business of the motel. It denied that the business of the motel was purely local since a good portion of its business was with people from other states.

Clark closed: "We . . . conclude that the action of the Congress in the adoption of the [Civil Rights] Act as applied here to a motel which concededly serves interstate travelers is within the power granted it by the Commerce Clause of the Constitution, as interpreted by this Court for 140 years. It may be argued that Congress could have pursued other methods to eliminate the obstructions it found in interstate commerce caused by racial discrimination. But this is a matter of policy that rests entirely with the Congress not with the courts. How obstructions in commerce may be removed—what means are to be employed—is within the sound and exclusive discretion of the Congress. It is subject only to one caveat—that the means chosen by it must be reasonably adapted to the end permitted by the Constitution. We cannot say that its choice here was not so adapted. The Constitution requires no more."

On the same day, the Court also ruled on a closely related case, *Katzenbach* v. *McClung*. The decision in this case, also written by Justice Clark, dealt with a Birmingham restaurant that mainly served a local clientele. It served African Americans but only at a takeout counter. About half the food the restaurant served came from out of state. The Court's opinion indicated that this fact was not crucial in its ruling. It took the stand that discrimination in a public accommodation such as a restaurant severely hindered interstate travel by African Americans.

In a concurring opinion, Justices William O. Douglas and Arthur J. Goldberg argued that the commerce clause was not the only constitutional support for the Court's view of interstate commerce, but also that the Fourteenth Amendment empowered Congress to impose the regulations provided in the Civil Rights Act of 1964.

DIRECTIONS: Answer the following questions on a separate sheet of paper.

1. What do you think the Court's decision in the Atlanta case required the motel to do?
2. Why do you think the Court chose to deal only with the commerce clause rather than the other two questions the motel had raised as well?
3. What did the Court's decisions in both the Atlanta and Birmingham cases have in common?
4. Justice Clark had a reputation for being a very conservative member of the Supreme Court. Do you think his rulings in the two cases described supported or detracted from this reputation?
5. Do you think the Court was correct in broadening its interpretation of the commerce clause? Explain.

Name _____ Date _____ Class _____

Supreme Court Case Study 41

The Rights of the Accused

Miranda v. Arizona, 1966

★★★★★★★★★★★★★★ **Background of the Case** ★★★★★★★★★★★★★★

Ernesto Miranda had been arrested at his home in Phoenix, Arizona, and accused of kidnapping and rape. Questioned at the police station by two police officers, he was not advised of his right to an attorney nor his right to remain silent. After two hours of interrogation, he signed a written confession to the crimes. At his trial, he was found guilty and sentenced to 20 to 30 years in prison. He took his case to the United States Supreme Court.

Constitutional Issue ★★★★★★★★★★★★★★★★★★★★★★★★★★★★★

The Fifth Amendment of the Constitution guarantees that "no person . . . shall be compelled in any criminal case to be a witness against himself. . . ." This right was made part of the Bill of Rights to prevent a tyrannical government from forcing accused persons to confess to crimes they may or may not have committed. Miranda's case before the Supreme Court was based on this Fifth Amendment protection. The Court accepted the case in order to explore and clarify certain problems arising from earlier decisions related to the rights of individuals taken into police custody. The precise question that the Court explored was under what circumstances an interrogation may take place so that a confession made during the interrogation would be constitutionally admissible in a court of law.

★★★★★★★★★★★★★★ **The Supreme Court's Decision** ★★★★★★★★★★★★★★

The Supreme Court overturned Miranda's conviction in a 5 to 4 decision. Chief Justice Earl Warren wrote the majority opinion. The Court's ruling centered on what happens when a person is taken into custody. No statement from the suspect, the Court held, may be used when it stems from custodial interrogation of the defendant unless it demonstrates the use of procedural safeguards effective to secure the privilege against self-incrimination. By custodial interrogation, we mean questioning initiated by law enforcement officers after a person has been taken into custody or otherwise deprived of his freedom in any significant way.

Warren noted that a suspect under interrogation is subject to great psychological pressures designed "to overbear the will," and that questioning often takes place in an environment "created for no other purpose than to subjugate the individual to the will of his examiner." In overturning Miranda's conviction, the Court intended "to combat these pressures and to permit a full opportunity to exercise the privilege against self-incrimination. . . ."

A person in police custody "or otherwise deprived of his freedom. . . must be warned prior to any questioning that he has the right to remain silent, that anything he says can be used against him in a court of law, that he has the right to the presence of an attorney, and that if he cannot afford an attorney, one will be appointed for him prior to any questioning if he so desires," Warren stated.

(continued)

Supreme Court Case Studies

Name _____ Date _____ Class _____

Supreme Court Case Study 41 *(continued)*

Once these warnings are given, the individual in custody may choose to stop answering questions, or may halt the interrogation until his attorney is present. Otherwise, he may waive his exercise of these rights. In such a case, there would be "a heavy burden . . . on the Government to demonstrate that the defendant knowingly and intelligently waived his privilege against self-incrimination and his right to . . . counsel."

The *Miranda* ruling applies only to interrogations. The Court emphasized that such safeguards were "not intended to hamper the traditional function of police officers in investigating crime. . . ." The ruling was not meant to bar "general on-the-scene questioning as to facts surrounding a crime or other general questioning of citizens in the fact-finding process. . . ." In addition, the Chief Justice declared, the Fifth Amendment does not bar voluntary statements from a person who, for example, enters a police station ". . . to confess to a crime, or a person who calls the police to offer a confession or any other statement he desires to make."

The *Miranda* ruling has led to the practice now followed routinely by arresting police officers and other law enforcement officials during which they read a suspect his or her *Miranda* rights.

★★★★★★★★★★★★★★★★★★★ **Dissenting Opinion** ★★★★★★★★★★★★★★★★★★★

Justices John Marshall Harlan, Tom C. Clark, Potter Stewart, and Byron White dissented. They saw no historical precedent for the majority position and feared the decision could weaken law enforcement. Justice White condemned the majority for creating law enforcement directives he viewed as inflexible, while at the same time leaving many unanswered questions.

DIRECTIONS: Answer the following questions on a separate sheet of paper.

1. How has the Supreme Court interpreted the Fifth Amendment's protection against self-incrimination to apply to all persons questioned in connection with a crime?

2. Suppose you were arrested as a suspect in a crime. The arresting officers rush you to a tiny room where they question you for 12 hours without a stop. Then, too weary to protest, you sign a confession. How would the Court's *Miranda* decision protect you in such a situation?

3. At the scene of a crime, a police officer questions witnesses about the details of a holdup. The officer suspects that some of the witnesses are connected with the crime. How does the *Miranda* decision apply in such an instance?

4. What do you think would happen if a person convicted of a crime proved that she or he was not informed of the *Miranda* rights when questioned by the police?

5. In recent years, the *Miranda* decision has been criticized by some persons as protecting the rights of criminals and neglecting the rights of crime victims. Do you agree or disagree with this point of view? Why?

Supreme Court Case Study 42

The Nature of a Fair Trial

Sheppard v. *Maxwell*, 1966

★★★★★★★★★★★★★ Background of the Case ★★★★★★★★★★★★★★

Dr. Samuel Sheppard was accused of murdering his pregnant wife at their home in a Cleveland, Ohio, suburb on July 4, 1954. Sheppard claimed that the murderer had been an intruder, with whom he had fought and by whom he had been knocked unconscious. At his trial Sheppard was convicted of the murder of his wife.

Events prior to his trial in October 1954 were described as a "publicity circus." Elements in the "circus" included extensive, sensationalist newspaper articles and editorials containing allegations unfavorable to Sheppard. Coverage included a reenactment of the events of the crime as Sheppard had described it, in front of police officials and news reporters, and a story that Sheppard refused to allow authorities to inject him with "truth serum." An inquest in a school auditorium climaxed in an attempt by Sheppard's lawyers to place into evidence some documents that were then forcibly thrown out of the room by the coroner.

Further, the trial began two weeks before the judge and the chief prosecutor were up for election. The Cleveland newspapers published the names and addresses of the 75 people named as prospective jurors. The jurors then received many letters and phone calls concerning the case.

At the trial, the courtroom was crammed with reporters, and the rest of the court building was largely given over to the media. During the trial, witnesses, lawyers, and jurors were constantly photographed entering and leaving the courtroom. Reporters were so noisy during the trial that the public address system proved inadequate. Information about deliberations that was supposed to remain secret from the jury was leaked and printed in newspapers accessible to the jurors. Jurors were permitted to hear and read all kinds of pretrial and trial publicity, much of it damaging to Sheppard.

The trial judge denied defense motions to delay the trial, move the trial to another location, declare a mistrial, and question the jurors as to their exposure to publicity.

Sheppard was convicted of second-degree murder. His appeals were all denied, including one to the United States Supreme Court.

Several years later, Sheppard filed a writ for *habeas corpus* directed against the warden of the prison where he had been serving his sentence. *Habeas corpus* refers to an order that a prisoner be brought before a court to determine whether he or she has been denied due process. Sheppard's petition was granted and then denied by successive federal courts. He then appealed his case to the United States Supreme Court, which granted relief; Sheppard was ordered released unless Ohio chose to retry him in an orderly proceeding.

*C*onstitutional Issue ★★★★★★★★★★★★★★★★★★★★★★★★★★★★★

   Every citizen accused of a crime is entitled to a fair trial. But just what does a "fair trial" mean? Was Sheppard denied a fair trial, in violation of the due process clause of the Fourteenth Amendment?

(continued)

Name _____ Date _____ Class _____

Supreme Court Case Study 42 *(continued)*

★★★★★★★★★★★★★ The Supreme Court's Decision ★★★★★★★★★★★★★★

The Court ruled for Sheppard in an 8 to 1 decision. (There was no opinion written by the one dissenting justice.) Justice Tom C. Clark wrote for the Court. Clark began by noting the historical importance of a free press in the administration of criminal justice. He stressed that "the press does not simply publish information about trials but guards against the miscarriage of justice by subjecting the police, prosecutors, and judicial processes to extensive scrutiny and criticism."

At the same time, Clark said, fair and orderly judicial administration requires that "the jury's verdict be based on evidence received in an open court, not from outside sources." In the *Sheppard* case, the trial judge had failed to control the manner of press coverage, to shield the jury from its onslaught, or to insulate witnesses from hearing one another's testimony.

Without forbidding press coverage, the trial judge might have taken actions such as preventing lawyers, witnesses, or court officials from discussing certain aspects of the case. He could also have requested that city and county officials regulate the dissemination of information by their employees. The press might also have been warned of the impropriety of publishing material that had not been part of the court proceedings. Had the judge, the other officers of the court, and the police placed the interests of justice first, the news media would have soon learned to be content with the task of reporting the case as it unfolded in the courtroom—not pieced together from extra-judicial statements. The Court concluded that due process had been violated in Sheppard's trial by the judge's failure "to protect Sheppard from the inherently prejudicial publicity which saturated the community and to control disruptive influences in the courtroom...." In the light of these factors, the Court granted Sheppard's *habeas corpus* petition and ordered his release unless the state retried him in an orderly fashion.

DIRECTIONS: Answer the following questions on a separate sheet of paper.

1. In what way had due process been violated in the *Sheppard* case?

2. What might the trial judge have done to insure that Sheppard received a fair trial?

3. If you had been one of the news reporters covering the trial, what might have been your reaction to the Supreme Court's decision?

4. Many trials are now being televised. Basing your answer on the Court's ruling, do you think televising a trial deprives a defendant of a fair trial?

5. Sheppard was given a new trial. In what way do you think the second trial probably differed from the first one?

84   Supreme Court Case Studies

Supreme Court Case Study 43

Evidence Obtained from a Bugged Telephone

Katz v. *United States*, 1967

★★★★★★★★★★★★★★★ Background of the Case ★★★★★★★★★★★★★★★

While gathering evidence for the prosecution of Charles Katz, the Federal Bureau of Investigation (FBI) "bugged" a telephone booth by attaching a microphone and tape recorder to the outside of the booth. This action was taken without a warrant. Based on the evidence the FBI secured from the bugged phone booth, Katz was convicted in a federal court in California for using telephone lines to transmit betting information from Los Angeles to Miami and Boston. This action violated federal communication statutes.

Katz sought review of his conviction by the United States Supreme Court on the grounds that a public telephone is a constitutionally protected area. Thus, he argued, evidence obtained by attaching an electronic listening device to a phone booth violates the user's right to privacy.

Constitutional Issue ★★★★★★★★★★★★★★★★★★★★★★★★★★★★★★★

Katz claimed that his right to privacy, a right that the Court had previously inferred from the Fourth Amendment's protection against unreasonable search and seizure, had been violated. The government, relying on rulings that had held electronic eavesdropping legal when no trespass (physical invasion of a protected area like the home) was involved, claimed that the FBI wiretap was legal because it was on the outside of the phone booth.

★★★★★★★★★★★★★★★ The Supreme Court's Decision ★★★★★★★★★★★★★★★

The Court decided 7 to 1 against the government. Justice Marshall did not participate in the vote. Justice Potter Stewart wrote the Court's decision. Although the government and Katz had both argued mostly over whether a phone booth was "a constitutionally protected area," the Court's decision followed a slightly different path. Stewart wrote that "the Fourth Amendment protects people, not places." Therefore, the government's argument of not actually penetrating the phone booth was beside the point.

Stewart continued "a person in a telephone booth may rely upon the protection of the Fourth Amendment [and] is surely entitled to assume that the words he utters into the mouthpiece will not be broadcast to the world." Given this reason, he continued, "it becomes clear that the reach of that Amendment cannot turn upon the presence or absence of a physical intrusion into any given enclosure."

Since Katz had "justifiably relied" on his privacy while using the telephone booth, the government's violation of that privacy constituted a search and seizure in violation of the Fourth Amendment. . . . In addition, the Court pointed out that the very "narrowly circumscribed" surveillance involved here could well have been authorized by a warrant. Not to have obtained a warrant ignored the central element of the Fourth Amendment, that is, justification before the fact and not afterward.

(continued)

Supreme Court Case Study 43 *(continued)*

In making this point, Stewart wrote, "The government stresses the fact that the telephone booth ... was constructed partly of glass, so that he [Katz] was as visible after he entered it as he would have been if he had remained outside. But what he sought to exclude when he entered the booth was not the intruding eye—it was the uninvited ear. He did not shed his right to do so simply because he made his calls from a place where he might be seen. No less than an individual in a business office, in a friend's apartment, or in a taxicab, a person in a telephone booth may rely upon the protection of the Fourth Amendment.... To read the Constitution more narrowly is to ignore the vital role that the public telephone has come to play in private communication."

In a concurring opinion, Justice John Marshall Harlan developed a test for determining what interests are protected: "First, that a person has exhibited an actual (subjective) expectation of privacy, and second, that the expectation be one that society is prepared to recognize as 'reasonable.'" This test became an accepted standard.

★★★★★★★★★★★★★★★★★★★ **Dissenting Opinion** ★★★★★★★★★★★★★★★★★★★

As the only voice of dissent in the case, Justice Hugo L. Black expressed the opinion that eavesdropping using electronic means did not constitute "search and seizure." He thought that the words of the Fourth Amendment quite literally applied only to "tangible things with size, form, and weight." He was referring to the phrasing of the Fourth Amendment that people had the right: "to be secure in their persons, houses, papers, and effects, against unreasonable searches and seizures...."

In concluding his dissent, Black wrote, "The Court talks about a constitutional 'right of privacy' as though there is some constitutional provision or provisions forbidding any law ever to be passed that might abridge the 'privacy' of individuals. But there is not."

Case Analysis Questions

DIRECTIONS: Answer the following questions on a separate sheet of paper.

1. Do you agree with Justice Stewart's opinion or with Justice Black's? Explain.

2. How do you think the FBI might have recorded Katz's conversation legally?

3. Suppose an individual has told friends that he knows his phone has been tapped. Yet, when he appeals a conviction based on information obtained from the wiretap, his appeal is denied. In what way did the individual fail to meet Justice Harlan's test?

4. Suppose you use a public telephone to discuss with a friend a plan to rob a bank. A police officer who happens to be standing outside the phone booth hears your conversation. The bank robbery takes place, and you are convicted for having participated in the robbery. The conviction is based in part on the police officer's testimony about your phone conversation. Do you think the Supreme Court's majority opinion would apply in your case? Explain.

5. In his dissent Justice Black wrote that the right of privacy is not provided for anywhere in the Constitution. By so believing, Justice Black has been described as applying a literal interpretation to the Constitution. What do you think this means?

Supreme Court Case Study 44

The Rights of Peaceful Protesters

Gregory v. *Chicago*, 1969

★★★★★★★★★★★★★★★ **Background of the Case** ★★★★★★★★★★★★★★★

Dick Gregory, an African American comedian and civil rights activist, helped lead a march protesting the slow pace at which Chicago's public schools were being desegregated. The march began at Chicago's City Hall and ended at Mayor Richard J. Daley's house, about five miles away.

The mayor's neighborhood of Bridgeport was an all-white area with a history of hostility to African Americans. A hostile neighborhood crowd soon gathered, attempting in various ways to harass the protesters, most of whom were African Americans. They, in turn, were under strict orders by march leaders to remain orderly and nonviolent, which they did. Over several hours the neighborhood crowd grew from about 150 to more than 1,000 people.

The police made valiant efforts to control the crowd, which had become increasingly violent, hurling eggs and rocks as well as racial abuse at the protesters. The police made repeated requests for Gregory to lead the marchers out of the neighborhood. Three marchers accepted the offer of a police escort from the area. Those who remained, Gregory included, were then arrested and removed in police vans. He and others were later convicted for disorderly conduct.

The Supreme Court of Illinois upheld the convictions. The Illinois court suggested that the demonstrators had been arrested not so much for marching but for refusing to obey the police request to disperse. Gregory took his case to the United States Supreme Court.

Constitutional Issue ★★★★★★★★★★★★★★★★★★★★★★★★★★★★★★★

Group protests, such as a march of a large number of people, about a public issue present the police with a challenge, especially when bystanders who oppose the marchers' cause taunt the marchers and even throw objects at them. If disorder then develops, the police may act in a manner that is possibly unconstitutional. Were the marchers' First Amendment rights to free speech and assembly, as applied to the states by the due process clause of the Fourteenth Amendment, violated in this case?

★★★★★★★★★★★★★★★ **The Supreme Court's Decision** ★★★★★★★★★★★★★★★

The Court ruled without dissent that the defendants had been deprived of their First Amendment rights. Chief Justice Earl Warren wrote for the Court.

Warren described the case as a simple one. "Petitioners' march," he wrote, "if peaceful and orderly, falls well within the sphere of conduct protected by the First Amendment." Since there was no evidence that the marchers had been disorderly, their conduct was constitutionally

(continued)

Supreme Court Case Study 44 (continued)

protected. In other words, the demonstrators, consistent with the First Amendment, could not be arrested and convicted for holding a march to express their views.

Warren also responded to the Illinois court's suggestion that the conviction was actually for Gregory's refusal to obey a police officer. "However reasonable the police request may have been and however laudable the police motives, petitioners were charged and convicted for holding a demonstration, not for a refusal to obey a police officer." Quoting an earlier Court decision, *Garner* v. *Louisiana*, he continued, "It is as much a denial of due process to send an accused [person] to prison following conviction for a charge that was never made as it is to convict him upon a charge for which there is no evidence to support that conviction."

Warren applauded the efforts of both the police and the marchers to maintain peace and order under the most trying circumstances. He cited specifics of the case that showed that Gregory and his group of marchers had maintained a peaceful attitude in the face of an angry mob. They had been told to stop singing at 8:30 that evening and had done so. In spite of the fact that the hostile crowd threw rocks and other objects at them, the marchers did not engage in any acts of violence toward the crowd. The Court agreed the marchers were well within their First Amendment rights.

In a separate opinion, Justice Hugo L. Black concurred. He found the disorderly conduct law itself to be unconstitutionally vague. He argued that a properly drawn statue could constitutionally protect both public order and demonstrators' First Amendment rights, "but under our democratic system of government, law-making is not entrusted to the moment-to-moment judgment of the policeman on the beat.... To let a policeman's command become equivalent to a criminal statute comes dangerously near to making our government one of men rather than of laws."

DIRECTIONS: Answer the following questions on a separate sheet of paper.

1. What fault did Chief Justice Warren find with the Illinois Supreme Court's reasoning?
2. What was Justice Black's main objection to the disorderly conduct statute?
3. What First Amendment right was reinforced by the Court's decision in the *Gregory* case?
4. Why do you think the Chicago police chose to ask Gregory and his followers to abandon their demonstration rather than arrest the people who were creating the disturbance?
5. Does the Court's decision make it illegal for a police officer to arrest demonstrators? Explain.

Supreme Court Case Study 45

Censorship Prior to Publication

New York Times v. United States, 1971

★★★★★★★★★★★★★★ **Background of the Case** ★★★★★★★★★★★★★★

During the turbulent years when the United States was engaged in the Vietnam War, protests against the war increased as the United States's role escalated.

One opponent of the Vietnam War, Daniel Ellsberg, a former Defense Department official, secured lengthy classified documents related to the war, including a "History of United States Decision-Making Process of Viet Nam [sic] Policy" and another document relating to the Gulf of Tonkin incident, which the government used to justify expanding its role in the war. These documents came to be known as the "Pentagon Papers." The government maintained that making the Pentagon Papers public might impose grave danger to the security of the United States.

Ellsberg turned the documents over to the *New York Times*, which planned to begin publishing them on July 13, 1971. The federal government sought to block publication and secured a temporary order from the Supreme Court which barred publication until the Court could hear and decide the case. The case was heard on June 26, 1971. On June 30, the Court lifted the stay and allowed the paper to go to press.

Constitutional Issue ★★★★★★★★★★★★★★★★★★★★★★★★★★★★★★

The First Amendment, as applied to the states through the due process clause of the Fourteenth Amendment, guarantees the freedoms of speech and the press. The question in this case was whether the government could prevent the publication of materials on the grounds that the national security was endangered.

As had happened before, the right to criticize the government in wartime became an issue. The Supreme Court had to decide whether the government had the right to prevent publication of material that the government regarded as harmful.

★★★★★★★★★★★★★★ **The Supreme Court's Decision** ★★★★★★★★★★★★★★

The Court ruled in favor of the *Times*, maintaining that the government had not met the "heavy burden of justification" for a prior restraint. The decision was issued only four days after the Court heard oral arguments. The justice writing the decision is not identified. All nine justices wrote opinions; 6 justices concurred with the Court's ruling, while 3 dissented.

In his concurring opinion, Justice Hugo L. Black wrote that the Court should not even have heard oral arguments in the case, and the government's injunction should have been automatically denied. "In my view, it is unfortunate that some of my Brethren are willing to hold that the publication of news may sometimes be enjoined. Such a holding would make a shambles of the First Amendment." To Black, by the First Amendment, "the press was protected so that it could bare the secrets of government and inform the people." In his view, the newspapers that

(continued)

Supreme Court Case Studies

Supreme Court Case Study 45 *(continued)*

published these papers "should be commended." In his concurring opinion, Justice William O. Douglas agreed with Black that prior restraints were never permissible.

Justice William J. Brennan also concurred, finding it noteworthy that "never before has the United States sought to enjoin a newspaper from publishing information in its possession." For him "only governmental allegation and proof that publication must inevitably, directly, and immediately cause the occurrence of an event kindred to imperiling the safety of a [troop] transport already at sea can support even the issuance of an interim restraining order." Justice Thurgood Marshall also agreed that restraint of publication was improper. Marshall emphasized the absence of statutory authorization for governmental action to enjoin a newspaper (but if there had been such a statute, its constitutionality could have been challenged).

Justice Potter Stuart agreed that sometimes secrecy in government is necessary, but it is entirely up to the executive branch to protect its secrets. He was convinced that the executive branch was correct with some of the documents involved in the case, but he could not say that "disclosure of any of them will surely result in direct, immediate, and irreparable damage to our Nation or its people."

★★★★★★★★★★★★★★★★★★★ Dissenting Opinion ★★★★★★★★★★★★★★★★★★★

Chief Justice Warren E. Burger dissented, rejecting the view that the First Amendment grants "absolute" privileges to the press. He wished for adequate time in which to consider the competing claims of press and government. Justice Harry A. Blackmun also complained that there had been no time for the Court to arrive at a reasoned judgment. He expressed concern that the publication of the Pentagon Papers might lead to battlefield casualties and diplomatic difficulties.

DIRECTIONS: Answer the following questions on a separate sheet of paper.

1. Why do you think each justice felt compelled to write a separate opinion?
2. Why did the case advance so rapidly through the appeals system?
3. Why is this case considered one of the most important in the Supreme Court's history?
4. What was the basis of Justice Black's opinion?
5. If you had been a justice of the Supreme Court considering this case, how would you have voted? Give reasons for your answer.

Supreme Court Case Study 46

The Extent of Equal Rights

Reed v. Reed, 1971

★★★★★★★★★★★★★★ **Background of the Case** ★★★★★★★★★★★★★★

Richard Lynn Reed, a minor who lived in Idaho, died without a will. Before he died, his adoptive parents, Cecil and Sally Reed, were separated. Although Richard's estate was small given his status as a minor, each of his adoptive parents separately sought to become the administrator of the estate. His mother first applied to the Idaho court. Before a hearing on her application could be held, the father also applied to become administrator.

The Idaho court then held a joint hearing on the two applications and ruled in favor of the father. It did so because Idaho law required that, if several persons who are equally entitled to administer an estate file a petition, "males must be preferred to females." Sally Reed then appealed this ruling to an Idaho district court, which held that the Idaho law violated the equal protection clause of the Fourteenth Amendment. Cecil Reed then appealed this decision to the Idaho Supreme Court, which reinstated the trial court's decision on the grounds that the distinction between the rights of men and women was required by Idaho law and that the lower court had no right to exercise its discretion in appointing the administrator of an estate. Sally Reed then appealed to the United States Supreme Court.

Constitutional Issue ★★★★★★★★★★★★★★★★★★★★★★★★★★★★★★

The Court had to rule on the question of whether a state law that favored a man over a woman of equal capabilities violated the Fourteenth Amendment's guarantee of equal protection of the law.

★★★★★★★★★★★★★★ **The Supreme Court's Decision** ★★★★★★★★★★★★★★

Chief Justice Warren Burger wrote the decision for a unanimous court. After reviewing the facts of the case, Justice Burger wrote that "Idaho does not, of course, deny letters of administration to women altogether. . . ." He pointed out that under law, a woman whose spouse dies has a preference over any male relative of the descendent. Burger explained that in the United States, presumably due to the greater life expectancy of women, a large proportion of estates are administered by surviving widows.

Justice Burger stated that "The Equal Protection Clause . . . does, however, deny to States the power to legislate that different treatment be accorded to persons placed by a statute into different classes on the basis of criteria wholly unrelated to the objective of that statute." Citing a previous Court decision, Burger wrote, "A classification 'must be reasonable, not arbitrary, and must rest upon some ground of difference having a fair and substantial relation to the object of the legislation, so that all persons similarly circumstanced shall be treated alike.'"

(continued)

Supreme Court Case Study 46 *(continued)*

Burger wrote that the Idaho Supreme Court, in upholding the Idaho law, concluded that its objective was to eliminate one possible source of conflict when two or more equally qualified persons apply to administer the same estate. Further, Burger noted that, "Clearly the objective of reducing the workload on probate courts by eliminating one class of contests is not without some legitimacy. The crucial question, however, is whether [the Idaho statute] advances that objective in a manner consistent with the command of the Equal Protection Clause. We hold that it does not. To give a mandatory preference to members of either sex over members of the other, merely to accomplish the elimination of hearings on the merits, is to make the very kind of arbitrary legislative choice forbidden by the Equal Protection Clause of the Fourteenth Amendment; . . ."

On these grounds the Court reversed the Idaho Supreme Court's decision.

DIRECTIONS: Answer the following questions on a separate sheet of paper.

1. If the dead son's estate was so small, why do you think each adoptive parent went to such expense and trouble to be appointed administrator of the estate?

2. On what grounds did the Idaho Supreme Court reverse the intermediate Idaho appellate court's decision?

3. Considering that decisions of the Court sometimes run to dozens or even hundreds of pages, the text of the Supreme Court's ruling in the *Reed* case was relatively brief. Why do you think this was?

4. Can you think of any grounds upon which a Supreme Court justice might have dissented in the *Reed* case?

5. What conclusion can you draw from the Court's decision in the *Reed* case?

Name _____ Date _____ Class _____

Supreme Court Case Study 47

The Rights of Religious Groups

Wisconsin v. Yoder, 1972

★★★★★★★★★★★★★★★ **Background of the Case** ★★★★★★★★★★★★★★★★

The First Amendment to the Constitution, which states that Congress may pass no law respecting the establishment of religion or prohibit the exercise of any religion, builds a wall between the government and religious groups. According to legal scholars who have interpreted the amendment, neither the national government nor state governments may pass laws that violate the beliefs of a religious group. Just how far does the First Amendment go in protecting people's religious rights? The case of *Wisconsin* v. *Yoder* illustrates how the Supreme Court has extended the protection of the amendment to a particular religious group.

The Amish, a Protestant sect that originated in Switzerland in the 1690s, immigrated to North America in the 1700s, settling first in Pennsylvania and later in several Midwestern states. They established farms, and even today most Amish are farmers who separate themselves from the modern world. They do not use motor-driven farm machinery or drive automobiles. They wear simple clothing, often homemade, fastened with common pins because the Amish believe that buttons and zippers are vain. Many Amish homes are lighted with kerosene lamps instead of electric lights. When travel is necessary, the Amish use horse-drawn, covered buggies. The Amish belief system and their rules, called *Ordnung*, forbid them to hold public offices, go to war, or swear oaths. To maintain their beliefs, tight-knit Amish communities operate their own elementary schools. Formal education ends when students finish the eighth grade.

Amish beliefs and customs brought them into conflict with Wisconsin state law. The case, however, had wider implications, not only because it affected Amish communities in 23 states, but also because the case tested the limits of the First Amendment. Wisconsin state law requires that all elementary school graduates attend high school until they are 16 years old. The Amish feared that attending a public high school might threaten the beliefs of their young people, and therefore refused to obey this law. Wisconsin brought suit, and a Wisconsin court convicted the Amish of violating the state education law. The Amish appealed the case to the Supreme Court.

*C*onstitutional Issue ★★★★★★★★★★★★★★★★★★★★★★★★★★★★★★★★

Does the First Amendment protect a group of people from being forced to send their children to public high schools if such attendance is contrary to their religious beliefs?

★★★★★★★★★★★★★★★ **The Supreme Court's Decision** ★★★★★★★★★★★★★★★

The court ruled 6-to-3 that the Amish, as a long-established religious group, may not be forced by the Wisconsin law to send their children to public high schools once they have completed the eighth grade. The Court based its decision on the religious rights provision of the First Amendment

(continued)

Supreme Court Case Studies 93

Name _____ Date _____ Class _____

Supreme Court Case Study 47 *(continued)*

and on the Fourteenth Amendment, which extended to the state level the protections granted to the national government by the Bill of Rights.

The Court reasoned that although a state has the power to impose reasonable regulations for the education of all children, a state's interest in universal education must be balanced against the freedom of religion provided for in the First Amendment, as well as the traditional interest of parents with respect to their religious convictions. The Court held that no matter how strong a state's interest in universal compulsory education may be, it is by no means absolute to the exclusion of all other factors.

The Court distinguished between members of legitimate religious groups and parents who held purely secular beliefs. The latter group, the Court held, did not have the right to interfere with a state's regulation of education. The Court described the Amish, on the other hand, as an identifiable religious sect with a long history of demonstrated, sincerely held religious beliefs.

In addition the Court found that the Amish had introduced convincing evidence to show that sending Amish children to public high schools might impair their physical or mental health and make them less likely to discharge their duties and responsibilities in the Amish community.

★★★★★★★★★★★★★★★★★★★ **Dissenting Opinion** ★★★★★★★★★★★★★★★★★★★

In his dissent Justice William O. Douglas agreed that the religious beliefs of the Amish are in conflict with compulsory high school education. He took issue with the majority opinion, however, on the grounds that parents' beliefs about education should not be imposed on their children. He stated that religion is an individual experience, and that, without knowing the position of the children involved, he could not agree with the majority decision.

DIRECTIONS: Answer the following questions on a separate sheet of paper.

1. Do you agree with the Supreme Court's majority opinion or with Justice Douglas's dissenting opinion? Explain.

2. Suppose a small religious group formed in the United States about five years ago. One of its beliefs was that children should not be educated beyond the sixth grade, so it operated religious schools from grades one through six. The laws of your state, however, require that children must attend school until they are 18 years old. The group refuses to obey this law. What would be the effect of the Court's decision on this group? Explain.

3. Orthodox Jews operate their own school systems that include high schools. Do you think Orthodox Jews would be affected by the Supreme Court's *Wisconsin* v. *Yoder* decision? Explain.

4. When the Supreme Court handed down its ruling in *Wisconsin* v. *Yoder,* some experts in constitutional law criticized it because the decision yielded too much authority to a religious group and weakened the state's power to regulate important educational matters. Do you agree or disagree with this criticism? Explain.

Name _____ Date _____ Class _____

Supreme Court Case Study 48

A Woman's Right to Abortion

Roe v. Wade, 1973

★★★★★★★★★★★★★★ **Background of the Case** ★★★★★★★★★★★★★★★

One of the most widely debated issues in recent times has been over whether a woman may legally have an abortion. Many religious groups have vigorously opposed abortion, while women's rights organizations and civil libertarians, as well as many unaffiliated individuals, have supported that right.

A unmarried pregnant woman, Jane Roe (a pseudonym), brought suit against District Attorney Wade of Dallas County, Texas. She challenged a Texas statute that made it a crime to seek or perform an abortion except when, in a doctor's judgment, abortion would be necessary to save the mother's life. Because Roe's life had not been threatened by her pregnancy, she had not been able to obtain an abortion in Texas.

Constitutional Issue ★★★★★★★★★★★★★★★★★★★★★★★★★★★★★★

Roe argued that her decision to obtain an abortion should be protected by the right of privacy, a right that stemmed from the Bill of Rights generally, and from the liberty interests guaranteed by the Fourteenth Amendment's due process clause. The state argued that the protection of life granted by the Fourteenth Amendment could not be applied to a fetus because a fetus was not a person in the eyes of the law.

★★★★★★★★★★★★★★ **The Supreme Court's Decision** ★★★★★★★★★★★★★★

The Court decided in Roe's favor. Justice Harry A. Blackmun wrote for the Court.

The Court, with one dissent, approached its decision by acknowledging the delicacy and depth of the issue before it. Nevertheless, it was the Court's task "to resolve the issue by constitutional measurement free of emotion and of predilection."

Justice Blackmun reaffirmed that there was a right to privacy that could be inferred from the First, Fourth, Fifth, Ninth, and Fourteenth Amendments. He said that "the right has some extension to activities relating to marriage . . ., procreation . . ., (and) contraception. . . ." Accordingly, "the right of privacy . . . is broad enough to encompass a woman's decision whether or not to terminate her pregnancy." Although specific and direct medical injury might follow a denial of choice, other injuries as well could result from an unwanted pregnancy. These include "a distressful life and future, psychological harm," and also the "distress . . . associated with the unwanted child, and . . . the problem of bringing a child into a family already unable, psychologically and otherwise, to care for it." Yet the Court concluded that the privacy right was not absolute; accordingly, the right could not support an absolute right to choose abortion and "must be [balanced] against important state interests in regulation."

The Court then turned to the question of whether a fetus is a person within the meaning of the Fourteenth Amendment. The Court decided that a fetus was not a person under the

(continued)

Supreme Court Case Studies

95

Supreme Court Case Study 48 (continued)

Fourteenth Amendment. In reaching this conclusion, Justice Blackmun wrote, "We need not resolve the difficult question of when life begins. . . . The judiciary, at this point in the development of man's knowledge, is not in a position to speculate as to the answer." Nonetheless, the state has valid interests to protect. One is "preserving and protecting the health of the pregnant woman" and the other is "in protecting the potentiality of human life."

To satisfy both sets of interests, the Court divided the term of pregnancy into two parts, based on medical knowledge. The first part is the first trimester, or three-month period of pregnancy. The Court identified this period as the point up to which fewer women died from abortions than in normal childbirth. In order to preserve and protect women during this period, a state may regulate abortion procedures in such areas as doctors' qualifications and licensing of facilities. Beyond that, however, the state may not go. In the first trimester, the abortion decision belongs to the woman and her doctor.

The point at which the state's compelling interest in preserving potential life begins when that life is viable, or capable of living outside the womb. During this period, approximately the third trimester, the state may constitutionally regulate and even forbid abortion, except when necessary to preserve a woman's life or health. Between the end of the first trimester and the beginning of the point of viability—not specified, but usually around the beginning of the third trimester—the state may "if it chooses, regulate the abortion procedure in ways that are reasonably related to maternal health," the Court concluded.

★★★★★★★★★★★★★★★★★★★ **Dissenting Opinion** ★★★★★★★★★★★★★★★★★★★

In Justice William H. Rehnquist's dissent, he questioned whether any constitutional right to privacy or liberty could be so broad as to include the complete restriction of state controls on abortion during the first trimester. In his view, "the Court's opinion will accomplish the seemingly impossible feat of leaving this area of the law more confused than it found it."

DIRECTIONS: Answer the following questions on a separate sheet of paper.

1. In what way did the Court break new ground in its ruling in the *Roe* case?
2. Explain the role of the state in abortion matters under the Court's ruling.
3. How did medical science play a role in the Court's ruling?
4. Where did Justice Rehnquist stand on the right to abortion?
5. Justice Rehnquist said the decision left the abortion area of the law more confused than it found it. What do you think he meant by that statement?

Name _____ Date _____ Class _____

Supreme Court Case Study 49

The President and Executive Privilege

United States v. Nixon, 1974

★★★★★★★★★★★★★★★ **Background of the Case** ★★★★★★★★★★★★★★★

During President Nixon's 1972 re-election campaign, several men were caught breaking into the Democratic National Committee's headquarters in the Watergate apartment and office complex in Washington, D. C. It turned out that the burglars were associated with the president's campaign. A nationwide political and public outcry mushroomed into what became known as the Watergate scandal.

The United States Department of Justice appointed a special prosecutor to carry out an independent investigation of the scandal. From the investigation, trials of various White House staff members, investigative newspaper reports, and televised Senate Select committee investigative hearings, a shocked nation learned that the White House was involved in planning and covering up the burglary.

When it was revealed that the president had taped many conversations in the White House Oval Office, both the Senate investigating committee and the special prosecutor attempted to secure the tapes. The president refused to release them, claiming separation of powers and executive privilege, the right of the president to keep his conversations confidential. The special prosecutor subpoenaed the tapes, and a federal judge ordered President Nixon to release them. Nixon refused and instead turned to the Supreme Court for a judgment on executive privilege.

Constitutional Issue ★★★★★★★★★★★★★★★★★★★★★★★★★★★★★★★

The question for the Court to decide was whether the president could refuse to surrender the tapes and other information to a federal court for possible use against those charged in connection with the Watergate break-in.

★★★★★★★★★★★★★★ **The Supreme Court's Decision** ★★★★★★★★★★★★★★

The Court agreed unanimously that the president had to turn over the tapes. Chief Justice Warren E. Burger wrote for the Court. President Nixon had argued that the courts had no jurisdiction over what he claimed was a dispute between the president and his subordinate, the special prosecutor. The Court responded that it was competent to decide the case, just as it had decided similar controversies between officers and branches of the government in the past. In addition, because the material was wanted for a normal federal criminal trial, the matter fell directly under the Court's jurisdiction through the judicial powers spelled out in Article III of the Constitution.

The president had also claimed that executive privilege shielded him from a subpoena for two reasons. First, it was necessary to protect the confidentiality of high-level presidential communications. Second, the principle of separation of powers protects the president through the independence of the executive branch.

(continued)

Supreme Court Case Studies   97

Name _____ Date _____ Class _____

Supreme Court Case Study 49 (continued)

The Court found this argument insufficient, depending merely on a broad and undifferentiated claim of public interest that such conversations remain confidential. It might have been different, the chief justice wrote, if this had been a claim to protect "military, diplomatic or sensitive national security secrets. . . ."

Chief Justice Burger further reasoned that the claim based on the separation of powers would work to impair the balance of those powers. He wrote: "To read the Article II powers of the President as providing an absolute privilege as against a subpoena essential to enforcement of criminal statutes on no more than a generalized claim of the public interest in the confidentiality of nonmilitary and nondiplomatic discussions would upset the constitutional balance of a 'workable government' and gravely impair the role of the courts under Article III."

Against the president's claim of executive privilege stood the Sixth Amendment rights of the accused to subpoena evidence and the Fifth Amendment guarantees against being deprived of liberty without due process of law. The Court weighed these claims and concluded, "without access to specific facts a criminal prosecution may be totally frustrated. The President's broad interest in confidentiality . . . will not be vitiated by disclosure of a limited number of preliminary conversations shown to have some bearing on the pending criminal cases." In short, the Court concluded, the president's claim "cannot prevail over the fundamental demands of due process of law in the fair administration of criminal justice."

Finally, the Court ordered certain safeguards on the handling of the tapes while in the possession of the district court. These safeguards included that they be examined by the judge in private; that only relevant material would be used; and that confidentiality would be preserved as far as possible and that the material would be safely returned.

When Nixon still hesitated to turn the tapes over to the Senate committee, the House recommended that the president be impeached. Nixon then released the tapes, which revealed his role in the cover-up, and four days later he resigned the presidency, the first president in the history of the U.S. to do so.

DIRECTIONS: Answer the following questions on a separate sheet of paper.

1. What reasons did the president give for justifying his claim of executive privilege?

2. Did the Court hold that there are no circumstances under which executive privilege might be asserted? Explain.

3. Do you agree or disagree with the Court's decision that a president must reveal material that he has recorded for his own use if it is needed as evidence in a criminal trial? Explain.

4. In what way did the Court's decision lead President Nixon to resign?

5. A constitutional scholar has written that the most important contribution of the Nixon case is "in its reaffirmation that even the highest officer of government is not beyond the reach of the law and the courts." Explain in your own words what this means and how this conclusion relates to the idea of a democratic government.

Supreme Court Case Study 50

Constitutionality of the Death Penalty

Gregg v. Georgia, 1976

★★★★★★★★★★★★★★ **Background of the Case** ★★★★★★★★★★★★★★★

The constitutionality of the death penalty is one of the most hotly debated issues the Supreme Court has dealt with because the Constitution does not directly address capital punishment. In fact, until well into the nineteenth century, capital punishment was widely accepted, and U.S. courts placed virtually no constitutional restrictions on the death penalty.

By the early twentieth century, the states had adopted laws requiring juries that found defendants guilty of murder to choose between life and death. Until the 1960s, death sentences were rather common, numbering about 200 a year. However, by then a large number of people began to raise moral and political questions about the death penalty and brought these concerns to the courts. In a 1972 case, the Court held that the death penalty as administered in the cases before it was unconstitutional, relying on the Eighth Amendment, which clearly forbids cruel and unusual punishment. In *Gregg* v. *Georgia* (1976), however, the Court, for the first time, concluded that the death penalty was not cruel and unusual.

Troy Leon Gregg and Floyd Allen, two hitchhikers, were picked up by Fred Simmons and Bob Moore. Later, the bodies of Moore and Simmons were discovered in a ditch. Following a description provided by a third hitchhiker who had been in the car for part of the journey, police found and arrested Gregg and Allen, who were driving Simmons's car. The .25 caliber pistol used in the slayings was found in Gregg's pocket.

Allen told the police that Gregg had intended to rob the two men all along, and that Gregg had done so after killing them. In his defense, Gregg claimed that he had fired in self-defense when he and Allen had been attacked by Moore and Simmons. A Georgia jury found Gregg guilty of armed robbery and murder.

In Georgia, persons convicted of murder and armed robbery were given presentencing hearings during which a jury would hear any "evidence in extenuation, mitigation, and aggravation of punishment . . .," including a previous criminal record or its absence. If the sentence was death, an appeals process was provided for, including expedited appeal to the Georgia Supreme Court. That court had to consider whether the death penalty had been imposed "under the influence of passion, prejudice or any other arbitrary factor," and whether the sentence was "excessive or disproportionate to the penalty imposed in similar cases, considering both the crime and the defendant."

The Georgia Supreme Court upheld Gregg's death sentence for murder, but not for armed robbery. Gregg petitioned the United States Supreme Court for review of his case.

Constitutional Issue ★★★★★★★★★★★★★★★★★★★★★★★★★★★★★★★

The question before the Supreme Court was whether Georgia's death penalty statute amounted to "cruel and unusual punishment" under the Eighth and Fourteenth Amendments.

Supreme Court Case Studies

Name _____ Date _____ Class _____

Supreme Court Case Study 50 (continued)

★★★★★★★★★★★★★ The Supreme Court's Decision ★★★★★★★★★★★★★★

The Court upheld Georgia's statute by a 7-to-2 vote, although a majority of justices could not agree on any one opinion. Justice Potter Stewart announced the Court's judgment. Stewart wrote that those who drafted the Eighth Amendment were primarily concerned "... with proscribing [banning] 'tortures' and other 'barbarous' methods of punishment." They did not, however, place the death penalty in these categories. Early Court decisions agreed: "the constitutionality of the sentence of death itself was not at issue. . . ." In fact, Stewart observed, the death penalty has long been accepted under United States law, and "it is apparent from the text of the Constitution itself that the existence of capital punishment was accepted by the Framers."

Stewart held that a death penalty conviction must accord with the "dignity of man" and must not be "excessive." Stewart continued: "First the punishment must not involve the unnecessary and wanton infliction of pain. . . . Second, the punishment must not be grossly out of proportion to the severity of the crime." The Court held that the death penalty still serves the socially necessary function of retribution. "This function may be unappealing to many, but it is essential in an ordered society that asks its citizens to rely on legal processes rather than self-help to vindicate their wrongs."

Finally, Justice Stewart stated that the death penalty in this circumstance was proportionate punishment. "When a life has been taken deliberately by the offender, we cannot say that the punishment is invariably disproportionate to the crime," he concluded. Given the carefully legislated guidelines under which Georgia imposes a capital sentence, the Court found that Gregg's death sentence was constitutional.

★★★★★★★★★★★★★★★★★ Dissenting Opinion ★★★★★★★★★★★★★★★★★★★

In one of two dissents, Justice Thurgood Marshall wrote that he would be willing to allow executions if they could show some useful purpose, such as deterring others from committing capital crimes. However, executing a criminal simply because society demands retribution is to deny him his "dignity and worth."

Justice William J. Brennan, in a second dissent, wrote that the death penalty treats "members of the human race as nonhumans, as objects to be toyed with and discarded."

DIRECTIONS: Answer the following questions on a separate sheet of paper.

1. What fate did Troy Leon Gregg face after the Supreme Court's decision in his case?
2. Under the Georgia statute, what would be one example of an aggravating circumstance?
3. Why is the *Gregg* case important in the history of the Supreme Court?
4. With what criteria did the Court find the death penalty to be valid?
5. Although two justices dissented, they did so for different reasons. Which of the dissents do you find more persuasive?

Supreme Court Case Study 51

Limitation on Affirmative Action

Regents of the University of California v. Bakke, 1978

★★★★★★★★★★★★★★★ **Background of the Case** ★★★★★★★★★★★★★★★

In the 1960s, many organizations established programs, called affirmative action, to improve opportunities for minorities and the disadvantaged. Objections to affirmative action arose when organizations, such as universities and colleges, set aside a certain number of places for minorities or disadvantaged persons. The question of the constitutionality of such practices came before the United States Supreme Court in the *Regents of the University of California* v. *Bakke* case.

In 1973 the Medical School of the University of California at Davis admitted 16 minority students through a special admissions process. This group of minority students collectively had substantially lower science grade point averages and Medical College Aptitude Test scores than those in the other group.

Alan Bakke, a white applicant, had a grade point average slightly below all the regular admission applicants, but his aptitude tests were substantially higher. When Bakke's 1973 and 1974 applications to the medical school were rejected, he sued the Regents, the university's governing board, for a place at the medical school. The California Superior Court found that the school's special admissions program violated the federal and state constitutions, Title VI, and the Civil Rights Act of 1964, but it declined to order Bakke admitted to the school, holding that Bakke had not proven that he "would have been admitted but for the existence of the special program."

Bakke appealed the decision to the California Supreme Court. Citing the equal protection clause of the Fourteenth Amendment, the court ordered him admitted to the medical school. The Regents then took their case to the United States Supreme Court.

*C*onstitutional Issue ★★★★★★★★★★★★★★★★★★★★★★★★★★★★★★★★★

The Supreme Court had to resolve two questions. First, did the establishment of special admissions criteria for minority students violate the equal protection clause of the Fourteenth Amendment? Second, are racial preference considerations always unconstitutional?

★★★★★★★★★★★★★ **The Supreme Court's Decision** ★★★★★★★★★★★★★

The Court held that the university's special admissions program for minorities violated the equal protection clause of the Fourteenth Amendment, although Justice Powell indicated that a properly devised program might well be constitutionally valid. Justice Lewis F. Powell, Jr., wrote for each of the two different five-member lineups.

(continued)

Supreme Court Case Studies

Supreme Court Case Study 51 *(continued)*

Powell explained that it is "no longer possible to peg the guarantees of the Fourteenth Amendment to the struggle for equality of one racial minority.... Although many of the Framers of the Fourteenth Amendment conceived of its primary function as bridging the vast distance between members of the Negro race and the white 'majority,' the Amendment itself was framed in universal terms, without reference to color, ethnic origins, or condition of prior servitude." He stated, "The guarantee of equal protection cannot mean one thing when applied to one individual and something else when applied to a person of another color. If both are not accorded the same protection, then it is not equal."

The Court refused to adopt the view that unless it could be shown that some proven constitutional or statutory violation existed, or that the government had some compelling justification in inflicting a burden on one individual in order to help another, the Court concluded, "the preferring members of any one group for no reason other than race or ethnic origin is discrimination for its own sake. This the Constitution forbids."

The University program failed this test because it "imposes disadvantages upon persons like respondent [Bakke], who bear no responsibility for whatever harm the beneficiaries of the special program are thought to have suffered." On the other hand, a university might well use racial criteria in an effort to insure diversity in its student body. Racial identity, however, could not be the sole criterion for admission. The University would still be free to devise an admissions program "involving the competitive consideration of race and ethnic origin" by making race one factor among others in the competition for all available places.

The Court concluded, "the fatal flaw in the petitioner's preferential program is its disregard of individual rights as guaranteed by the Fourteenth Amendment. Such rights are not absolute. But when a State's distribution of benefits or imposition of burdens hinges on ancestry or the color of a person's skin, that individual is entitled to a demonstration that the challenged classification is necessary to promote a substantial state interest."

DIRECTIONS: Answer the following questions on a separate sheet of paper.

1. On what grounds did the Court reject the university's affirmative action program?

2. What did the Court suggest as a way for the university to use racial criteria and not violate the Constitution?

3. Was the Court ruling a victory for Bakke? Explain.

4. If you were an African American applying for admission to the university's medical school, would you stand a better chance for admission under the system that Bakke attacked or under the program suggested by the Court? Explain.

5. Some people complained that the Court's ruling in the *Bakke* case marked the end of affirmative action. Do you agree with this judgment? Give reasons for your answer.

Supreme Court Case Study 52

Racial Preference in Employment

Kaiser Aluminum and Chemical Corporation (and United Steelworkers of America) v. Weber, 1979

★★★★★★★★★★★★★★★ **Background of the Case** ★★★★★★★★★★★★★★★

Title VII of the 1964 Civil Rights Act made it unlawful to discriminate in the hiring and firing of employees on the basis of race, color, religion, sex, or national origin. Title VII also made it unlawful to "limit, segregate, or classify" employees in such a way as to deny them employment opportunities on any of those same grounds. Title VII further provided that "Nothing contained in this title shall be interpreted to require any employer . . . labor organization . . . to grant preferential treatment to any individual or to any group because of . . . race, color, religion, sex, or national origin . . . on account of an imbalance which may exist with respect to the total number or percentage of persons of any race, color, religion, sex, or national origin employed by any employer. . . ." Title VII covered training, retraining, and apprenticeship programs.

In 1974 the United Steelworkers of America (USWA) and Kaiser signed a labor agreement that included a plan to open Kaiser's Gramercy, Louisiana, nearly all-white skilled craftwork positions to African American employees. Under this plan, instead of following its usual practice of hiring from the outside, Kaiser would retrain its own workers for skilled craftwork positions. Trainees would be selected on the basis of job seniority, but 50 percent of all trainees were to be African Americans. This would continue until the percentage of African Americans among Kaiser's skilled craftworkers had risen to 39 percent, which was the percentage of blacks in the local labor force.

One effect of the plan was that African Americans with less seniority than white employees were taken into the retraining program. Brian Weber was among a group of white employees who had been rejected for retraining although he had greater seniority than some of the African American employees selected. Weber sued, claiming that he had been discriminated against in violation of Title VII. The federal district court agreed with Weber. Kaiser and the union then appealed to the United States Court of Appeals, which again held in Weber's favor. The company and the union then took their case to the United States Supreme Court.

Constitutional Issue ★★★★★★★★★★★★★★★★★★★★★★★★★★★★★★★★★★★★★★★

The Court had to decide whether Title VII permitted a racially conscious affirmative action plan.

★★★★★★★★★★★★★★★ **The Supreme Court's Decision** ★★★★★★★★★★★★★★★

The Court voted 5 to 2 against Weber, with Justice William J. Brennan writing for the Court. (Justices Powell and Stevens did not participate in the decision.) Brennan specified the question as "the narrow statutory issue of whether Title VII *forbids* private employers and

(continued)

Name _____ Date _____ Class _____

Supreme Court Case Study 52 *(continued)*

★★★★★★★★★★★★★★ The Supreme Court's Decision ★★★★★★★★★★★★★★

unions from voluntarily agreeing upon bona fide affirmative action plans that accord racial preferences in the manner and for the purpose provided in the Kaiser-USWA plan."

The Court observed that Weber's "argument is not without force." However, Brennan wrote, "It is a familiar rule that a thing may be within the letter of the statute and yet not within the statute, because [it is] not within its spirit, nor within the intention of its makers."

In Brennan's opinion Congress drafted the statue in question because it "feared that the goals of the Civil Rights Act could not be achieved unless this trend [in employment discrimination based on race] was reversed." In reviewing the debates that took place in Congress when the Civil Rights Act was being considered, the Court was convinced that Congress had not intended "to prohibit private and voluntary affirmative action efforts as one method of solving this problem."

The Court found that "the purposes of the plan mirror those of the statute. Both were designed to break down old patterns of racial segregation and hierarchy. Both were structured to 'open employment opportunities for Negroes in occupations which have been traditionally closed to them.'" Finally, the Court noted that nothing in the plan would result in white workers being fired to make room for African Americans, nor were whites completely unable to obtain retraining. "Moreover," Brennan wrote, "the plan is a temporary measure; it is not intended to maintain racial balance, but simply to eliminate a manifest racial imbalance."

★★★★★★★★★★★★★★★★★ Dissenting Opinion ★★★★★★★★★★★★★★★★★

Chief Justice Warren E. Burger wrote one dissent, in which he held that the Kaiser-USWA plan embodied the very discrimination the Civil Rights statute was designed to forbid. He declared that the "statute was conceived and enacted to make discrimination against *any* individual illegal, and I fail to see how 'voluntary compliance' with the no-discrimination principle that is the heart and soul of Title VII . . . will be achieved by permitting employers to discriminate against some individual to give preferential treatment to others."

DIRECTIONS: Answer the following questions on a separate sheet of paper.

1. Why did the Court think a literal reading of the Civil Rights Act was misleading?

2. Do you think it was proper for Justice Brennan to take into account the debates that took place while Congress was considering the Civil Rights Act? Give reasons for your answer.

3. Do you agree with Justice Brennan's majority opinion or Chief Justice Burger's dissent? Explain.

4. The *Kaiser-USWA* v. *Weber* decision supported the company-union's affirmative action plan. Without this decision, what might have occurred?

5. Would you be willing to temporarily surrender an employment opportunity to a member of a group that has historically been denied access to such an opportunity? Explain.

Supreme Court Case Study 53

The Right to Search Students

New Jersey v. *T.L.O.*, 1985

★★★★★★★★★★★★★★ **Background of the Case** ★★★★★★★★★★★★★★

A New Jersey high school teacher discovered a 14-year-old freshman, whom the courts later referred to by her initials, T.L.O., smoking in a school lavatory. Since smoking was a violation of school rules, T.L.O. was taken to the assistant vice-principal's office.

When questioned by the assistant vice-principal, T.L.O. denied that she had been smoking. The assistant vice-principal then searched her purse. There he found a pack of cigarettes along with rolling papers commonly used for smoking marijuana. He then searched the purse more thoroughly and found marijuana, a pipe, plastic bags, a large amount of money, an index card listing students who owed T.L.O. money, and "two letters that implicated T.L.O. in marijuana dealing."

The assistant vice-principal notified the girl's mother and turned the evidence of drug dealing over to the police. T.L.O. was charged, as a juvenile, with criminal activity. T.L.O., in turn, claimed the evidence of drug dealing found in her purse could not be used in court as evidence because it had been obtained through an illegal search and seizure. T.L.O.'s attorneys claimed that the Fourth Amendment protects against unreasonable search and seizure. They maintained that the Fourth Amendment requirements for a warrant and probable cause applied to T.L.O. while in high school as a student. After appeals in lower courts, the case eventually reached the United States Supreme Court.

Constitutional Issue ★★★★★★★★★★★★★★★★★★★★★★★★★★★★★★★★★

T.L.O.'s case raised the question of whether the Fourth Amendment required school officials, when conducting searches of students' property in school, to meet the same strict standards as police officials. In most instances police officers must have probable cause to believe that the subject of a search has violated or is violating the law, and generally must obtain a warrant issued by a neutral judicial officer. If these standards are not met by the police, evidence they have gathered from a search can be excluded as evidence of guilt in a criminal trial.

★★★★★★★★★★★★★★ **The Supreme Court's Decision** ★★★★★★★★★★★★★★

Justice Byron R. White wrote the Court's 6-to-3 decision, which ruled against T.L.O. The Court concluded that the Fourth Amendment ban on unreasonable searches and seizures applies to searches conducted by school officials but that the search of T.L.O. was reasonable. The Court also ruled that school officials do not have to meet the same standards as police officers when conducting searches.

Justice White wrote that students have a real need to bring personal property into school and have "legitimate expectations of privacy" while in school. At the same time, however, "against the child's interest in privacy must be set the substantial interest of teachers and

(continued)

Supreme Court Case Study 53 (continued)

administrators in maintaining discipline in the classroom and on school grounds." The Court devised a plan to ease for school officials the Fourth Amendment requirements for a lawful search. Because of the significance of the school's interests, the Court ruled that school officials need not obtain a search warrant before searching a student who is under their supervision. "The warrant requirement," the Court held, "is unsuited to the school environment . . . [and] would unduly interfere with the maintenance of the swift and informal disciplinary procedures needed in the schools."

Next, the Court ruled that school officials do not have to be held to the same strict probable cause standard that applies to the police when conducting searches. In earlier cases the Court had ruled that "probable cause" meant that the police must have solid information that there is a real chance the person being searched has violated or is violating the law. Declining to apply this standard to public school officials, the Court said that school officials may search a student as long as "there are reasonable grounds for suspecting that the search will turn up evidence that the student has violated or is violating either the law or the rules of the school." Thus, the Court replaced the "probable clause" requirement with a "reasonableness" requirement.

★★★★★★★★★★★★★★★★★★ **Dissenting Opinion** ★★★★★★★★★★★★★★★★★★

Justices William Brennan and two other justices disagreed strongly with letting school officials use a reasonableness standard instead of the same probable cause standard required of the police. Justice Brennan wrote that this [idea] "finds support neither in precedent nor policy and . . . [could lead to] a dangerous weakening of the purpose of the Fourth Amendment to protect the privacy and security of our citizens."

DIRECTIONS: Answer the following questions on a separate sheet of paper.

1. In what way does the Court differentiate between the standard set for a school official and that for a police officer regarding a search and seizure?
2. Why did the Court give school officials more freedom than the police to conduct searches?
3. Do you think the assistant vice-principal's search was "reasonable"? Explain.
4. Under the Court's ruling, do you think a school official has the right to search a student any time he or she wishes? Give reasons for your answer.
5. Do you agree with the Court's decision or with the dissenting opinion? Explain.

Supreme Court Case Study 54

Prayer in the Public Schools

Wallace v. *Jaffree*, 1985

★★★★★★★★★★★★★★ Background of the Case ★★★★★★★★★★★★★★★

In the 1980s, after the Supreme Court had declared many forms of prayer in the schools unconstitutional, 25 states passed laws they hoped would meet the Court's standards for constitutionality. These were the so-called moment-of-silence laws. The laws were designed to promote a new type of school prayer. The moment-of-silence laws varied slightly, but in general they allowed teachers to set aside a moment in each public school classroom each day for students to engage in silent meditation. Often the intent of these laws was to give each student the opportunity to pray during the moment of silence.

Alabama had a law that authorized a one-minute period of silence in all public schools "for meditation or voluntary prayer." Ishmael Jaffree, a parent of three school children in the public schools of Mobile County, Alabama, challenged the state's moment-of-silence law. He claimed that the law violated the First Amendment prohibition against the establishment of religion.

Constitutional Issue ★★★★★★★★★★★★★★★★★★★★★★★★★★★★★★

The question for the Court to decide was whether a state law authorizing a daily period of silence in all of Alabama's public schools for the purpose of meditation or voluntary prayer violated the establishment clause of the First Amendment.

★★★★★★★★★★★★★ The Supreme Court's Decision ★★★★★★★★★★★★★★

By a 6-to-3 vote the Court ruled that the Alabama law was an endorsement of religion in the public schools and thus violated the First Amendment.

Justice John Paul Stevens wrote the majority opinion. He noted that the history of the Alabama law clearly indicated that the state "intended to change existing law and that it was motivated by the . . . purpose . . . to characterize prayer as a favored practice." Such an endorsement, Stevens argued, "is not consistent with the established principle that the government must pursue a course of complete neutrality toward religion."

Stevens explained that whenever government itself "speaks on a religious subject, one of the questions that we must ask is 'whether the government intends to convey a message of endorsement or disapproval of religion.'" In Alabama the Court found that the state legislature had passed the moment-of-silence law "to convey a message of state approval of prayer activities in the public schools. . . ." The law, the Court held, did not have a valid secular purpose, but rather one that sought to return prayer to the public schools.

Two of the justices, Sandra Day O'Connor and Lewis F. Powell, Jr., wrote concurring opinions that noted that some moment-of-silence laws might be constitutional. O'Connor argued that "a state-sponsored moment of silence in the public schools was different from

(continued)

Supreme Court Case Studies   **107**

Name _____ Date _____ Class _____

Supreme Court Case Study 54 *(continued)*

state-sponsored vocal prayer or Bible reading." First, she wrote, "a moment of silence is not inherently religious. Silence, unlike prayer or Bible reading, need not be associated with a religious exercise."

Second, a pupil who participated in a moment of silence need not compromise his or her beliefs. During a moment of silence, O'Connor wrote, "a student who objects to prayer is left to his or her own thoughts, and is not compelled to listen to the prayers or thoughts of others." Nevertheless, she concluded that the Alabama law was unconstitutional because it was very clear from the official history of the law that its "sole purpose" was "to return voluntary prayer to the public schools." In addition, O'Connor noted that the state legislature clearly wanted to use the law to encourage students to choose prayer over other alternatives during the moment of silence. Thus, the message actually conveyed to students and teachers was that "prayer was the endorsed activity during the state-prescribed moment of silence."

★★★★★★★★★★★★★★★★★★ **Dissenting Opinion** ★★★★★★★★★★★★★★★★★★

Chief Justice Warren E. Burger, Justice William H. Rehnquist, and Justice Byron R. White each wrote dissenting opinions. Chief Justice Burger captured the main dissenting idea when he stated, "It makes no sense to say that Alabama has 'endorsed prayer' by merely enacting a new statute . . . that voluntary prayer is *one* of the authorized activities during a moment of silence."

Thus, Burger went on to suggest that if using the word *prayer* in a moment-of-silence law unconstitutionally endorses religion, then deliberately omitting the word in a similar law "manifests hostility toward religion." Burger maintained, "The Alabama legislature has no more 'endorsed' religion than a state or the Congress does when it provides legislative chaplains, or than this Court does when it opens each session with an invocation to God."

Justice Rehnquist reviewed the history of the First Amendment and concluded that the Framers of the Constitution intended "to prohibit the designation of any church as a national one. . . . Nothing in the establishment clause, however, requires government to be strictly neutral between religion and irreligion." Thus, according to Rehnquist, the Constitution did not prohibit Alabama from making a "generalized endorsement of prayer" by passing a moment-of-silence law that would promote prayer "as a favored practice."

DIRECTIONS: Answer the following questions on a separate sheet of paper.

1. Why did Alabama pass its moment-of-silence law?

2. On what grounds did the Supreme Court declare the Alabama law unconstitutional?

3. In Justice O'Connor's view, if the Alabama legislature had not related the moment-of-silence law to religion, do you think she would have declared it unconstitutional? Explain.

4. What was the basis of Chief Justice Burger's dissent?

5. Do you agree with Justice Stevens's opinion or with Chief Justice Burger's? Explain.

Supreme Court Case Study 55

Rights of Students to Free Speech

Bethel School District v. Fraser, 1986

★★★★★★★★★★★★★★★ **Background of the Case** ★★★★★★★★★★★★★★★

Matthew Fraser, a student at Bethel High School in Pierce County, Washington, gave a speech to a school assembly nominating a fellow student for elective office. About 600 high school students elected to attend the assembly. Throughout his speech Fraser used "an elaborate, graphic, explicit sexual metaphor" to describe his candidate.

The assembly was a regular part of a school-sponsored educational program in self-government. Students were required to attend the assembly or report to a study hall.

Fraser had discussed his speech in advance with two of his teachers. Both warned him that the speech was "inappropriate" and that he "probably should not deliver it." They warned him that giving the speech might have "severe consequences" for him.

Fraser chose to ignore this advice. His speech disrupted the assembly. Students "hooted and yelled." Others appeared to be embarrassed. As a result, under the school's disruptive conduct rule, school officials suspended Fraser from school for three days and removed his name from a list of possible graduation speakers.

The school's rule prohibited conduct that "materially and substantially interferes with the educational process . . . including the use of obscene, profane language or gestures." Fraser challenged the constitutionality of the school's punishment under this rule. He claimed the school's punishment violated his right to free speech as guaranteed by the First Amendment. Eventually the case made its way to the United States Supreme Court.

*C*onstitutional Issue ★★★★★★★★★★★★★★★★★★★★★★★★★★★★★

Controversies over First Amendment rights to free speech often arise from unexpected sources and circumstances, and a common question is whether these rights apply to certain individuals—for example, children.

The First Amendment does not specify whether the rights of free speech are limited to persons of any particular age. Does this mean that adults have greater freedom to use whatever language they choose than young people? Do students in high school have the same freedom as older people? Does the First Amendment protection of free speech prevent school officials from limiting obscene or vulgar speech that could disrupt the educational process?

★★★★★★★★★★★★★★ **The Supreme Court's Decision** ★★★★★★★★★★★★★★

By a vote of 7 to 2 the Court ruled that, under the First Amendment, school officials have the authority to discipline students for lewd or indecent speech at school events. Chief Justice Warren E. Burger wrote the decision.

(continued)

Supreme Court Case Study 55 *(continued)*

Burger began by observing that the schools have a basic responsibility to prepare students for citizenship. Thus, it was appropriate for schools to prohibit the use of vulgar language in public discourse in school. Burger wrote, "The undoubted freedom to advocate unpopular and controversial views in schools and classrooms must be balanced against the society's countervailing interest in teaching students the boundaries of socially appropriate behavior."

The Court noted that the First Amendment gives wide freedom to adults in matters of political speech. However, the Court stated, "It does not follow, however, that simply because the use of an offensive form of expression may not be prohibited to adults making what the speaker considers a political point, the same latitude must be permitted to children in a public school."

Indeed, Burger observed that "nothing in the Constitution prohibits states from insisting that certain modes of expression are inappropriate and subject to sanctions." Instead, Burger explained, "the determination of what manner of speech in the classroom or in school assembly is inappropriate properly rests with the school board."

In the Supreme Court decision *Tinker* v. *Des Moines*, the Court had protected the rights of students under the First Amendment to wear black armbands to school to protest the Vietnam War. In that decision, the Court ruled that students do not "shed their constitutional rights to freedom of speech or expression at the schoolhouse gate." Was using obscene speech to nominate a fellow student the same as using armbands to convey a political message about the Vietnam War?

In the *Tinker* case the Court had ruled that when school officials punished students for wearing black armbands, they were censoring students' political ideas about the Vietnam War. In Fraser's case, however, Burger pointed out that the school's penalties "were unrelated to any political viewpoint." Thus, Burger concluded that "the First Amendment does not prevent the school officials from determining that to permit a vulgar and lewd speech such as [Fraser's] would undermine the school's basic educational mission."

DIRECTIONS: Answer the following questions on a separate sheet of paper.

1. According to the Court, how did the school's responsibility for citizenship education affect students' First Amendment rights?

2. How did the Court distinguish between the *Tinker* case and the *Fraser* case?

3. Suppose Fraser had given the same speech to a group of students away from the school grounds but had nevertheless been punished by school officials. How do you think the Court would have ruled in that case? Give reasons for your answer.

4. What did the Court say about the difference between adults' rights under the First Amendment and students' rights under the same amendment?

5. Do you agree or disagree with the Court's ruling in the *Fraser* case? Give reasons for your answer.

Name _____ Date _____ Class _____

Supreme Court Case Study 56

Students' First Amendment Rights

Hazelwood School District v. *Kuhlmeier*, 1988

★★★★★★★★★★★★★★★ **Background of the Case** ★★★★★★★★★★★★★★★★

In May 1983 the principal of Hazelwood East High School in St. Louis County, Missouri, ordered that two pages from an issue of *Spectrum*, a student newspaper, be deleted. The two pages included an article on students' experiences with pregnancy and another about the impact of divorce on students at the school.

The principal objected to the story on pregnancy because he believed the girls described in the story could easily be identified even if their names were left out of the story. In addition, he said, the references in the story to sexual activity were not suitable for the younger students at the school.

The principal objected to the story on divorce because it named a student who complained about her father's behavior. The principal believed the parents should have been given a chance to respond to the story.

The school paper was written and edited by the school's journalism class as part of the school curriculum. The principal also said he had "serious doubts" that the two articles fit the journalistic rules of fairness and privacy taught in the course. Three former students who worked on the student paper in 1983 then filed a suit against the principal, the school district, and other school officials. They claimed that the principal's action had violated their First Amendment rights to free speech.

In May 1985 a federal district court judge ruled against the students. In July 1986, however, a federal appeals court overturned that ruling. The appeals court said the *Spectrum* was a public forum for student expression and was fully protected by the First Amendment. In 1987 the United States Supreme Court agreed to hear the case.

*C*onstitutional Issue ★★★★★★★★★★★★★★★★★★★★★★★★★★★★★★★★★

Clashes between high school students and school administrators are not uncommon. Students tend to resent being told what they cannot do or say. In some instances, such disputes reach the courts, as in the case of *Bethel School District* v. *Fraser*. In that case the Supreme Court ruled that under the circumstances of the case, the students were not protected by the First Amendment right of free speech.

In the *Hazelwood* case, the principal's decision to censor the school newspaper raised a basic constitutional question. Does the First Amendment guarantee of freedom of speech prevent school administrators from regulating student speech in school-sponsored publications, such as newspapers and yearbooks?

★★★★★★★★★★★★★★★ **The Supreme Court's Decision** ★★★★★★★★★★★★★★★

The Court ruled 5 to 3 against the students. (The Court had only 8 justices during this time.) Justice Byron R. White wrote the majority opinion.

(continued)

Supreme Court Case Study 56 (continued)

White stated that the First Amendment rights of students in public schools are not exactly the same as the rights of adults in other settings. White explained that a school "must be able to set high standards for student speech ... under [its] auspices—standards that may be higher than those demanded by some newspaper publishers and theatrical producers in the 'real' world—and may refuse to ... [publish] student speech that does not meet those standards."

In the case of *Tinker* v. *Des Moines* in 1969, the Court had ruled the First Amendment gave students the right to wear black armbands to school to protest the Vietnam War. Justice White said that while the *Tinker* decision protected students' rights to personally express their political ideas, speech in school-sponsored newspapers was different because it occurred "as part of the school curriculum."

A school newspaper like the *Spectrum*, the Court decided, was not "a forum for public expression" but rather a tool for teaching and learning. As a result, "educators are entitled to exercise greater control over this form of student expression to assure that participants learn whatever lessons the activity is designed to teach." Thus, the Court held "that educators do not offend the First Amendment by exercising editorial control over the style and content of student speech in school-sponsored expressive activities...."

★★★★★★★★★★★★★★★★★★★ **Dissenting Opinion** ★★★★★★★★★★★★★★★★★★★

Justice William H. Brennan, joined by Justices Marshall and Blackmun, dissented. Brennan noted that the *Tinker* decision said school officials could limit student speech only if the speech threatened to "materially disrupt" schoolwork or violate the rights of others. He argued, "*Tinker* teaches us that the state educator's undeniable ... mandate to inculcate moral and political values is not a general warrant to act as 'thought police' stifling discussion of all but state-approved topics and advocacy of all but the official position."

Brennan added that "instead of teaching children to respect the diversity of ideas that is fundamental to the American system ... the Court today teaches youth to discount important principles of our government as mere platitudes."

School officials across the nation praised the Court's decision. They believed it gave them more authority to regulate student conduct. One official said the decision meant that schools, like "any other publisher, have the right to decide what will and will not be published." Civil libertarians, on the other hand, viewed the decision as an unwarranted curtailment of students' rights.

Case Analysis Questions

DIRECTIONS: Answer the following questions on a separate sheet of paper.

1. What reason did the Court give for allowing school officials to censor the school paper?
2. How did the Court distinguish between its decision in the *Tinker* case and the present case?
3. What danger did Justice Brennan see in the Court's decision?
4. If you had been the principal in the Hazelwood school, how would you have reacted after seeing the articles the students wished to publish? Give reasons for your answer.

Supreme Court Case Study 57

Rights of Employees

Skinner v. Railway Labor Executives Association, 1989

★★★★★★★★★★★★★★★ **Background of the Case** ★★★★★★★★★★★★★★★

For many years railroads have prohibited operating employees from possession of alcohol and from consuming alcohol while on duty or on call for duty. This prohibition has been extended to include the use of other drugs as well. An employee found in violation of this rule can be dismissed from his or her job.

As strict as the rules had been, the Federal Railroad Administration (FRA) recognized that alcohol and drug use by railroad employees continued to occur. After a review of accident investigations, the FRA found that between 1972 and 1983, there were a minimum of 21 significant train accidents involving 25 fatalities, with alcohol or drug use as probable causes.

In 1985, in an attempt to curb these accidents, the FRA issued new regulations that required mandatory blood and urine testing of all railroad crew members involved in major train accidents—any accident involving a fatality; "the release of hazardous material accompanied by an evacuation or reportable injury"; or damage to railroad property of $50,000 or more would mandate the new testing.

Railway labor organizations filed suit against these FRA regulations, claiming that employees' Fourth Amendment protection against unreasonable searches would be violated by the mandatory testing program. A trial in a federal district court ended with a decision in favor of the FRA, but the Court of Appeals reversed that decision. The case was then heard by the United States Supreme Court.

Constitutional Issue ★★★★★★★★★★★★★★★★★★★★★★★★★★★★★★★

Being intoxicated or under the influence of alcohol or drugs while in a position that can cause harm to oneself or others is a serious problem, and most levels of government have laws that severely punish offenders. Drunken drivers are a major cause of death on the highways. The question before the Court was whether the FRA regulation requiring mandatory blood and urine testing after a major accident was an unreasonable search under the Fourth Amendment.

★★★★★★★★★★★★★★ **The Supreme Court's Decision** ★★★★★★★★★★★★★★

Justice Anthony M. Kennedy delivered the opinion of the Court. The Court first held that the Fourth Amendment was applicable to drug and alcohol testing mandated or authorized by FRA regulations. Nevertheless, the Court next held that the drug and alcohol tests mandated by the regulations were reasonable under the Fourth Amendment even though there was no proof that any particular employee was impaired or might be impaired. This conclusion was justified, the Court held, because the compelling government interest served by the regulations outweighed employees' privacy concerns.

(continued)

Supreme Court Case Study 57 *(continued)*

Justice Kennedy wrote, "In light of . . . the surpassing safety interests served by toxicological tests in this context . . . we hold that the alcohol and drug tests contemplated by . . . the FRA's regulations are reasonable within the meaning of the Fourth Amendment. The judgment of the Court of Appeals is accordingly reversed."

★★★★★★★★★★★★★★★★★★★ **Dissenting Opinion** ★★★★★★★★★★★★★★★★★★★

Justice Thurgood Marshall, joined by Justice Brennan, delivered a dissent from the Court's opinion. He wrote, "In permitting the Government to force entire railroad crews to submit to invasive blood and urine tests, even when it lacks any evidence of drug or alcohol use or other wrongdoing, the majority today joins those shortsighted courts which have allowed basic constitutional rights to fall prey to momentary emergencies."

Marshall particularly objected to the fact that the Court's decision seemed to ignore the probable cause requirement for search and seizure under the Fourth Amendment. He spoke out against any exception, in this case defending the rights of all railroad employees who showed no evidence of drug or alcohol abuse and would be forced to be tested anyway.

The issue of invasion of privacy and the intrusive nature of the blood and urine tests also concerned Marshall. He wrote, "I find nothing minimal about the intrusion on individual liberty that occurs whenever the Government forcibly draws and analyzes a person's blood and urine." Marshall felt that some corroborating evidence such as the observance by a coworker of impaired behavior should be required before testing. He also felt that only those workers should be tested who could reasonably be suspected of impaired behavior and whose specific actions could have caused the accident. He concluded, "Ultimately, today's decision will reduce the privacy all citizens may enjoy. . . . I dissent."

DIRECTIONS: Answer the following questions on a separate sheet of paper.

1. What circumstances forced the FRA to issue its new regulations?

2. How did the Court balance the rights of employees against the rights of the government and railroad operators?

3. If you were a railroad passenger, which opinion would you be most likely to favor, Justice Kennedy's or Justice Marshall's?

4. What alternatives did Justice Marshall offer that in his opinion would identify offenders and still preserve employees' rights under the Fourth Amendment?

5. Do you believe that the Court's decision weakens the guarantees of the Fourth Amendment's search and seizure provisions? Explain your answer.

Supreme Court Case Study 58

The Right to Die

Cruzan v. Director, Missouri Department of Health, 1990

★★★★★★★★★★★★★★★ Background of the Case ★★★★★★★★★★★★★★★

After being involved in an automobile accident, Nancy Cruzan sustained injuries that resulted in permanent brain damage. Medical specialists in a Missouri state hospital where she was taken after the accident determined that she was in a "persistent vegetative state" with no operational brain functions. There were no medical expectations that she would ever recover.

Cruzan's parents therefore requested that she be allowed to die. They asked that she be taken off artificial nutrition and hydration systems, but hospital employees refused.

Cruzan's parents then asked a state court to authorize the hospital to take their daughter off the life-support systems. After a trial the court ruled that a person in Nancy Cruzan's condition had a fundamental right under the state and federal constitutions to choose whether to prolong her life through artificial means. The court based this ruling on the statements of Cruzan's former housemate, who testified that Nancy Cruzan said she would not want to be kept alive by artificial means if she were injured to the point where she could not live "at least halfway normally."

The defendant in the case, the Missouri Department of Health, appealed the decision to the state supreme court, which reversed the lower court's ruling. The Missouri Supreme Court ruled that the state's "living will" statute expressed "a state policy strongly favoring the preservation of life." Cruzan's parents did not have the right to terminate their daughter's medical treatment. The state high court concluded that "no person can assume the choice [death] for an incompetent in the absence of the formalities required under Missouri's living will statutes or the clear and convincing, inherently reliable evidence absent here." The court also ruled that Cruzan's statements to her housemate were "unreliable for the purpose of determining her intent." The Cruzan family then took the case to the United States Supreme Court.

Constitutional Issue

The Court had to decide whether the Constitution protects the right of seriously ill patients to be free from life-sustaining medical treatment. A related issue was whether Nancy Cruzan's parents had the right to act in her behalf to end medical treatment. Such issues arose in the public's minds with increasing frequency during the latter decades of the twentieth century as advanced medical technology made it possible to maintain the life of seriously ill or injured patients even though they had little chance of resuming a normal life.

★★★★★★★★★★★★★ The Supreme Court's Decision ★★★★★★★★★★★★★

The Court by a 5-to-4 vote affirmed the decision of the Missouri Supreme Court that the judgment of family members in this situation was not sufficient to end life-sustaining treatment.

Chief Justice William H. Rehnquist wrote for the Court. The Court held first that the United States Constitution did not forbid Missouri from requiring clear, convincing evidence of an

(continued)

Supreme Court Case Study 58 *(continued)*

incompetent's wishes to the withdrawal of life-sustaining treatment. Further, the Court concluded that the state high court was entitled to apply the clear and convincing standard of proof because that standard protected the state's interest in protecting life while allowing the state's interest to be overcome only in the face of substantial proof. Next, the Court concluded that the state supreme court did not "commit constitutional error" in finding that the evidence of Cruzan's parents was not clear and convincing. In addition, due process did not require the state to accept the judgment of a family member on this matter without substantial proof that his or her views were those of the patient. On this last point, if a living will document had been completed by Nancy to the effect that she would allow her parents to carry out her wish to be taken off life-supporting systems, this document would have served as "substantial proof."

Sympathizing with Nancy's parents while defending the Court's decision, Rehnquist wrote, "No doubt is engendered by anything in this record but that Nancy Cruzan's mother and father are loving and caring parents. If the State were required to repose a right of 'substituted judgment' with anyone, the Cruzans would surely qualify. But we do not think the due process clause requires the State to repose judgment on these matters with anyone but the patient herself."

★★★★★★★★★★★★★★★★★ **Dissenting Opinion** ★★★★★★★★★★★★★★★★★

Justice William J. Brennan wrote one of the dissenting opinions. He wrote, "The State has no legitimate general interest in someone's life, completely abstracted from the interest of the person living that life, that could outweigh the person's choice to avoid medical treatment." He concluded, "Because I believe that Nancy Cruzan has a fundamental right to be free of unwanted . . . [medical treatment] . . . , which right is not outweighed by any interests of the State, and because I find that the improperly biased procedural obstacles imposed by the Missouri Supreme Court impermissibly burden that right, I respectfully dissent. Nancy Cruzan is entitled to die with dignity."

DIRECTIONS: Answer the following questions on a separate sheet of paper.

1. What did the Court's ruling mean for Nancy Cruzan?
2. Did the Court completely rule out the right of a terminally ill patient to terminate life-support systems? Explain.
3. In Justice Brennan's opinion, what constitutional provision was involved in this case?
4. Some people believe that it is immoral to arrange for a person's death, even though the person has no chance to live a normal life. Why do you think the Court did not address this question?
5. Do you agree or disagree with the Court's ruling? Explain.

Supreme Court Case Study 59

Limits on Government's Right to Search

California v. Acevedo, 1991

★★★★★★★★★★★★★★★ **Background of the Case** ★★★★★★★★★★★★★★★

On October 28, 1987, a federal drug enforcement agent in Hawaii called Officer Coleman of the Santa Ana, California, Police Department. The agent told Coleman that he had seized a Federal Express package containing marijuana which was addressed to a man named J. R. Daza living in Santa Ana. The agent sent the package to Coleman, who took it to the Federal Express office in order to arrest the person who came to claim it.

Three days later, on October 31, "a man, who identified himself as Jamie Daza," claimed the package. Police officers followed him as he drove to his apartment and took the package inside. Shortly after, another man left the apartment carrying a knapsack that appeared to be half full. Police officers "stopped him as he was driving off, searched the knapsack, and found 1½ pounds of marijuana." About a half hour later, Acevedo arrived and went into the apartment. He reappeared carrying a full brown paper bag, which he deposited in the trunk of his car. Police officers then stopped Acevedo, opened the trunk and the bag, and found marijuana. They arrested Acevedo.

Acevedo "was charged in state court with possession of marijuana for sale." He demanded that evidence that the marijuana had been found in the car trunk be suppressed. The court denied his motion. Acevedo "then pleaded guilty but appealed the denial of the suppression motion" to the California Court of Appeals. The appellate court ruled that the evidence concerning the marijuana found in Acevedo's trunk should have been suppressed. The court referred to an earlier case which held that the police needed a warrant to conduct a search of the bag. Police officers could have seized the bag and held it, but could not open it without first obtaining a warrant to do so. The State of California then appealed this decision to the California Supreme Court, which refused to review the case. California then asked the United States Supreme Court to review the state appellate court decision, and it agreed to do so.

Constitutional Issue ★★★★★★★★★★★★★★★★★★★★★★★★★★★★★★★★

The Fourth Amendment protects "the right of the people to be secure in their persons, houses, papers, and effects, against unreasonable searches and seizures. . . ." The amendment, however, does not explain what is meant by "unreasonable" searches and seizures. The Court must consider the constitutional rights of accused persons without losing sight of society's right to be protected from criminal acts.

★★★★★★★★★★★★★★★ **The Supreme Court's Decision** ★★★★★★★★★★★★★★★

Justice Harry Blackmun delivered the opinion of the Court. The decision held that the police may search a container in an automobile without a warrant if there is probable cause to search the container. There does not have to be probable cause to search the entire automobile. Blackmun wrote for the Court, "The line between probable cause to search a vehicle and probable cause to

(continued)

Supreme Court Case Studies

117

Supreme Court Case Study 59 *(continued)*

search a package in that vehicle is not always clear. . . ." The search, however, must be limited to the container. The vehicle cannot be searched unless separate probable cause exists to support such action.

In a concurring opinion Justice Antonin Scalia wrote, "The Fourth Amendment does not by its terms require a prior warrant for searches and seizures; it merely prohibits searches and seizures that are 'unreasonable.' . . . In my view, the path out of this confusion should be sought by returning to the principle that the 'reasonableness' requirement of the Fourth Amendment affords the protection that the common law [the legal system that relies on previous court decisions and custom rather than on statutes] afforded." In essence, then, the Court ruled that the police had probable cause to seize the bag in Acevedo's car and search it.

The Court's decision in this case has done much to clarify the question of when a police search and/or seizure is or is not legal, and has enabled the police to conduct warrantless searches or seizures without being concerned that their actions are illegal.

★★★★★★★★★★★★★★★★★ **Dissenting Opinion** ★★★★★★★★★★★★★★★★★

Justice John Paul Stevens argued for a stricter interpretation of the Fourth Amendment and the need for a warrant in circumstances such as found in the *Acevedo* case. He wrote: "Our decisions have always acknowledged that the warrant requirement imposes a burden on law enforcement. And our cases have not questioned that trained professionals normally make reliable assessments of the existence of probable cause to conduct a search. We have repeatedly held, however, that these factors are outweighed by the individual interest in privacy that is protected by advance judicial approval. The Fourth Amendment dictates that the privacy interest is paramount, no matter how marginal the risk of error might be if the legality of warrantless searches were judged only after the fact."

Stevens continued to express grave concern about the Court's decision: "It is too early to know how much freedom America has lost today. The magnitude of the loss is, however, not nearly as significant as the Court's willingness to inflict it without even a colorable [plausible] basis for its rejection of prior law. I respectfully dissent."

Case Analysis Questions ★★★★★★★★★★★★★★★★★★★★★★★★★★★★★★★

DIRECTIONS: Answer the following questions on a separate sheet of paper.

1. What was the reason California's appeal in the *Acevedo* case was successful?
2. Assume you are driving a car home through a city neighborhood known for drug trafficking. You stop at a store to buy a soda. On your return to your car, the police say they want to search you and your car. How would the *Acevedo* decision apply in this instance?
3. With which Supreme Court justice's opinion do you most agree? Explain.
4. On balance, who do you think benefited most from the Court's majority opinion, individual citizens or the police? Give reasons for your answer.
5. In what way do you think the wording of the Fourth Amendment was clarified by the Court's opinion?

Name _____ Date _____ Class _____

Supreme Court Case Study 60

Exclusion of Women from Employment

International Union, UAW v. *Johnson Controls, Inc.*, 1991

★★★★★★★★★★★★★★★ **Background of the Case** ★★★★★★★★★★★★★★★

In the early years of industrialization in the United States, little attention was paid to protecting workers from dangerous work environments. Gradually individual states passed legislation regarding industrial safety. Then in 1970, with the passage of the Occupational Safety and Health Act, the federal government started setting safety and health standards for industry.

Meanwhile, the women's movement in the United States worked to end discrimination against women in employment so that more women were hired for jobs that had historically not been open to women.

Johnson Controls, Inc., manufactured batteries in which lead is an ingredient in the manufacturing process. Exposure to lead involves health risks, including possible harm to the fetuses of pregnant female employees. Before the Civil Rights Act of 1964, known as Title VII, Johnson Controls did not employ any women in battery manufacturing. In 1977 the company announced a policy stating that a woman who is expecting a child should not choose a job which exposed her to lead. This policy warned that women exposed to lead had a higher rate of abortion and that it was, "medically speaking, just good sense not to run that risk...."

Then in 1982 the company instituted a policy excluding all female employees medically capable of bearing children from any job that involved actual or potential lead exposure exceeding OSHA standards. Female employees who had medical proof that they could not bear children were the only women allowed to hold jobs exposing them to lead.

A group of employees, including men as well as women, filed a class action suit against the company, claiming that the company policy constituted sex discrimination in violation of the Civil Rights Act of 1964. Among those employees were Mary Craig, who had chosen to be sterilized in order to keep her job, and Elsie Nason, a 50-year-old divorcee who had suffered a loss in pay when she was transferred out of such a job. Both a federal district court and a court of appeals ruled in favor of Johnson Controls. The women, through their union, appealed the case to the United States Supreme Court.

*C*onstitutional *Issue* ★★★★★★★★★★★★★★★★★★★★★★★★★★★★★

The question before the Court was whether Johnson Controls' policy was discriminatory in violation of employees' civil rights as put forth in the Civil Rights Act of 1964. Under Title VII, could an employer lawfully exclude a female employee from certain jobs because of the company's concern for the health of the children the woman might bear?

★★★★★★★★★★★★★★★ **The Supreme Court's Decision** ★★★★★★★★★★★★★★★

The Court decided without dissent 6 to 3 in favor of the employees. Justice Harry A. Blackmun wrote the principal opinion of the Court, which held that an employer could not exclude a female employee from certain jobs because of concern for the health of a fetus she might conceive.

(continued)

Supreme Court Case Study 60 (continued)

Justice Blackmun wrote: "The bias in Johnson Controls' policy is obvious. Fertile men, but not fertile women, are given a choice as to whether they wish to risk their reproductive health for a particular job." The company policy violated the Civil Rights Act of 1964, which "prohibits sex-based classifications in terms of conditions of employment, in hiring and discharging decisions, and in other employment decisions that adversely affect an employee's status." Title VII mandates that "decisions about welfare of future children must be left to the parents who conceive, bear, support, and raise them rather than to the employers who hire those parents."

Justice Blackmun also cited the Pregnancy Discrimination Act, which made it clear that "... discrimination based on a woman's pregnancy is, on the face of it, discrimination because of her sex." Further, "It is no more appropriate for the courts than it is for individual employers to decide whether a woman's reproductive role is more important to herself and her family than her economic role. Congress has left this choice to the woman as hers to make."

In regard to the safety issue, Blackmun wrote, "Our case law, therefore, makes clear that the safety exception is limited to instances in which sex or pregnancy actually interferes with the employee's ability to perform the job." Further, "Fertile women, as far as appears in the record, participate in the manufacture of batteries as efficiently as anyone else."

Justice Byron R. White wrote a concurring opinion in which he said that "a fetal-protection policy would be justified [under Title VII] . . . if, for example, an employer could show that exclusion of women from certain jobs was reasonably necessary to avoid substantial tort [personal injury] responsibility." He took the position that employers could be sued for damages by children who suffered prenatal injuries and that companies should be able to protect themselves to some extent. He agreed, however, that the policy of Johnson Controls was unacceptable.

Justice Antonin Scalia also had some reservations about the majority's reasoning, although he concurred in the judgment. He wrote, "I think, for example, that a shipping company may refuse to hire pregnant women as crew members on long voyages because the on-board facilities for foreseeable emergencies, though quite feasible, would be inordinately expensive."

DIRECTIONS: Answer the following questions on a separate sheet of paper.

1. Why did Johnson Controls order that women could not hold jobs that exposed them to lead?

2. How did the company's policy violate the Civil Rights Act of 1964?

3. In the Court's view, who should decide whether a woman was to work at a job that exposed her to lead?

4. Justice White mentioned a possible reason why employers might want to exclude women from certain jobs. What was that reason?

5. Do you agree or disagree with the Court's ruling? Give reasons for your answer.

Supreme Court Case Study 61

Considering Victim Impact in Sentencing Procedures

Payne v. *Tennessee*, 1991

★★★★★★★★★★★★★★★ **Background of the Case** ★★★★★★★★★★★★★★★

Pervis Tyrone Payne was convicted by a jury of killing a 28-year-old woman and her two-year-old daughter and stabbing her three-year-old son in an apartment in Millington, Tennessee, in June 1987.

In the sentencing phase of the trial, Payne's lawyer called on Payne's mother and father, his girlfriend, and a clinical psychologist. The girlfriend testified that Payne was a very caring person who devoted much time to her three children, that he did not drink or take drugs, and that it was inconsistent with his character to have committed the crimes of which he had been found guilty. Payne's parents likewise testified to his good character. The psychologist testified that Payne was mentally handicapped and that he "was the most polite prisoner he had ever met."

The state called the mother of the adult victim, who testified that her grandson, who had survived the stabbing, cried for his mother and his dead sister; and the prosecution, in its closing argument, emphasized the likely longtime deleterious effects on the boy.

The jury sentenced Payne to death, a sentence that he appealed first to the Tennessee Supreme Court and, when that court affirmed both his convictions and death sentences, then to the United States Supreme Court.

*C*onstitutional Issue ★★★★★★★★★★★★★★★★★★★★★★★★★★★★★★★★

In serious criminal cases in federal courts and in the courts of many states, a jury's responsibility does not end with deciding whether an accused person is guilty. The jury is also required to hear arguments from the prosecution and the defense as to the kind of punishment it should impose or recommend. Typically, the prosecution emphasizes the seriousness of the crime and recommends the most severe punishment. The defense attorney tries to convince the jury that a less severe sentence such as life without parole would be appropriate. In addition, in recent years, both the defense and the prosecution also call witnesses who did not testify at the trial [the guilt/innocence phase of a capital proceeding]. For the prosecution, "victim impact evidence," relating to the emotional impact of the crime on the victim or on the victim's family, is presented. Defense witnesses, on the other hand, may try to convey to the jury that the accused had a difficult childhood, was kind to his or her relatives, and to present other evidence that puts the defendant in a favorable light.

When, despite the defense's effort, the jury in a murder case recommends the death sentence, the defense may appeal to higher courts on the grounds that cruel and unusual punishment has been inflicted, as prohibited by the Eighth Amendment. In two such cases in the 1980s the Supreme Court ruled that the Eighth Amendment did in fact bar the admission of victim impact evidence during the penalty phases of a trial for murder. In the *Payne* case, the Supreme Court once again was asked to rule on the admissibility of victim impact evidence.

(continued)

Name _____ Date _____ Class _____

Supreme Court Case Study 61 (continued)

★★★★★★★★★★★★★ The Supreme Court's Decision ★★★★★★★★★★★★★

The Court ruled 6 to 3 to uphold Payne's convictions and death sentences, and in doing so overruled two of its earlier decisions. Chief Justice Rehnquist wrote the majority opinion, much of which was devoted to explaining why the Court believed that the decisions in two earlier cases relating to the inadmissibility of victim impact statements in capital cases were wrong. In these cases, the Court had held that the Eighth Amendment prohibits a capital sentencing jury from considering victim impact evidence. Rehnquist wrote that "a State may properly conclude that for the jury to assess meaningfully the defendant's moral culpability and blameworthiness, it should have before it at the sentencing phases evidence of the specific harm caused by the defendant." He went on to point out that there is nothing unfair about allowing the jury to bear in mind the harm caused by a defendant's killing at the same time it hears mitigating evidence introduced by the defendant. "We thus hold," Rehnquist went on, "that if the State chooses to permit the admission of victim impact evidence and prosecutorial argument on that subject, the Eighth Amendment erects no *per se* bar. A state may legitimately conclude that evidence about the victim and about the impact of the murder on the victim's family is relevant to the jury's decision as to whether or not the death penalty should be imposed."

Overruling earlier decisions of the Court is a serious matter. The Court generally proceeds on the basis of a doctrine called *stare decisis*, a Latin term meaning "let the decision stand." Rehnquist took pains to defend the Court's action in not abiding by stare decisis in this case. He pointed out that "in the past twenty terms, [the Court had overruled] 33 of its previous constitutional decisions." Further, he noted, the cases which it was now overruling were decided by very narrow margins and were accompanied by "spirited" dissents.

DIRECTIONS: Answer the following questions on a separate sheet of paper.

1. What is the meaning of the term "victim impact evidence"?

2. What two responsibilities do juries carry out in capital murder cases in federal courts and in the courts of many states?

3. In the sentencing phase of Payne's trial, how much weight do you think the jury gave to the testimony of Payne's witnesses? Defend your answer.

4. If you were one of the dissenting justices, what arguments would you present for your position?

5. Why is it important for the Supreme Court to be careful in overruling its previous decisions?

122   Supreme Court Case Studies

Supreme Court Case Study 62

"Coerced" Confessions

Arizona v. *Fulminante*, 1991

★★★★★★★★★★★★★★★ **Background of the Case** ★★★★★★★★★★★★★★★

After Oreste Fulminante's 11-year-old stepdaughter Jeneane was murdered in Arizona, he left the state. He was later convicted of an unrelated federal crime and imprisoned in the state of New York. A fellow inmate named Anthony Sarivola was a paid informant of the FBI who befriended Fulminante.

Fulminante was the target of tough treatment from other inmates, who had heard that he was a possible child murderer. Sarivola offered Fulminante protection from other inmates if he would tell him the truth. Fulminante agreed and told Sarivola that he had, indeed, killed his stepdaughter. He provided convincing details of the crime, which he also confessed to Sarivola's wife after he was released from prison.

On the basis of these confessions, Fulminante was indicted in Arizona for first-degree (capital) murder. Fulminante protested that his Fifth Amendment privilege against self-incrimination and his Fourteenth Amendment due process rights had been violated because his confession to Sarivola had been "coerced." Therefore he claimed his confession should not be admissible as evidence of his guilt. A 1967 Supreme Court ruling had said that a coerced confession can never be considered "harmless error" and was always grounds for overturning a conviction.

The trial court, however, denied Fulminante's motion to suppress the confessions and found that both confessions had been voluntary. The state introduced both confessions as evidence at trial, and Fulminante was convicted of murder and sentenced to death. The Arizona Supreme Court, however, reversed Fulminante's conviction and ordered him to be retried without the use of the first confession, which the court judged to be coerced. Arizona successfully petitioned the United States Supreme Court to review the state supreme court's ruling.

*C*onstitutional Issue ★★★★★★★★★★★★★★★★★★★★★★★★★★★★★

When is a confession of guilt by an accused person considered to be acceptable evidence in a trial? The matter for the Supreme Court to judge was whether in fact Fulminante's confessions were coerced, depriving Fulminante of his constitutional rights.

★★★★★★★★★★★★★★★ **The Supreme Court's Decision** ★★★★★★★★★★★★★★★

Justice Byron R. White delivered one of the principal opinions of the Court, affirming the judgment of the Arizona Supreme Court. He wrote: "The Arizona Supreme Court ruled in this case that respondent Oreste Fulminante's confession, received in evidence at his trial for murder, had been coerced and that its use against him was barred by the Fifth and Fourteenth Amendments to the United States Constitution. . . . We affirm the judgment of the Arizona court, although for different reasons than those on which that court relied."

(continued)

Name _____ Date _____ Class _____

Supreme Court Case Study 62 *(continued)*

Further explaining the Court's decision, Justice White agreed with the Arizona Supreme Court that there was "a credible threat of physical violence unless Fulminante confessed and that was sufficient to support a finding of coercion." White made the point that without the confessions, which relied on one another for their effect on the jury, Fulminante likely could not have been convicted. He noted that the physical evidence at the scene of the crime and other circumstantial evidence would not have been enough to convict Fulminante. White wrote, "The transcript discloses that both the trial court and the State recognized that a successful prosecution depended on the jury believing the two confessions." He concluded: "Because a majority of the Court has determined that Fulminante's confession to Anthony Sarivola was coerced and because a majority has determined that admitting this confession was not harmless beyond a reasonable doubt, we agree with the Arizona Supreme Court's conclusion that Fulminante is entitled to a new trial at which the confession is not admitted. Accordingly the judgment of the Arizona Supreme Court is affirmed."

Justice Anthony Kennedy wrote in a concurring opinion: "In the interests of providing a clear mandate to the Arizona Supreme Court in this capital case, I deem it proper to accept in the case now before us the holding of the five justices that the confession was coerced and inadmissible. I agree with a majority of the Court that admission of the confession could not be harmless error when viewed in light of all the evidence; and so I concur in the judgment to affirm the ruling of the Arizona Supreme Court."

The key point in this case, in spite of the fact that Fulminante did receive a new trial, is that a majority of the justices agreed that a coerced confession is subject to harmless-error analysis—that is, that a coerced confession in itself does not necessarily mean that a decision of guilty must be reversed. This ruling implicitly overruled the 1967 ruling described on page 123. The ruling in the *Fulminante* case set a new precedent: that a coerced confession introduced at trial does not necessarily reverse a conviction.

DIRECTIONS: Answer the following questions on a separate sheet of paper.

1. What was the ruling of the original trial court? Of the Arizona Supreme Court?
2. What is the meaning of "harmless error"?
3. What was Fulminante's argument to the Supreme Court?
4. What is the difference between the Supreme Court's 1967 ruling on coerced confessions and its ruling in the *Fulminante* case?
5. Do you agree or disagree with the Court's 1967 ruling that presenting a coerced confession at trial is always grounds for overturning a conviction?

Supreme Court Case Study 63

Race-based Congressional Districts

Shaw v. Reno, 1993

★★★★★★★★★★★★★★★ **Background of the Case** ★★★★★★★★★★★★★★★

From the earliest days of the federal republic, parties in power in state legislatures organized congressional districts in their states so that the parties would be certain to have their represetatives elected to Congress. Manipulating the boundaries of congressional districts by the political party in power, or political gerrymandering as it came to be known, was accepted as a normal part of state politics.

The physical size and shape of congressional districts became an issue after the Voting Rights Act of 1965 and its later amendments. The act had been passed to eliminate the practices that had kept African Americans and other minorities from voting. In the South particularly, registration by African Americans increased dramatically as a result of the act. Nevertheless, the impact of increased voting by African Americans tended to be diluted by including African American voters in congressional districts that were heavily white. As a result, relatively few African Americans were elected to Congress from states with large African American populations.

States covered by the Voting Rights Act—such as North Carolina—cannot change any electoral practice, i.e., they cannot redistrict, without receiving preapproval from either the attorney general or the United States District Court for the District of Columbia. When the state became entitled to a twelfth congressional district as a result of the 1990 census, it needed preapproval in order to redraw its congressional map to reflect 12 rather than 11 districts.

The North Carolina legislature adopted a redistricting plan in which 1 of the 12 congressional districts had a majority African American voting population. The state submitted this plan to the attorney general for preapproval. However, the attorney general declined to approve the plan because he believed that North Carolina should create 2 majority African American congressional districts rather than 1.

The North Carolina legislature responded by enacting a redistricting plan which contained 2 majority African American districts—Districts 1 and 12. Five white North Carolinians sued the state and federal governments over the design of the Twelfth District. The district spanned 160 miles in a snake-like pattern to include exclusively African American neighborhoods along Interstate 85. The five whites argued that the white population's constitutional rights had been violated under the redistricting.

*C*onstitutional Issue ★★★★★★★★★★★★★★★★★★★★★★★★★★★★★★★

The legality of the redistricting turned on the Fourteenth Amendment's equal protection clause. The people who filed the suit believed that the way the Twelfth District was redrawn was a racial gerrymander and violated their right to equal protection under the law.

Supreme Court Case Studies 125

Name _____ Date _____ Class _____

Supreme Court Case Study 63 (continued)

★★★★★★★★★★★★★★ The Supreme Court's Decision ★★★★★★★★★★★★★★

The Supreme Court ruled in a 5-to-4 decision that states with irregularly shaped electoral districts, drawn with the intention of creating minority districts, could be challenged on equal protection grounds. Justice Sandra Day O'Connor, writing for the Court, stated that the "bizarre" shape of the Twelfth District resembled the "most egregious racial gerrymanders of the past" which had excluded African Americans.

Justice O'Connor stated that there are legitimate reasons for states to provide minority districts. She believed, however, that "traditional districting principles" in regard to compactness, contiguity, and respect for political divisions must be utilized. The justice drew a comparison between linking a geographical area together on the basis of skin color to that of a "political apartheid." She was referring to the former policy of South Africa that was used to legally separate and discriminate the races.

★★★★★★★★★★★★★★★★★ Dissenting Opinion ★★★★★★★★★★★★★★★★★★

The four dissenting justices believed that white voters had not been harmed by the redrawing of the Twelfth District. The dissent also criticized the emphasis on the shape of the district. They believed discriminatory gerrymandering could take place in a regularly shaped district as easily as in an oddly shaped district.

Justice John Paul Stevens stated that "the duty to govern impartially is abused when the group with power over the election process defines electoral boundaries to enhance its own political strength at the expense of any weaker groups. However, the duty to be impartial is not violated when the majority acts to facilitate the election of such a member of a group that lacks such power."

In another dissent, Justice David Souter held that legislators have to take race into account when drawing district lines in order to avoid the dilution of the minority vote. He believed that if redistricting harms participation in the election process, then the Fourteenth Amendment is violated. He held that because no one's participation had been harmed, the redrawing of the Twelfth District did not violate the Fourteenth Amendment.

DIRECTIONS: Answer the following questions on a separate sheet of paper.

1. Why had the Twelfth District been created by the state legislature?

2. What was the constitutional basis on which some white citizens of the Twelfth District brought the case to court?

3. What was the Court's position on redrawing congressional districts to promote minority interests?

4. On what grounds did Justice Stevens base his dissent?

5. What is your opinion of the practice of creating congressional districts to facilitate the election of minorities to Congress?

Supreme Court Case Study 64

Illegal Anti-abortion Activity

National Organization for Women (NOW) v. Scheidler, 1994

★★★★★★★★★★★★★★★ Background of the Case ★★★★★★★★★★★★★★★

In the 1973 case of *Roe* v. *Wade*, the Supreme Court ruled that a woman's right to choose abortion is protected by the Constitution. The Court's decision sparked a 25-year debate between supporters and opponents of abortion rights.

The debate, however, has not always been peaceable. Some anti-abortion activists appear to have resorted to intimidation and violence in championing their cause. In addition to picketing the homes of doctors who performed abortions, they have tried to physically restrain women from entering abortion clinics, and even murdered a physician who performed abortions.

The National Organization for Women (NOW), one of the largest and most active women's rights organizations, filed a civil lawsuit against individuals and groups for their violent anti-abortion activities. NOW claimed that these individuals and groups had used criminal tactics, including extortion and threats, in their protests. The defendants included Joseph Scheidler, who led the Pro-Life Action League; Randall Terry, leader of Operation Rescue; the Pro-Life Direct Action League; and Project Life. Activists belonging to these groups had been charged with robbery, defacing property, throwing fire bombs at abortion clinics, and threatening doctors.

The main issue in the case was whether the anti-abortion activists and groups could be held liable under a 1970 anti-crime law known as the Racketeer Influenced and Corrupt Organizations Act (RICO). RICO makes it illegal for "an enterprise" to conduct its activities by using a pattern of racketeering—criminal activity such as bribery or extortion. Proof of two or more statutorily enumerated criminal acts constitutes a pattern of racketeering. It is also a crime to conspire to violate RICO.

A federal district court dismissed NOW's case. It stated that the language used in RICO required an "economic motive." The plaintiffs had not proven that the anti-abortion defendants it accused of racketeering had "some profit-generating purpose." The court of appeals upheld the district court's ruling, and the case was appealed to the United States Supreme Court.

The case had taken on additional importance because the Supreme Court had ruled earlier, in January 1993, that pro-choice groups could not use civil rights laws to stop anti-abortion activities. This meant that some other means had to be found to challenge the more aggressive tactics of anti-abortion protesters. The newly installed Clinton administration filed a brief in support of NOW, in part because it also wished to use RICO against terrorists who might not be motivated by monetary gain.

(continued)

Supreme Court Case Study 64 (continued)

Constitutional Issue ★★★★★★★★★★★★★★★★★★★★★★★★★★★★★★★★★

The question before the Court was whether a civil RICO violation required proof that the defendant's pattern of racketeering had an economic motive.

★★★★★★★★★★★★ The Supreme Court's Decision ★★★★★★★★★★★★★

On January 24, 1994, the Supreme Court ruled unanimously that abortion-rights groups could use the RICO law. Chief Justice William H. Rehnquist wrote the Court's decision. He stated that there was no question that pro-choice groups could sue anti-abortion groups and demonstrators who had supposedly organized violent and criminal acts against abortion clinics and doctors who performed abortions.

Rehnquist stated that RICO could also be used in the case, even if the group involved did not have any financial motive. He went on to say that "the fact that RICO has been applied in situations not expressly anticipated by Congress does not demonstrate ambiguity." In his view, the law was not ambiguous, but was capable of handling a wide variety of cases.

In a concurring opinion, however, Justices David Souter and Anthony Kennedy sounded a note of caution. They urged courts applying RICO to use prudence because of the "First Amendment interests that could be at stake."

The Court's decision allowed NOW to refile its lawsuit in a district court.

Case Analysis Questions ★★★★★★★★★★★★★★★★★★★★★★★★★★★★★★★

DIRECTIONS: Answer the following questions on a separate sheet of paper.

1. What was the original intent of the RICO Act?
2. Do you believe the Court should have enforced the statute as written, or should it have enforced the intent of Congress? Explain.
3. What was the basis of the Court's ruling?
4. Did the Court's decision punish Scheidler and the other defendants? Give reasons for your answers.
5. What caution did the concurring justices urge in the application of RICO?

Supreme Court Case Study 65

Aid to Parochial Schools

Agostini v. *Felton*, 1997

★★★★★★★★★★★★★★★ **Background of the Case** ★★★★★★★★★★★★★★★

The Supreme Court has considered many cases which involved questions of government aid to parochial schools. Such aid is most often challenged on the basis of the First Amendment's ban on laws respecting the establishment of religion. The Court has found reasons to allow such aid when the circumstances seemed to warrant it. In 1947, for example, the Court ruled that a New Jersey law authorizing local school boards to reimburse parents for the cost of transportation to both public and private schools was constitutional. The Court reasoned that the law was designed to protect *all* students equally and was not aid to church-related schools.

On the opposite side of the aid-to-parochial schools question was the Court's ruling in a 1985 case, *Aguilar* v. *Felton*. Here the Court ruled that under a federal law that provided supplemental, remedial instruction to disadvantaged children, such aid could not be given on parochial school premises. In 1997 the question of aid to religious schools resurfaced, and the Court had to decide whether its 12-year-old ruling was still valid.

Under Title I of the Elementary and Secondary Education Act of 1965, disadvantaged children who needed remedial help were entitled to publicly funded services, whether they went to public or private schools. Many public school systems provided such help to parochial school children by having public school teachers give such instruction in parochial and other private schools.

After the Court made its 1985 *Aguilar* ruling banning aid to disadvantaged children on the premises of parochial schools, many public school systems provided the remedial instruction off-site. In some systems, parochial school students were bussed to public schools for the remedial instruction. The New York City public schools spent millions of dollars leasing vans to serve as mobile classrooms which were parked on public streets near parochial schools. Parochial school children then walked to the vans, where they were instructed by public school teachers. About 20,000 parochial school students a year were taught in the mobile classrooms.

In 1995 parents of children (including the Agostinis) who received such instruction and the New York City Board of Education asked the federal district court to rule that the *Aguilar* decision was no longer good law. The district court ruled that the Supreme Court's ruling in the *Aguilar* case was still a binding decision. The case was argued in the United States Supreme Court in April 1997, and the Court handed down its ruling in June 1997.

𝒞onstitutional Issue ★★★★★★★★★★★★★★★★★★★★★★★★★★★★★

Did the 1985 decision in the *Aguilar* ruling for remedial instruction still apply in 1995, or should the Court reverse the ruling since it had ruled in earlier cases that neutral, non-religious programs did not violate the establishment clause of the Constitution?

(continued)

Supreme Court Case Studies

Name _____ Date _____ Class _____

Supreme Court Case Study 65 *(continued)*

★★★★★★★★★★★★★★ The Supreme Court's Decision ★★★★★★★★★★★★★★★

Justice Sandra Day O'Connor wrote for the Court's 5-to-4 majority. Justice O'Connor wrote that the Court could no longer accept the premises of the *Aguilar* decision. The Court had used three presumptions for deciding whether the establishment clause of the First Amendment was applicable. These were: (1) "any public employee who works on the premises of a religious school is presumed to inculcate religion"; (2) "the presence of public employees on private school premises creates a symbolic union between church and state"; (3) "any and all public aid that directly aids the education function of religious schools impermissibly finances religious indoctrination. . . ." The Court rejected these presumptions in the *Agostini* case. In Justice O'Connor's words, "No evidence has ever shown that any New York City Title I instructor teaching on parochial school premises attempted to inculcate religion in students." She also wrote, ". . . a federally funded program providing supplemental, remedial instruction to disadvantaged children on a neutral basis is not invalid under the establishment clause when such instruction is given on the premises of sectarian schools by government employees pursuant to a program containing safeguards such as those present here."

★★★★★★★★★★★★★★★★★★ Dissenting Opinion ★★★★★★★★★★★★★★★★★★★

Justice David Souter wrote the dissent in which he claimed the Court's ruling would "authorize direct state aid to religious institutions on an unparalleled scale, in violation of the establishment clause's central prohibition against religious subsidies by the government. . . . There is simply no line that can be drawn between the instruction paid for at taxpayers' expense and the instruction in any subject that is not identified as formally religious."

DIRECTIONS: Answer the following questions on a separate sheet of paper.

1. What was the effect of the Court's ruling in the *Agostini* case?

2. Why would the mayor of New York City call the decision "very wise" and say the precedent that the decision overruled was "irrational"?

3. On what grounds did the Court reverse itself on the question of aid to religious schools?

4. How do you think the Supreme Court is likely to rule in future cases involving aid to parochial school children?

5. Do you agree or disagree with the Court's decision? Give reasons for your answer.

Supreme Court Case Study 66

Evidence Obtained in a Stop and Frisk

Illinois v. *Wardlow*, 2000

★★★★★★★★★★★★★★ Background of the Case ★★★★★★★★★★★★★★

On September 9, 1995, police officers Nolan and Harvey were working in the special operations section of the Chicago Police Department. Driving in a four-car caravan, they converged on an area known for heavy narcotics trafficking. As their car passed 4035 West Van Buren, Nolan observed a man holding an opaque bag standing next to the building. The officers turned their car southbound and watched the man as he ran through the gangway and an alley. The officers stayed in their vehicle but pursued the man. When they cornered him on the street, Nolan exited his car and stopped the suspicious person. The officer conducted a pat-down search for weapons because it was common to find weapons in the area where narcotics transactions occurred.

During the frisk, Officer Nolan squeezed the bag and felt an object similar to the shape of a gun. He proceeded to open the bag and discovered a .38-caliber handgun with five live rounds of ammunition. The officer arrested Wardlow.

Wardlow's attorney filed a motion to suppress the evidence. The Illinois trial court denied the motion, finding that the gun was recovered during a lawful stop and frisk. Wardlow was convicted of unlawful use of a weapon by a felon. Wardlow appealed the decision, and the State Appellate Court reversed the lower court. The State Appellate Court said that, under *Terry* v. *Ohio*, Nolan did not have reasonable suspicion to make the stop. On appeal by Illinois, the State Supreme Court upheld the ruling, determining that sudden flight in a high crime area does not create a reasonable suspicion justifying a "*Terry* stop," because flight may simply be an exercise of the right to "go on one's way."

*C*onstitutional Issue ★★★★★★★★★★★★★★★★★★★★★★★★★★★★★★★★

In *Terry* v. *Ohio*, the Supreme Court had held that an officer may, consistent with the Fourth Amendment, conduct a stop and frisk when the officer has a reasonable suspicion that there is criminal activity going on. In this case, the issue is whether the mere act of fleeing from the police meets the "reasonable suspicion" requirement for a stop and frisk. If the stop and frisk meets this standard, the evidence discovered may be admitted in court.

★★★★★★★★★★★★★★ The Supreme Court's Decision ★★★★★★★★★★★★★★

The United States Supreme Court granted certiorari, and Chief Justice Rehnquist delivered the majority opinion. The justices found that the officers' actions did not violate the Fourth Amendment. Rehnquist referred to the case of *Terry* v. *Ohio*, under which an officer who has a "reasonable, articulable suspicion that criminal activity is afoot may conduct a brief, investigatory stop." While an individual's presence in a "high crime area" is not enough to support a reasonable suspicion of criminal activity, a location's characteristics are relevant in helping determine whether the circumstances warrant further investigation. In this case, Wardlow's

(continued)

Supreme Court Case Studies

Supreme Court Case Study 66 (continued)

unprovoked flight aroused the officers' suspicions. "Nervous, evasive behavior is another pertinent factor in determining reasonable suspicion, . . . and headlong flight is the consummate act of evasion." Because the courts do not have scientific standards of reasonable suspicion to review an officer's decision, it must be based on commonsense judgments and inferences about human behavior.

The Court said that Officer Nolan was justified in suspecting that Wardlow was involved in criminal activity and, therefore, in investigating further. Any individual, when approached, has a right to ignore the police and go about his business, but unprovoked flight is the exact opposite of "going about one's business." "Allowing officers confronted with such flight to stop the fugitive and investigate further is quite consistent with the individual's right to go about his business or to stay put and remain silent in the face of police questioning." The Court agreed that there is a risk that officers may stop innocent people, but *Wardlow* recognized that officers can detain individuals to resolve ambiguities in their conduct. In such instances, *Wardlow* requires that the officer be able to articulate more than an "inchoate and unparticularized suspicion or 'hunch' of criminal activity." Unprovoked flight is, however, not a mere refusal to cooperate.

DIRECTIONS: Answer the following questions on a separate sheet of paper.

1. What role did the area where Wardlow was standing play in the way the Court viewed the chase and stop?
2. Why did the lower courts believe that the stop and frisk were not consistent with the Fourth Amendment?
3. How would you define "reasonable suspicion"?
4. Should the fact that Wardlow was found to be carrying a weapon have been taken into consideration by any of the courts? Why or why not?
5. How will the decision in this case affect future conduct by police officers?

Name _____ Date _____ Class _____

Supreme Court Case Study 67

Challenge to English as the Official Language
Alexander v. Sandoval, 2001

★★★★★★★★★★★★★★★ Background of the Case ★★★★★★★★★★★★★★★

Martha Sandoval wanted to take her driver's license test, but she could not take it because she did not speak English. Alabama, her home state, had stopped allowing people to take such tests in languages other than English after it amended its constitution in 1990. The amendment that made English the official language of the state was used to justify requiring all driver's license exams to be administered in English.

From the 1970s to 1991, Alabama had administered the driver's license test in 14 different languages. Sandoval, who spoke Spanish and understood a few English phrases, wanted to learn English and was enrolled in classes for a while, but working two jobs to support her children meant she had to drop the classes. Without a driver's license, Sandoval was limited in her ability to go to the grocery store or pharmacy, take her children to school, or even find a good job.

On December 31, 1996, Sandoval filed a federal class action suit against the Alabama Department of Public Safety. She alleged a violation of Title VI of the Civil Rights Act of 1964, which prohibits discrimination by recipients of federal money, such as Alabama's Department of Public Safety. The federal district court ruled against Director James Alexander and the State of Alabama, finding that the English-only policy "singles out resident non-English speaking applicants by requiring them to take their examination in English only, without the aid of interpreters or translators." It also said that "the regulation had impermissible disparate impact on the basis of national origin in violation of Title VI."

An 11th Circuit Court of Appeals panel affirmed the lower court's decision. Then the Alabama Attorney General (Alexander) petitioned the U.S. Supreme Court for a writ of certiorari. He claimed that while Title VI bars intentional discrimination, it is not clear whether Congress intended to allow private people to sue their state for policies that have a discriminatory impact when the state is not intentionally discriminating and the discrimination is not related to the purpose of the federal funding. The attorney general wrote, "These cases show that the concern that this Court expressed some 34 years ago in *Washington* v. *Davis*, that disparate impact claims would threaten 'a whole range of tax, welfare, public service, regulatory, and licensing statutes,' is not misplaced." He concluded, "This case presents this court with a clear opportunity to resolve this question."

*C*onstitutional Issue ★★★★★★★★★★★★★★★★★★★★★★★★★★★★★★

> In 1964 Congress passed a Civil Rights Act to stop discrimination. Title VI of that act prohibits discrimination on the basis of national origin. The issue in this case was whether Title VI created a "private right of action" against unintentional discrimination. A Department of Justice regulation earlier implied that policies that have the effect of discriminating, even if that is not their purpose, should be considered as discrimination. Based on Title VI, could private citizens sue state agencies for administering federal grants in a manner that has the effect of discriminating on the basis of ethnicity (national origin)?

(continued)

Supreme Court Case Studies 133

Name _____ Date _____ Class _____

Supreme Court Case Study 67 *(continued)*

★★★★★★★★★★★★★★ The Supreme Court's Decision ★★★★★★★★★★★★★★

On September 26, 2000, the U.S. Supreme Court granted certiorari in the case. On April 24, 2001, a divided Court held 5–4 that private individuals, such as Martha Sandoval, may not recover damages under Title VI of the federal Civil Rights Act from states whose rules they consider racially or ethnically discriminatory. Justice Antonin Scalia wrote for the majority, "Neither as originally enacted nor as later amended does Title VI display an intent to create a freestanding private right of action to enforce (such) regulations." The Court held that Sandoval could not properly invoke the regulation. Because Title VI imposed requirements beyond those specifically contemplated by Congress, the regulation could not form the basis for a private suit.

The decision clarified that individuals can sue for federal civil rights violations if there is a state-sponsored intentional discrimination. Scalia said the difference here is that the provision of the Civil Rights Act (section 602) did not focus on the individual being protected from discrimination or on the funding that state agencies receive from the federal government, but on the state agencies themselves. "So far as we can tell," wrote Scalia, "this authorizing portion of §602 reveals no congressional intent to create a private right of action."

★★★★★★★★★★★★★★★★★ Dissenting Opinion ★★★★★★★★★★★★★★★★★

Writing the dissenting opinion, Justice John Paul Stevens criticized the majority for creating an important exception "unfounded in our precedent and hostile to decades of settled expectations." Stevens conceded that the Court had "never said in so many words that a private right of action exists to enforce the disparate-impact regulations" promulgated under the federal Civil Rights Act. Stevens observed, however, that the Court had effectively ruled in prior decisions that a private right of action exists. He added that he believed the majority's decision was the "unconscious product of the majority's profound distaste for implied causes of action rather than an attempt to discern the intent of the Congress that enacted Title VI of the Civil Rights Act of 1964."

DIRECTIONS: Answer the following questions on a separate sheet of paper.

1. Why did the State of Alabama require that all driver's license exams be given in English?

2. Why did Martha Sandoval believe that the state policy discriminated against her?

3. On what grounds did the majority of the Supreme Court rule against Sandoval?

4. What criticism did Justice Stevens level at the majority's decision?

5. In your opinion, is a state's decision to adopt English as the official language a form of discrimination?

Supreme Court Case Study 68

Congress Delegates Authority to Federal Agencies

Whitman v. American Trucking Associations, 2001

★★★★★★★★★★★★★★★★ **Background of the Case** ★★★★★★★★★★★★★★★★

Congress created the Environmental Protection Agency (EPA) to oversee environmental legislation. In 1997 the administrator of the Environmental Protection Agency revised the ozone and particulate matter national ambient air quality standards (NAAQS). Private parties and several states challenged the revised NAAQS on several grounds. Most important was the charge that the administrator had assumed powers that the Constitution delegates to Congress alone.

The District of Columbia Circuit Court heard the case. It reviewed the EPA administrator's interpretation of the relevant law that instructs the EPA to set standards "the attainment and maintenance of which . . . are requisite to protect the public health" with "an adequate margin of safety." The Circuit Court said that Congress, in breach of the Constitution, had delegated legislative power to the administrator. The Court of Appeals also ruled that the EPA may not consider implementation costs in setting the NAAQS.

Constitutional Issue ★★★★★★★★★★★★★★★★★★★★★★★★★★★★★★

May Congress delegate its lawmaking power to the administrative branch? In *Whitman v. American Trucking Associations*, the Supreme Court addressed the issue of whether Congress had wrongfully delegated lawmaking power to the Environmental Protection Agency. The justices reviewed a provision of the Clean Air Act that authorized the EPA to write air quality regulations that "are requisite to the public health." The case presented the following questions: (1) Did the Clean Air Act delegate legislative power to the administrator of the Environmental Protection Agency? (2) May the administrator consider the costs of implementation in setting national ambient air quality standards? (3) Does the Court of Appeals have jurisdiction to review the EPA's interpretation of the Clean Air Act with respect to implementing the revised ozone NAAQS? (4) If so, was the EPA's interpretation permissible?

★★★★★★★★★★★★★★★ **The Supreme Court's Decision** ★★★★★★★★★★★★★★★

The lower court had said that because the statutory term "public health" was so vague, the Clean Air Act allowed the EPA to enact whatever rules it wanted. The Supreme Court conceded that Congress cannot simply delegate all its authority to federal agencies. It cannot pass the buck for matters of basic public policy to bureaucrats. The Supreme Court, however, overturned the lower federal court ruling that a provision of the Clean Air Act was unconstitutional. The justices unanimously recognized that Congress lacks the time and expertise to write all of the administrative laws needed to govern our complex society. The Court held that when Congress gave the EPA general guidelines, it satisfied its constitutional duty and provided the EPA with sufficient guidance to do its job.

(continued)

Name _____ Date _____ Class _____

Supreme Court Case Study 68 (continued)

Justice Scalia delivered the unanimous opinion, stating that the Court agreed with the Solicitor General that the text of the Clean Air Act "at a minimum requires that [f]or a discrete set of pollutants and based on published air quality criteria that reflect the latest scientific knowledge, [the] EPA must establish uniform national standards at a level that is requisite to protect public health from the adverse effects of the pollutant in the ambient air."

The ruling in *American Trucking* was important because it rejected a view that could have paralyzed federal regulatory agencies. Some people believe that limiting Congress's ability to delegate rule-making authority to federal agencies would return power from the agencies to Congress. However, such a view would thwart the regulatory power of Congress. The legislature does not have the capacity to do the job currently done by the agencies.

Historically, courts have tended to support the notion that a federal agency must interpret the laws Congress requires the agency to administer. Provided that the agency's approach is "reasonable," a court usually upholds it. The agency's ruling carries the force of law.

This decision was not the Supreme Court's final word on the issue. Following the *Whitman* decision, the Court ruled in *United States* v. *Mead Corp.* that an agency's ruling does not carry the force of law unless there is some affirmative indication that Congress intended to give the agency that power. Taken together, the Court's rulings in *American Trucking* and in *Mead Corp.* show that the Court will give Congress wide latitude to accomplish goals that are within its powers. To accomplish these goals, Congress may delegate power to administrative agencies if the legislation specifies the areas in which those agencies' decisions will have the force of law.

DIRECTIONS: Answer the following questions on a separate sheet of paper.

1. What duty and responsibility of the legislative branch was in question in this case?

2. Why did two lower courts rule that the EPA administrator's actions were unconstitutional?

3. What did the majority of the Supreme Court believe in regard to the power that Congress gave the EPA?

4. Why must Congress be careful in writing laws that will be enforced by federal administrative agencies?

5. How does this decision help federal regulatory agencies?

Answer Key

★ CASE STUDY 1

Marbury v. Madison, 1803

1. The *Marbury* v. *Madison* case established the right of the Supreme Court to rule on the constitutionality of laws.

2. It provided a way to check the powers of Congress and the president, and thus more effectively balanced the powers of all three branches of the federal government.

3. On the one hand, Marshall declared the Judiciary Act unconstitutional because the power for Congress to pass such an act was not mentioned in the Constitution. Yet at the same time he believed the Supreme Court had the power to declare a law unconstitutional, even though this power was not specifically mentioned in the Constitution.

4. Answers will vary. Students who favor the Court's power may say that it provides a check on Congress and more equally balances the power of the three branches of government. Students who oppose the Court's power may say that since Congressional representatives are elected, they represent the will of the people, so the laws passed by Congress should stand and not be subjected to a review by a Court of appointed judges.

5. Answers will vary. Students who think the influence of personal politics on Court rulings is improper may say that legal opinions should be based on a legal interpretation of the Constitution law and not on politics. Students who accept political influence on Court rulings as proper may say that it often reflects the will of the majority.

★ CASE STUDY 2

McCulloch v. Maryland, 1819

1. The *McCulloch* case established the principle that Congress has implied powers not specifically stated in the Constitution.

2. The "necessary and proper" clause gives Congress the authority to make any laws that are required to carry out its enumerated tasks.

3. The Court ruled that the United States Bank was immune to the Maryland tax because as an arm of the federal government it is not required to pay state taxes.

4. Federalists believed in a strong national government, and the *McCulloch* decision reflects that point of view in that it limited the power of the states to tax any part of the federal government.

5. The *McCulloch* decision greatly enlarged the powers of the federal government by stating that it is "supreme within its sphere of action," and has powers that are not specifically set forth in the Constitution.

★ CASE STUDY 3

Dartmouth College v. Woodward, 1819

1. Dartmouth College remained a private institution and was protected under Article I, Section 10 of the Constitution from interference by the state. The trustees were reinstated to administer the college, and the college records, the corporate seal, and other corporate property were returned to the trustees by the state treasurer.

2. Chief Justice Marshall explained that if a state or other sovereign—here the British crown—granted a charter of incorporation, the charter has "every ingredient of a complete and legitimate contract."

3. The *Dartmouth* case established that a corporate charter granted by the state comes under the protection of the contract clause that prohibits states from making any laws which impair the obligation of a contract. Therefore, businesses could flourish without being subjected to interference by the state.

4. If states wanted to provide higher education, they had to provide publicly funded institutions because the *Dartmouth* decision prohibited the states from taking over private institutions.

5. The *Dartmouth* decision weakened the power of the states by ruling that even though states have the power to charter corporations, corporations are protected from interference by the states because they are protected under the contract clause in Article 1, Section 10 of the Constitution, which prohibits states from making any laws that impair the obligations of a contract.

★ CASE STUDY 4

Gibbons v. Ogden, 1824

1. A trucking company operating between San Francisco and Portland would be regulated by both federal and state governments. Each state, for example, could impose taxes on the company's purely in-state business, but the federal government could set safety standards for vehicles using the interstate highway system.

2. Unless he defined navigation as a part of commerce, he would not have been able to deal with the question of interstate commerce in the United States.

3. Jackson said Marshall expanded federal power over commerce to a breadth never exceeded, because the *Gibbons* decision opened the way for Congress to regulate interstate commerce, which now constitutes the great bulk of commerce in this country. Marshall also laid the groundwork for regulating activities that are indirectly, as well as directly, involved in interstate commerce.

4. Both cases gave the federal government powers than are not spelled out literally in the Constitution; thus both decisions diminished states' powers and increased those of the federal government.

5. Answers will vary. Students agreeing with the *Gibbons* decision may say that the federal government is needed as a power greater than the states to make decisions about issues involving more than one state. Students opposed to the *Gibbons* decision may say a state has the right to regulate business within its boundaries, so the federal government should not have interfered with New York's right to assign an exclusive ferryboat license for a New York port.

★ CASE STUDY 5

Dred Scott v. Sandford, 1857

1. When the Supreme Court ruled that the Missouri Compromise was unconstitutional, it held that Congress had no power to ban slavery in the territories. Thus Scott's claim that he had been in free territory where slavery was not permitted was invalid.

2. The *Dred Scott* decision severely hampered legal efforts to end slavery through court procedures.

3. Slave holders were obviously pleased with the decision because it foreclosed legal efforts by abolitionists to end slavery.

4. The Court said that since African Americans were not citizens of the United States, they did not have the legal right to sue in a federal court.

5. The *Dred Scott* decision is important because although it was intended to settle the question of slavery, it adopted an extreme view and unleashed a storm of protest against the Court, which ultimately became a factor in the coming of the Civil War.

★ CASE STUDY 6

Ex Parte Milligan, 1866

1. The Court concluded that neither Congress nor the president could grant the military authority to try civilians, so long as civilian courts were still functioning.

2. General Hovey probably thought a military court would declare Milligan guilty, whereas a civilian court might find him not guilty.

3. According to the Court's ruling, military rule would take precedence over civilian authority when civilian courts were not operating.

4. Four Justices thought Congress should be responsible for deciding in special circumstances whether a military court could try civilians.

5. Habeas corpus is an important part of the Constitution because it prevents authorities from legally holding a prisoner as long as they wish without filing formal charges against that individual. This was in keeping with the spirit of the Bill of Rights, which restricted governments from denying personal freedoms.

★ CASE STUDY 7

Slaughterhouse Cases, 1873

1. The Court ruled that the protections of the Thirteenth and Fourteenth Amendments did not apply to the butchers in the *Slaughterhouse* Cases. The Court stated that the amendments were designed only for the protection of formerly enslaved people.

2. The ruling in the *Slaughterhouse* cases nullified the *Dred Scott* decision.

3. The Court's decision meant that as a butcher, you would not have been able to supply meat in New Orleans unless you did business as part of the licensed monopoly.

4. State governments gained more than the federal government from the Court's decision in the *Slaughterhouse* cases, since the Court ruled that the protections of the Thirteenth and Fourteenth Amendments did not curb Louisiana's power to grant a monopoly.

5. Answers will vary. Students who agree with the Court's majority opinion might say that the Fourteenth Amendment makes the states responsible for enforcing laws that protect the rights of citizens, and that since the state granted the monopoly, it was legal. Students who oppose the decision might point out that if the butchers were denied work because of the monopoly, they would be forced to work for the monopoly, which could be considered forced servitude, illegal under the Thirteenth Amendment.

★ CASE STUDY 8

Reynolds v. United States, 1879

1. Chief Justice Waite supported Congress's right to legislate against religious practices that might have a harmful effect on the social order. In the *Reynolds* case, polygamy was so viewed. Congress, therefore, had the right to prohibit such a practice.

2. Polygamy was one aspect of the Mormon religion, as ritual murder might be in another religion, contrary to the mores of Western society. The Court did not believe the religious protections of the First Amendment should include behaviors offensive to civilized society.

3. The Court recognized that there are sometimes circumstances when the freedoms guaranteed by the First Amendment must be curtailed to avoid anarchy or other social chaos.

4. The Court could justify regulating marriage because in addition to being "a sacred obligation," marriage also involves a civil contract that needs to be regulated by law.

5. Answers will vary. Students might justify the actions of government authorities in singling out one person to prosecute because society wanted polygamy stopped, and the authorities probably felt that prosecuting one person would do so. Students who feel the action is unjust might say that choosing only one person for prosecution left others who had committed the same crime unpunished.

★ CASE STUDY 9

Plessy v. Ferguson, 1896

1. The majority opinion of the Supreme Court claimed that the Fourteenth Amendment aimed to establish the equality of the races, but was not intended to abolish distinctions based on color or to enforce social equality. Furthermore, they stated the Louisiana law was reasonable because states could legally segregate the races in the exercise of their police powers.

2. The separate-but-equal principle means segregation is legal as long as equal facilities are provided for each race.

3. Justice Harlan dissented from the majority opinion on the grounds that segregation based on race was inconsistent with the freedoms and equality established by the Constitution.

4. Plessy based his appeal in part on the Thirteenth Amendment because it banned "involuntary servitude," and segregation of railroad cars was a form of such servitude.

5. The *Plessy* decision affirmed the legality of segregation practices in the southern states. Although the Court's decision required equality of public facilities, the southern states made no effort to carry out this requirement.

★ CASE STUDY 10

Northern Securities v. United States, 1904

1. The Court's decision extended the meaning of the word *commerce* to apply to companies not directly engaged in interstate commerce but which nevertheless controlled such commerce.

2. Justices Brewer and Harlan agreed that Northern Securities Company was guilty of unlawful restraint of trade and had thus violated the Sherman Antitrust Act. Justice Brewer did not agree with the rest of Justice Harlan's reasoning, including the idea that a combination need not be directly involved in commerce in order to restrain it or to have the potential to restrain it.

3. The fact that the railroads operated in several states brought them into the category of interstate commerce, which the Constitution gave Congress the power to regulate.

4. Members of the majority differed on several points: whether the word *commerce* should have a broad or narrow interpretation and what constituted restraint of trade.

5. The Court's decision clearly established the principle that the ownership of an interstate business as well as its direct operation fell within the definition of *commerce* and thus within the power of Congress to regulate it.

★ CASE STUDY 11

Weeks v. United States, 1914

1. The Supreme Court ordered that Weeks's papers be returned to him because they had been illegally seized and could not be used as evidence against Weeks in court.

2. The exclusionary rule bars evidence that is obtained illegally from being used in a trial.

3. The Court's ruling in the *Weeks* case increased the likelihood that police officers would obtain a warrant prior to searching for and seizing evidence that could be relevant to the case they were investigating.

4. Common law held that relevant evidence could be submitted in court no matter how it had been obtained. The *Weeks* ruling overturned this common practice and established that illegally obtained evidence, no matter how relevant, could be excluded at a trial.

5. Students who agree with the Court's ruling might say that a trial would not be fair if illegally seized evidence was admitted and that it is just as necessary in a civilized society for law enforcement officers to obey the law as it is for other citizens. Students taking the opposite position may say that the exclusionary rule allows guilty persons to go free and that all relevant evidence should be allowed at trial, no matter how it was obtained.

★ CASE STUDY 12

Schenck v. United States, 1919

1. The Espionage Act was passed to discourage people from interfering with the government's efforts to build an army to fight World War I.

2. The clear and present danger principle meant that under dangerous circumstances, such as falsely calling "fire" in a crowded theater or trying to undermine the nation's efforts to raise an army during a war, free speech may be curtailed.

3. Holmes accepted the limitations on Schenck's freedom of speech only because the nation was at war.

4. Students' answers will vary. Some may say that the government has a right to take action against anyone or anything that might interfere with the war effort. Others will argue that First Amendment rights have to be upheld in all circumstances because not to do so would seriously diminish the protections guaranteed by the Bill of Rights.

5. Holmes's subsequent dissent reveals that he greatly respected the First Amendment's guarantee of freedom of speech and that he was willing to limit those guarantees only in times of crisis when a real and definite danger threatened the nation and the clear and present danger principle could be applied.

★ CASE STUDY 13

Gitlow v. New York, 1925

1. The Court did not explain why it applied the First Amendment protections to the states; rather it assumed the application of these rights to the states under the Fourteenth Amendment due process clause.
2. No. The Court held that a state could constitutionally prohibit an entire class of subversive speech, and it was not necessary to prove that such speech would produce a specific result.
3. The Court did not prohibit the reading of any so-called subversive literature.
4. Answers will vary. Students who agree with the majority opinion may say that states have a right to make and enforce laws against those individuals who advocate the overthrow of an elected government by force, violence, or anarchy. Students who agree with Holmes's dissent may say that although Gitlow's radical ideas were unpopular, there was no evidence they were effective in influencing others to bring about a violent uprising, so Gitlow presented no clear and present danger to the government and should not have been prosecuted.
5. Answers will vary. Students who agree with unlimited freedom of speech and press may draw a distinction between speech and actions, saying that individuals should only be prosecuted for violent or unlawful actions, not unpopular ideas or speech. Students who think there should be some limitations on speech and the press may cite examples in which what is said or written may incite hatred of a specific group or be dangerous to the public, such as providing instructions for bomb making.

★ CASE STUDY 14

Whitney v. California, 1927

1. Whitney was convicted of criminal syndicalism for being a member of the Communist Labor Party; the party was found to have been organized to advocate, teach, and abet criminal syndicalism.
2. The Court ruled that the Communist Labor Party to which Whitney belonged endangered the government of California and the public peace and security.
3. Brandeis, unlike Sanford, held that merely holding opinions that were offensive to the government, even though they may result in some violence or the destruction of property, is no reason for prohibiting freedom of speech.
4. Students' opinions will vary. Some will say that membership in such an organization may lead to acts that threaten the government and should therefore be banned. Others may say that membership should not be punished because it involves only agreement with the aims of the organization and is therefore a belief, which is protected by the First Amendment.
5. The justices may have held that if the defendant performed no criminal act, the defendant should not be punished for his or her beliefs. (This is what the Court held in the 1969 case of *Brandenburg* v. *Ohio*.)

★ CASE STUDY 15

Olmstead v. United States, 1928

1. The majority of justices on the Court felt that the Fourth Amendment applied only to things, not to hearing or sight, so the amendment did not apply to telephone wiretaps, which involve hearing.
2. The Court said that the means by which evidence is obtained is unimportant as long as the evidence is pertinent.
3. Under the *Olmstead* ruling, the evidence would be admissible since the Court indicated that it did not matter how evidence was secured as long as the evidence was pertinent.
4. Brandeis was commenting on the fact that the majority of justices were willing to accept an illegal seizure of evidence to achieve a socially desired end, the conviction of Olmstead.
5. Answers will vary. Students who agree with the Court's decision may say that telephone speech is not the same as a person's house, papers, or effects and is therefore not protected by the Fourth Amendment. Students who disagree with the decision may say that telephone speech is just as personal as letters, property, and other effects and should, therefore, be protected by the Fourth Amendment and, in turn, by the Fifth Amendment which protects a citizen from incriminating oneself. In addition, they may support the requirement of government prosecutors to follow the law scrupulously when building cases against defendants.

★ CASE STUDY 16

Near v. Minnesota, 1931

1. No. Censorship may be permitted in times of war or against obscene publications.
2. The Fourteenth Amendment applies the freedoms of the First Amendment to the states.
3. The lawyer should claim that, according to the *Near* decision, prior censorship of the press is not legal. The press can only be held responsible for the truth of their information after publication, not before.
4. The mayor could sue the paper for libel if he/she could prove that the paper published information it knew to be false.
5. The *Near* decision is important because it bans prior censorship of the press.

★ CASE STUDY 17

Powell v. Alabama, 1932

1. The defendants' guilt was not an issue for the Court to decide. Whether a defendant is guilty or innocent is a matter for a jury or a trial court, sitting as the fact finder, to decide. As a general rule, the Supreme Court rules only on whether the trial met constitutional standards.
2. The Fourteenth Amendment's requirement of due process of the law was at the heart of the Court's examination of the *Powell* case.
3. Answers may vary. One possibility is that the trial court behaved as though it believed that Powell and his friends, as African Americans, were not entitled to anything more than a brief, routine hearing in court, and that the defendants were probably guilty anyway.
4. The trials were so speedy that they took only one day each, a very short time for capital cases. The defendants had little time to prepare their defense and no attorney to help them conduct their case.
5. Without a lawyer, it is assumed that a defendant does not have the ability to defend himself, even if the defendant is otherwise well educated; hence the saying that any person, even a lawyer, who attempts to defend himself or herself has a fool for a client.

★ CASE STUDY 18

DeJonge v. Oregon, 1937

1. Answers may vary. One possibility is that the right to assemble peacefully is foundational to United States civil and political freedoms in much the same way as are free press and free speech.
2. The decision applied to the states the freedoms of the Bill of Rights through the Fourteenth Amendment.
3. Probably not, because the facts show that it had been widely advertised as organized by the Communist Party.
4. Not only the defendant but also the American people in general, because the Court's decision reaffirmed their fundamental right to assemble and to speak at such assemblies.
5. Possible answers: Students who favor limits may say that the right to assemble should be limited when there is a danger of a riot or other dangerous circumstances. Students who support no limits may say that the right to assemble peacefully is such a basic right that any lawful limitation might encourage other limitations.

★ CASE STUDY 19

West Coast Hotel v. Parrish, 1937

1. The economic conditions of the 1930s forced the justices to rethink their attitudes toward the constitutionality of social and economic legislation.
2. The majority based its decision on the belief that enacting legislation that protects women and other workers whose economic bargaining position may be

weak from unscrupulous and overreaching employers is a legitimate use of government power.

3. The Court overruled a previous decision that had been regarded as a controlling precedent.

4. The constitutional scholar was saying that support for the judicial philosophy expressed by the dissent essentially had ended because of the economic realities during the 1930s and that this case marked the end of the period when the Court ruled against the constitutionality of laws that sought to regulate business.

5. Students' answers will vary. Some students may say that if the *West Coast Hotel* case is typical of the Court's attitudinal change about social and economic regulations, the Court probably will decide that regulating business is permissible in the future. Other students may say that it is impossible to forecast how the Court is likely to rule in future cases.

★ CASE STUDY 20

Minersville School District v. *Gobitis*, 1940

1. The flag salute helped form a sense of patriotism, or "cohesive sentiment," which is at the basis of a free society.

2. The Court should not overrule the wisdom of the legislature, and the court room is not the place to debate issues of educational policy.

3. Answers may vary. One possibility is that the Court would support an individual's right to salute or not salute the flag in accordance with the individual's personal beliefs.

4. Student answers will vary. Students who say they would have protested may support their protest by recalling that all of our liberties have been won through individual or group protests against government restrictions. Students who say they would not have protested may agree with the Court that it is important to build a cohesive society and that saluting the flag is one way to accomplish that end.

5. To civil libertarians, the *Gobitis* decision seemed to be a wrongheaded decision based on a very limited understanding of the Fourteenth Amendment guarantees.

★ CASE STUDY 21

Betts v. *Brady*, 1942

1. Earlier law could be interpreted as allowing, but not requiring, that an indigent defendant be represented by counsel.

2. The Sixth Amendment applies to federal, not state, jurisdiction. Matters related to the state must be viewed in the light of the due process clause of the Fourteenth Amendment.

3. Justice Black based his dissent on the ruling in the *Powell* case and that the right to counsel is fundamental to the Sixth and Fourteenth Amendments.

4. In the *Powell* case, a capital crime had been involved, so the lack of proper counsel along with other elements violated every principle of fairness; the *Betts* case, on the other hand, was not a capital case. Roberts's judgment on the question of providing counsel was that each case had to be decided on its own merits. He thought that to deny counsel might be "shocking to the universal sense of justice" in one case but not in another.

5. Roberts emphasized that "Every court has power . . . to appoint counsel where that course seems to be required in the interest of fairness." Students who agree with Justice Roberts may say that an impartial judge, who represents the people, should have the authority to decide how to spend the people's tax money and which defendants do or do not need legal counsel to provide a fair trial. Students who do not agree with Justice Roberts's position may say that all defendants are considered innocent until found guilty and that they all should be guaranteed counsel to protect their legal rights while preparing for and during their trial.

★ CASE STUDY 22

West Virginia State Board of Education v. *Barnette*, 1943

1. The flag salute was considered to be a form of utterance, or speech, so the freedoms guaranteed in the First Amendment would apply to the flag salute as well as to speech.

2. In the *Gobitis* case, the Court ruled that the state's flag salute requirement was constitutional because there were situations in which freedom of religion could be restricted; in the *Barnette* case, the Court ruled that the state's flag salute requirement was unconstitutional because it violated the principles of the First Amendment that limited government.

3. The Court held that "to believe that patriotism will not flourish if patriotic ceremonies are voluntary and spontaneous instead of a compulsory routine is to make an unflattering estimate of the appeal of our institutions to free minds. . . ."

4. Answers may vary. Students may mention that freedoms are sometimes restricted during times of war, national unrest, or natural disasters.

5. Student answers will vary, but they should include the idea that the rights guaranteed by the Bill of Rights, in this case the First Amendment, apply to all beliefs, whether they are accepted by the majority or only by a minority.

★ CASE STUDY 23

Endo v. *United States*, 1944

1. The Court focused on the fact that Mitsuye Endo was an American citizen whose loyalty had never been questioned.

2. Other Japanese Americans could have sued successfully for their release on the grounds that they were American citizens and that their Japanese ancestry did not preclude them from being loyal to the United States.

3. Justice Murphy believed that the whole internment program was unconstitutional, whereas Douglas defended the relocation, but argued that the authority to detain a citizen or place conditions on the person's release, as protection against espionage or sabotage, is exhausted when that person's loyalty is conceded.

4. Students' answers will vary. Probably most students, more than half a century after World War II, will agree with Justice Murphy. Some students, however, may agree with Douglas on the grounds that the internment program, as unfair as it was, was an attempt by the government to protect the nation.

5. Students may speculate that, as is often true in important cases that involve constitutional questions, some other person or organization opposed to the government's internment program on constitutional grounds paid the legal costs involved.

★ CASE STUDY 24

Korematsu v. *United States*, 1944

1. The evacuation orders were based on the war powers of the president and Congress.

2. Answers will vary. Students will probably express outrage that his or her patriotism could have been so severely questioned.

3. Black's stand in this case did not enhance his reputation as a defender of people's rights.

4. Justice Murphy argued that the Japanese Americans had been deprived of equal protection of the law and procedural due process guaranteed by the Fifth Amendment.

5. Answers will vary. Students who agree with the description may say that the government's use of the military against its own citizens is definitely alarming. Students who disagree with the description may say that during times of war, the government sometimes needs to approve restrictions that would never be considered in ordinary times.

★ CASE STUDY 25

Everson v. *Board of Education*, 1947

1. There was concern that denying benefits to students attending parochial schools would be seen as discrimination against religion.

2. Yes, the Court's ruling would probably apply to such schools as well since the reasoning was that paying for transportation is similar to providing police and fire protection.

3. Justice Rutledge argued that the cost of transportation was part of the cost of education, and since the instruction was

primarily religious, reimbursement for transportation costs was not allowable.

4. Probably not, since paying the teachers was clearly part of the cost of parochial school education.

5. Answers will vary. Students who agree with Justice Black may say that tax-subsidized transportation to schools falls into the same category as police and fire protection and should therefore be available to all children, not just to those in public school. Students who agree with Justice Rutledge may stress that the purpose of reimbursing transportation costs is to defray costs, and that the cost of transportation is no less a part of religious instruction than teachers or textbooks. In order to maintain the separation of church and state, the state must withhold what the Constitution forbids it to give.

★ CASE STUDY 26

McCollum v. Board of Education, 1948

1. on the grounds that religion and government should be separate from each other

2. Frankfurter meant that the separation between religion and government is so important that it should not be easily disregarded.

3. the customs of the people

4. Answers may vary. One possibility students may suggest is that the justices all wanted to go on record in a decision that varied so markedly from the *Everson* decision.

5. Answers will vary. Students who agree with the decision will probably stress the separation of church and state in the constitution. Those who disagree with the decision may argue that religious education is positive for the community and the country and is supported by a majority of people. Therefore religious instruction should be allowed in public schools as long as all religions are provided equal access.

★ CASE STUDY 27

Dennis v. United States, 1951

1. The Smith Act had to pass the clear and present danger test.

2. Vinson claimed that only the existence of a conspiracy need be proved, while Black and Douglas held that overt acts were necessary to convict, and that only speeches and publications had been proven.

3. Under the Court's reasoning, you might have been found guilty because, according to the Smith Act, it was illegal to advocate the overthrow of the government by force or violence.

4. Students' answers will vary. Students who favor protection may say that freedom of speech and thought are protected by the First Amendment, and it has been well established that these protections are especially important for those who advocate unpopular positions. Students who oppose protections may point out that groups who want to change the government already have recourse to do so peacefully; they need not conspire to overthrow a legal government by force or violence.

5. The Court might have agreed with Justices Douglas and Black that advocacy alone is not sufficient to prove illegality.

★ CASE STUDY 28

Feiner v. New York, 1951

1. Justice Vinson said the police acted properly to prevent public disorder.

2. Justice Black saw the majority decision as subjecting all speeches, political or otherwise, to the supervision and censorship of the local police, which he viewed as a long step toward totalitarian authority.

3. Students who agree with Justice Vinson's ruling may reason that police need the power to protect public safety even if their actions interfere with an individual's right to free speech. Students who agree with Justice Black's dissent may express concern about the possibility of overzealous police officers censoring public speech, especially speech that they consider offensive, instead of protecting speakers from unsympathetic audiences.

4. Justices Black, Douglas, and Minton thought the job of the police in this situation was to protect freedom of speech, so their most important task would be to protect the speaker, especially one who was espousing unpopular ideas.

5. Speakers would probably be careful not to say anything that might incite their listeners to riot.

★ CASE STUDY 29

Brown v. Board of Education of Topeka, Kansas, 1954

1. Recognizing the psychological impact that segregation had on children was necessary in order to show that segregation violated the equal protection clause of the Fourteenth Amendment.

2. The *Brown* decision affected all public schools, both in the North and the South, so it probably directly affected more people than any other Court decision.

3. Students who agree with the *Brown* decision may point out that segregated schools violate the basic principles of equality upon which the United States is founded. Students who disagree with the Brown decision may point out that African American students in integrated schools may have to fit into a setting that is dominated by the white culture, whereas they may learn better in a cultural setting that is more familiar to them.

4. Students' answers may vary. One possible answer is that many people in the South loudly denounced the *Brown* decision with a determination not to obey the Court's ruling.

5. The justices may have realized that a ruling either way in the *Brown* case was bound to be controversial, so they may have planned a show of unanimity in order to decrease public dissension on the issue.

★ CASE STUDY 30

Yates v. United States, 1957

1. Advocacy is merely supporting a cause or proposal; incitement is urging or encouraging others to take action in support of a cause or proposal.

2. The Court held that the trial judge's instructions were inadequate because he had not informed the jury that to convict under the Smith Act, the prosecution needed to prove not only that the defendants had advocated overthrowing the government, but also that they had intended to incite people to such action.

3. In *Dennis*, the Court made no distinction between advocacy and incitement; in the *Yates* case, the Court did make that distinction.

4. The *Yates* case determined that persons who simply advocate communism are not guilty of violating the Smith Act.

5. Students who agree with the *Yates* decision may say that the First Amendment protects unpopular speech, so people who advocate Communist causes should be protected unless they take or incite others to take some illegal action in support of their cause. Students who disagree with the decision may point out that elected governments need laws to help protect the public interest by prosecuting groups like the Communists, who not only advocate the forcible overthrow of the government but are also well organized enough to act illegally in support of their beliefs.

★ CASE STUDY 31

Barenblatt v. United States, 1959

1. The Court ruled that the First Amendment does not give a witness the right to resist governmental inquiry in all circumstances, and when competing individual and the governmental interests are at stake, a balance must be struck in favor of the government.

2. The Court assumed that the committee did have a specified purpose and that its work conformed with Congress's intentions because Congress had regularly provided appropriations for the committee's work and had raised it to a standing committee.

3. All dissenting judges agreed that Barenblatt's First Amendment rights had been violated.

4. Since the Court defended the committee against all the attacks made on it by Barenblatt, there was no reason why the committee would have to change how it operated.

5. Students who agree with the Court's decision may say that the Communist Party was a dangerous threat to this country, so Congress had a right to thoroughly investigate its members even if some of their First Amendment and Fifth Amendment protections had to be relinquished. Students who agree with the dissent may say that Congress should never, under any circumstances, ignore the protections provided citizens by the Bill of Rights. To do so is to violate the Constitution.

★ CASE STUDY 32

Mapp v. Ohio, 1961

1. Illegally seized evidence violates the constitutional right to privacy.
2. Convicting a criminal by using illegally seized evidence can undermine a government's authority and determination to observe its own laws.
3. The illegally seized evidence in the *Mapp* case was so-called obscene material.
4. Evidence rejected as illegally seized in a federal case was acceptable in a state court.
5. Students who agree with the *Mapp* decision may emphasize the idea that the authority of government is weakened by failure to observe its own laws. Students who disagree with the decision may say that too many criminals are set free because of the legal technicalities created by the exclusionary rule.

★ CASE STUDY 33

Baker v. Carr, 1962

1. The case did not involve a political question; it presented a "case" or "controversy" and if the appellants were correct, the federal courts had the authority and ability to fashion a remedy. The case was therefore justiciable or subject to review by a federal court under Article III, Section 2 of the Constitution.
2. The practice of states refusing to reapportion legislative districts to reflect changes in the distribution of their population.
3. The *Baker* decision stated that a citizen in the state can ask a federal court to consider whether the legislative districts of the state are proper.
4. Students who agree with Justice Brennan may say that the Court had the right to require states to undergo redistricting every ten years according to provisions in the Constitution so as to eliminate inequities and maintain fairness in legislative representation. Students who agree with Frankfurter's dissent may say that federal courts should not be deciding questions involving the internal policies of the states.
5. Answers may vary. Possible answer: The *Baker* decision reinforced the democratic principle that every citizen's vote should carry the same weight.

★ CASE STUDY 34

Engel v. Vitale, 1962

1. The justices decided that it was unconstitutional for the government to prescribe prayer or governmentally sponsored religious activity because such action violates the establishment clause.
2. Students who agree with Justice Black's opinion may say that any prayer as part of a governmental program, whether or not the prayer is compulsory, breaches the separation between Church and State. Students who agree with Justice Potter's dissent may say that the Court has interfered with the free exercise of religion.
3. The Hyde Park schools had to abandon their practice of reciting a daily prayer.
4. Students' answers will vary, but they should understand that the Founders were not against religion and that the motto on the bills is nothing more than a statement, not an activity.
5. Student opinions will vary, but they should show thoughtful consideration of the implications of the *Engel* decision.

★ CASE STUDY 35

Abington School District v. Schempp, 1963

1. The Bible may be read and discussed in public schools as literature or in a historical context.
2. Laws must neither advance nor inhibit religion and must have a legitimate secular purpose.
3. The states held that Bible reading promoted moral values, contradicted materialistic trends, and perpetuated our institutions and the teachings of literature.
4. Students who agree with the *Abington* ruling may say that it is appropriate to read the Bible for historical or literary studies, but that promoting religious activity in a public school violates the First Amendment. Students who agree with the dissent may say that the ruling denied the rights of children who want to take part in religious prayer.
5. No, for the same reason that Bible reading was ruled unconstitutional; civil authority and religious activity must remain separate. Government must maintain strict neutrality, neither aiding nor opposing religion.

★ CASE STUDY 36

Gideon v. Wainwright, 1963

1. The Court felt that Gideon, as well as most other people, did not have the legal expertise to defend himself adequately in a criminal proceeding, and that legal counsel for a defendant is necessary to insure a fair trial.
2. No, a defendant can act as his or her own lawyer if he or she is mentally competent, or the Court will appoint a lawyer for the defendant.
3. The Court said its judgment in the *Betts* case was wrong because it broke with precedents established in earlier cases, such as the *Powell* case.
4. The Court ruled that lawyers for defendants in criminal cases are necessities not luxuries.
5. The *Gideon* decision put poor defendants on the same legal plane as those defendants who can afford to hire their own criminal attorneys.

★ CASE STUDY 37

Escobedo v. Illinois, 1964

1. A lawyer must be provided when police shift from investigation to accusation.
2. Goldberg referred to the right of a person accused of a crime to be advised of his/her Fifth Amendment protection against self-incrimination.
3. Many police officers would probably object to the Court's ruling on the grounds that it interfered with their ability to obtain confessions and would thus make convicting criminals more difficult.
4. Justices Harlan and Stewart thought that the Court's decision gave too many advantages to the criminal and thwarted legitimate functions of the police.
5. Students' answers will vary. Students who agree with the ruling may say that it is important to protect the rights of innocent people who might find themselves being interrogated by the police and that convicting the guilty can and should be accomplished without sacrificing those rights. Students who agree with the dissent may say that the ruling allows criminals to go unpunished because it interferes with the ability of the police to obtain the necessary information and confessions to successfully prosecute dangerous criminals.

★ CASE STUDY 38

Reynolds v. Sims, 1964

1. The Court had to decide whether the state apportionment system in Alabama met the equal protection standards of the Fourteenth Amendment.
2. The Court rejected the comparison for two reasons: First, giving each state two seats in the United States Senate was a necessary compromise to create the United States as a nation. Second, the original states, unlike the Alabama counties, are independent and sovereign and so might be treated more favorably than a state might treat its counties.
3. The *Reynolds* v. *Sims* ruling would force states to redistrict to assure that each voting district in the state contained the same number of voters.
4. Students' answers may vary. One possible answer is that since heavily populated

areas like cities had been underrepresented in the Alabama state legislature, city dwellers would probably be pleased with the Court's ruling.
5. Students' answers may vary. One possible answer is that the "one person, one vote" principle insures that each person's vote carries the same weight, so that everyone has an equal voice in government, as a true democracy requires.

★ CASE STUDY 39

Wesberry v. Sanders, 1964

1. The Court's decision says that the state would have to reapportion its congressional districts so that each district had about the same number of people.
2. According to Justice Black, Article I, Section 2, of the Constitution means that all electoral districts must have essentially the same number of people. Representation must reflect the population.
3. Black said the Founders intended that the districts within each state would have essentially the same population, except that a state would always have at least one representative no matter how small.
4. Justice Harlan would say that there is nothing unconstitutional about the population distribution described in question 1.
5. Students' answers will vary. Students who agree with the decision may say that in a democracy one person's vote in an election should be worth as much as another person's and that the Court has a responsibility to see that this happens. Students who disagree with the decision may say that the Court had no jurisdiction to rule in this case because according to the Constitution the states have control of their elections, subject only to the supervising power of Congress, not that of the Supreme Court.

★ CASE STUDY 40

Heart of Atlanta Motel v. United States, 1964

1. The Court's decision required the motel to accept African American guests or, if it chose not to do so, to close its business.
2. The Court felt that accepting the constitutionality of the interstate commerce question was sufficient to deny the motel's appeal.
3. Both decisions said that the commerce clause was sufficient authority for Congress to enact the Civil Rights Act.
4. Students' answers will vary. One possible answer is that Justice Clark's reputation as a conservative was probably weakened because conservatives normally apply strict interpretations to the Constitution, whereas the Court's interpretation in this decision broadened the power of the commerce clause.
5. Students' answers will vary. Students who agree with the Court's interpretation may say that the government needs to ban discrimination whenever and wherever it exists. Students who disagree with the Court's interpretation may say that owners of private businesses should have the right to choose their customers and how to operate their businesses as they wish without government interference.

★ CASE STUDY 41

Miranda v. Arizona, 1966

1. The Supreme Court held that if a person has not been informed of his or her right to remain silent under interrogation, his or her Fifth Amendment rights have been violated.
2. Unless an accused person has been informed of his or her *Miranda* rights and has waived those rights, a confession cannot be used as evidence against that person in a trial.
3. Before questioning someone about his or her involvement in a crime, a police officer must inform the person of his or her *Miranda* rights. However, if the officer is just gathering information about the crime, the officer may take witnesses' statements without informing them of their *Miranda* rights.
4. The conviction would probably be overturned.
5. Students' answers will vary. Students who agree may say that justice is not served by warning a criminal that he or she should not speak without the presence of a lawyer. In some cases a criminal might be inclined to confess to a crime but will not do so if he or she is warned not to. Students who disagree may say that a person in police custody is under severe pressure and emotional stress and, therefore, may have a reduced capacity for good judgment. For this reason having counsel present during an interrogation is vital in order to protect the person's legal rights.

★ CASE STUDY 42

Sheppard v. Maxwell, 1966

1. The pretrial publicity and the circus atmosphere made it impossible for Sheppard to receive a fair trial, thus depriving him of his due process rights protected by the Fourteenth Amendment.
2. The Supreme Court said that the trial judge might have prevented lawyers and others from discussing certain aspects of the case, might have warned the press about publishing material that had not been part of the court's proceedings, might have shielded the jury from the onslaught of press coverage, and might have asked local officials to regulate the dissemination of information by their employees.
3. Students' answers will vary. One possible answer is that a truly professional reporter probably would have welcomed the Court's decision because the responsibility of the press is to publish facts about a trial, not to focus on the sensational aspects surrounding a high-profile case. A reporter only interested in publishing sensational stories would probably have resented the decision.
4. Students' answers will vary. Some students may say that televising trials helps to educate the public about the justice system. Others may say that television can increase the public's interest in a trial to the point that public reaction might influence the outcome and, therefore, the fairness of a trial.
5. Sheppard's second trial was probably conducted in a more orderly, restrained fashion.

★ CASE STUDY 43

Katz v. United States, 1967

1. Students' answers will vary. Students who agree with Justice Stewart's opinion may say that the Fourth Amendment protects individuals' right to privacy and that police should not in any way violate this constitutional right in order to gather evidence. Students who agree with Justice Black's opinion may say that the Fourth Amendment guarantees protection for people to be secure in their persons, houses, papers, and effects against unreasonable searches and seizures, but the amendment does not protect telephone conversations in public booths.
2. The FBI could have applied for, and on the facts of this case, almost certainly would have obtained a warrant to record Katz's telephone conversations.
3. The individual did not meet Harlan's first test: that he expected the conversation to be private.
4. The Court's decision probably would not apply since no wiretap was involved and the police officer did not plan to overhear the conversation.
5. A literal interpretation means that Justice Black looked only at the words of the Constitution and not for their broader implications in the modern world.

★ CASE STUDY 44

Gregory v. Chicago, 1969

1. Chief Justice Warren found that Illinois mistakenly assumed the marchers were charged with refusal to obey a police officer when they were actually charged with holding a demonstration.
2. Justice Black charged that the disorderly conduct statute was unconstitutionally vague.
3. The Court's decision supported the First Amendment's protection of the right to free speech and peaceable assembly.
4. Students' answers may vary. One possible answer is that the police may have believed that if the demonstration

stopped, the violence by the neighborhood crowd would also stop.
5. No. The police, for example, could have arrested the marchers if they had responded to the neighborhood crowd by attacking them physically.

★ CASE STUDY 45

New York Times v. United States, 1971

1. Answers will vary. Justices may have felt that the reasoning behind their individual conclusions was important, not only to the public, but also in future cases with similar issues. Because many war protesters mistrusted the government and believed officials were withholding information from the public with regard to the war, the justices may have felt a need to reaffirm the public's confidence that constitutional guarantees still protected their rights.
2. The case advanced rapidly because the *Times* had already begun preparations for publishing the Pentagon Papers, and if publication was to be stopped permanently, the case would have to be decided quickly.
3. This case is important because it established the First Amendment's near-absolute ban on official restriction before the act of publication.
4. Justice Black said that even the original injunction should have been denied on First Amendment grounds because the press was protected so that it could bare the secrets of government and inform the people.
5. Students' answers will vary. Students who support the *New York Times* may say that freedom of the press needs to be protected so that the press can report the facts behind the government's actions and can keep the people informed. Students who agree with the government's position may say that secrecy in government is necessary, and that disclosure of government secrets sometimes can cause difficulties.

★ CASE STUDY 46

Reed v. Reed, 1971

1. Students' answers will vary. Possible answers might be that the hostility between the parents was so intense that each would go to almost any length to outdo the other. Another answer might be that some outside organization saw in this case the possibility of overturning yet another example of discrimination against women. (This in fact was true, since several briefs by "friends of the court" were filed by representatives of civil liberties organizations and women's groups.)
2. The Idaho Supreme Court reversed the intermediate appellate court on the grounds that the choice of men over women was required by Idaho law and that the statute gave courts no discretion to depart from its terms.
3. Students' answers may vary. One likely possibility would be that no extended discussion was required because the facts of the case bore out a clear violation of the equal protection clause of the Fourteenth Amendment.
4. Students' answers may vary. One possibility may be that the justices might have ruled that the Court should not interfere with the administrative requirements of a state.
5. Students' answers may vary. A possible conclusion may be that the Supreme Court of 1971 was very forthright in ruling against any form that a violation of equal rights might take.

★ CASE STUDY 47

Wisconsin v. Yoder, 1972

1. Students' answers will vary. Those who agree with the Court's decision may say that the state's power to impose educational regulations must be balanced against the traditional interests of long-established religious groups, as these groups are protected from governmental interference by the First and Fourteenth Amendments. Students who agree with Justice Douglas's dissenting opinion may note that Douglas raised another issue in the case when he argued that parents' beliefs about education should not be imposed on their children. The class may want to discuss the role of parents versus the state in education and also whether Douglas's statement that religion is an individual experience means that parents do not have the right to impose religious beliefs on their children.
2. Students' answers will vary. One possible answer is that the Court's decision may not protect this religious group from government regulation because the group has only a five year history, whereas the Amish, about which the Court made its decision, were a religious sect with a long history of demonstrated beliefs.
3. Students' answers may vary. One possible answer is that the *Wisconsin* v. *Yoder* decision defined some limits on the government's power to regulate religious schools, especially those schools representing a long history of demonstrated religious beliefs. Since the schools administered by Orthodox Jews also represent a long history of demonstrated religious beliefs, the Court's decision would probably strengthened the position of those Orthodox Jews who are opposed to governmental interference in their educational system.
4. Students' answers will vary. Those who agree with critics of the *Wisconsin* v. *Yoder* decision may say that in a democracy, it is in a state's interest to have educated citizens; therefore, the state's education requirement should apply to all citizens, and that the Court's decision set a precedent which gave one group the authority to defy the state's education requirements, thus weakening the state's authority in educational matters. Students who disagree with the critics may say that freedom of religion is a basic right guaranteed by the First and Fourteenth Amendments and that the state should not interfere with a parent's legitimate right to provide his or her child with a religious education.

★ CASE STUDY 48

Roe v. Wade, 1973

1. The Court extended an individual's constitutional right to privacy to include activities related to marriage, procreation, contraception, and the termination of a pregnancy.
2. A state may regulate procedures and conditions under which abortions are performed after the first trimester and before fetal viability. At the point when the fetus is capable of living outside the womb, the state may forbid abortions unless the life of the mother is threatened.
3. The reasoning underlying the Court's decision was based on medical knowledge that divided a woman's pregnancy into trimesters and evidence showing abortion early in pregnancy is safer than childbirth.
4. Justice Rehnquist doubted that the constitutional rights of liberty were so broad that they prohibited a state from regulating abortion during the first trimester.
5. Students' answers will vary. Possible answer: Some key definitions related to the abortion issue were not resolved by the Court's decision, such as when life begins, when the "point of viability" occurs, and what constituted exceptions to the prohibition or regulation of late-term abortions "to preserve maternal health," because maternal health is also not defined.

★ CASE STUDY 49

United States v. Nixon, 1974

1. The president claimed a need to protect the confidentiality of high-level communications and to protect the independence of the executive branch through the separation of powers.
2. No, the Court held that executive privilege may be invoked for situations in which the president needs to protect "military, diplomatic, or sensitive national security secrets."
3. Students' answers will vary. Students who agree that a president must reveal material for a criminal trial may say that an individual cannot receive a fair trial unless he or she has access to all relevant information and evidence concerning the crime. Students who disagree may say that a president needs to be able to keep conversations with others confidential, otherwise advisers will be hesitant to speak freely and to provide the president with needed information and advice.

4. The Court forced President Nixon to turn the tapes over to the federal trial court, and their contents revealed that he had violated federal laws through his efforts to withhold and cover up information pertinent to a federal crime.

5. The statement means that in our government even a president is not above the law and that this case reinforced the democratic nature of our government.

★ CASE STUDY 50

Gregg v. *Georgia,* 1976

1. Gregg faced execution.

2. Students' answers may vary. One possible answer is that the defendant's previous conviction for capital murder or a history of serious assaultive criminal convictions."

3. In the *Gregg* case the Court squarely upheld the death penalty.

4. The Court found it to be valid if the punishment did not involve the unnecessary and wanton infliction of pain and was proportionate in severity with that of the crime.

5. Students' answers will vary. Justice Marshall argued that capital punishment served no useful purpose because it did not deter crime. Justice Brennan argued that the death penalty treated members of the human race as nonhumans. Students who view the issue in its practical implications might agree with Justice Marshall and conclude that the death penalty should then be allowed if and when it is proven to deter crime. Those who view capital punishment from a more moralistic viewpoint would probably agree with Justice Brennan's view that the practice violates human dignity. Some students might argue that Brennan's arguments are more persuasive because Marshall's arguments allow for circumstances in which he might find capital punishment acceptable, should it be proven to deter crime.

★ CASE STUDY 51

Regents of the University of California v. *Bakke,* 1978

1. The Court ruled that the university's special admissions program was unconstitutional because it gave preference to a group of individuals based solely on the individual's race or ethnic origin.

2. The Court suggested that the medical school devise an admissions program that makes race one factor among others in a competition for all available places.

3. The Court ruling was a victory for Bakke because he finally could be admitted to the medical school.

4. Students' answers may vary. One possibility is that an African American student would probably stand a better chance under the medical school's original plan because that plan used a separate admission process that favored minority students, while under the Court's plan, race would be only one criterion used for admission.

5. Students' answers will vary. Students who deny that the Court's ruling was a death blow to affirmative action may say that the Court still allowed for racial and ethnic criteria to be used for admissions purposes but not as the sole criterion. Other students may say that before the Court's decision, minority students were accepted at many schools for the purpose of racial balance and fairness; if schools do not pursue this as a goal, their need to include minority students will diminish.

★ CASE STUDY 52

Kaiser Aluminum and Chemical Corporation (and United Steel Workers of America) v. *Weber,* 1979

1. A literal reading of Title VII did not take into account the spirit of the law and the intention of Congress, which was to break down the old patterns of racial segregation and hierarchy in employment and to provide opportunities for African Americans in occupations which had been traditionally closed to them.

2. Students' answers will vary. Students who support Justice Brennan's actions may say that it was important for him to understand Congress's intention in passing the law before he made a decision about the case. Students who think Justice Brennan's opinion was incorrect and inappropriate may say that Congress's intentions were not relevant, that the case should have been decided solely on what was said or not said in the statute.

3. Students' answers will vary. Students who agree with the majority opinion may say that the company's plan broadened opportunities for African Americans by offering them opportunities that had been traditionally closed to them, and that any adverse aspects of the plan for other individuals were only temporary. Students who agree with the dissent may say that the company's plan was unconstitutional because it discriminated against some individuals by giving preferential treatment to others.

4. Students' answers will vary. One possible answer is that without the decision the company's attempts to open employment opportunities to all would have slowed or been deferred.

5. Students' answers will vary. Some students may be willing to sacrifice their own opportunity because achieving racial balance in employment is extremely important to the future of the country as a whole. Other students may say that they would not support discrimination under any circumstances, even for a greater good.

★ CASE STUDY 53

New Jersey v. *T.L.O.,* 1985

1. Police officers usually must have probable cause, while school officials need only have reasonable grounds for a search.

2. The Court felt that school officials must have the authority to maintain order and discipline in the schools.

3. Students' answers will vary. Students who think the search was reasonable may say that T.L.O. was caught violating the school smoking rule, so it was reasonable for the assistant vice-principal to search her purse in order to confiscate any cigarettes she might still have. Students who think the search was unreasonable may say that T.L.O. should have been punished for smoking in school but that her privacy should not have been invaded.

4. No, school officials need to have reasonable grounds for suspecting that the search will turn up evidence that the student has violated or is violating either the law or the rules of the school.

5. Students' answers will vary. Students who agree with the Court's decision may say that school officials need the flexibility to deal with problem students immediately in order to maintain order and discipline. To ensure the safety of the other students, they sometimes cannot wait for search warrants and other legal procedures before taking action. Students who agree with the dissent may say that students are citizens and, as such, are entitled to the same rights and protections as other citizens.

★ CASE STUDY 54

Wallace v. *Jaffree,* 1985

1. The Alabama law was intended to provide public school students a daily opportunity to pray silently in the classroom on a voluntary basis.

2. The Court ruled that the Alabama law was an effort to promote prayer in the public schools and thus violated the First Amendment.

3. Justice O'Connor probably would not have objected to Alabama's law on constitutional grounds if the law had not mentioned religion because she believes that a moment of silence without the stated purpose of promoting religion is, in itself, not unconstitutional.

4. Chief Justice Burger maintained that the only reason the Court found Alabama's law unconstitutional was that the law used the word *prayer* and that the intended purpose of the Alabama law was no more unconstitutional than the use of chaplains in state legislatures and Congress.

5. Students' opinions will differ. Students who agree with Justice Stevens may say that government should be completely neutral toward religion and that Alabama's law clearly sent a message of approval for prayer, which is an inappro-

priate message to be given to public school students. Students who agree with Chief Justice Burger's dissent may say that the Alabama legislature did not endorse religion because voluntary prayer was only one of the authorized activities during the moment of silence. The law allowed students freedom to pray or not to pray and that as Justice O'Connor pointed out: "During a moment of silence, a student who objects to prayer is left to his or her own thoughts, and is not compelled to listen to the prayers or thoughts of others."

CASE STUDY 55

Bethel School District v. Fraser, 1986

1. The Court ruled that schools have a basic responsibility to prepare students for responsible citizenship; thus, the Court considered it appropriate for school officials to insist that students stay within the boundaries of socially appropriate behavior.

2. Unlike *Tinker* in which students wore armbands to school to protest the Vietnam War, the *Fraser* case involved a student's objectionable and disruptive, but essentially nonpolitical, speech.

3. Students' answers may vary. One possibility is that the Court would probably have ruled that school authorities would have no right to punish a student for speech or action that did not disrupt the school's basic educational mission.

4. The Court ruled that students do not necessarily have the same First Amendment rights as adults because freedom of speech must be balanced against society's countervailing interest in teaching students the boundaries of socially appropriate behavior.

5. Students' opinions will differ. Students who agree with the Court's ruling may say that school teachers and administrators need to be able to prevent or to discipline student behavior that undermines the school's basic educational mission. Students who disagree may say that the First Amendment should apply to all citizens regardless of their ages or occupations and that by putting age limitations on the protection of speech, the Court has weakened the First Amendment.

CASE STUDY 56

Hazelwood School District v. Kuhlmeier, 1988

1. The Court reasoned that a school newspaper is part of the school curriculum rather than a public forum and, as a result, needs to be under the control of the school officials.

2. In the *Tinker* case the students were expressing their own political opinions about the Vietnam War, while in the *Hazelwood* case the student newspaper was part of the school curriculum and was a tool for teaching and learning.

3. Justice Brennan feared that the decision would teach students to discount the important principles of our government as mere platitudes instead of teaching them to respect the diversity of ideas that is fundamental to the American system.

4. Students' answers will vary. One possibility is that the principal might have discussed his "serious doubts" about the articles with the journalism teacher and students in an effort to reach a consensus about how to solve the privacy and ethical problems before publication.

CASE STUDY 57

Skinner v. Railway Labor Executives Association, 1989

1. The FRA issued new regulations after drunkenness and the use of drugs by railroad employees while on the job continued despite earlier regulations against the use of intoxicants while on the job.

2. The Court ruled that the public's right to safety outweighed the employees' privacy rights.

3. Railroad passengers would most likely favor Justice Kennedy's opinion because it gave greater weight to public safety, including passenger safety, than Justice Marshall's opinion.

4. Justice Marshall suggested that fellow workers might provide evidence of impaired behavior or that only workers who showed some signs of impairment should be tested.

5. Students' answers will vary. Some students may say that the Court ruling weakens Fourth Amendment protections but that public safety is more important than the rights of a few railroad workers. Other students may say that Fourth Amendment guarantees against search and seizure have been severely weakened because railroad authorities are not required to show probable cause or even individualized suspicion prior to requiring a search, and that blood and urine testing allowed by the ruling is especially invasive.

CASE STUDY 58

Cruzan v. Director, Missouri Department of Health, 1990

1. The Court ruling meant that the hospital would continue to keep Nancy Cruzan alive on life-support systems.

2. No. The Court stated that a living will executed by a patient would permit the withdrawal of the life-support systems.

3. None. Justice Brennan believed that there was a fundamental right to be free of unwanted medical treatment.

4. The Court deals only with constitutional issues and does not enter into the realm of morality.

5. Students' answers will vary. Some students may say that it is immoral to prolong a person's life using artificial means if the person is in a persistent vegetative state without any hope of recovering, and that, in the absence of a living will, the family, not the state, should be making decisions for a loved one. Other students may say that the state should not allow family members the legal right to make life-ending medical decisions without some prior written permission from the patient or some other substantial proof that the family member's views are the same as the patient's.

CASE STUDY 59

California v. Acevedo, 1991

1. The Court believed that the police officers' search of the bag in Acevedo's car without a warrant did not violate Acevedo's Fourth Amendment protections because they had probable cause, so their search was reasonable and their seizure of the bag of marijuana was legal.

2. Unless the police had probable cause to suspect you of carrying illegal materials on your person or in your car, they could not legally search you or your car.

3. Students' answers will vary. Students who agree with Justice Blackmun may say that once probable cause is established, the police should be able to search and, if necessary, seize both the contents of the automobile and the contents of any container found in the automobile. Students who agree with Justice Scalia may say that the Fourth Amendment does not require a prior warrant for searches and seizures; it only prohibits searches and seizures that are unreasonable; and the police should be able to conduct searches or seizures for which they have probable cause and which they consider reasonable. Students who agree with Justice Stevens may say that an individual's privacy is most important, and that according to the Fourth Amendment, police need to obtain a warrant before they have the legal right to search an individual's house or property.

4. Students' answers will vary. Students who think that police benefited from the decision may say it has enabled the police to conduct searches or seizures without being concerned that their actions are illegal and that they can now search and seize evidence without getting a prior warrant as long as the search is considered reasonable—which generally means being supported by probable cause. Students who think that individuals benefited from the decision may say that the decision has done much to clarify when a police search and/or seizure is or is not legal, and it will limit police searches and seizures to only those in which the police have probable cause for their actions.

5. Students' answers will vary. One possible answer is that the Court began to make clear what the term *unreasonable*, as stated

in the Fourth Amendment, means because the Court ruled in this specific case that the police explanation of probable cause for their search and seizure was reasonable.

★ CASE STUDY 60

International Union, UAW v. Johnson Controls, Inc., 1991

1. Johnson Controls, Inc. knew that lead exposure might harm a woman's unborn fetus.

2. The Civil Rights Act of 1964 prohibits sex discrimination in hiring policies, and Johnson Controls excluded fertile females but not fertile males from holding a certain type of job.

3. The Court said the woman herself, and not the employer, should make the decision whether she should work at a lead-exposing job.

4. Judge White thought that companies might want to exclude women from certain jobs to avoid being sued by workers or their children who have been harmed because of hazardous working conditions.

5. Students' answers will vary. Students who agree with the Court's ruling may say that it is illegal for a company to discriminate against women in its hiring policies and women, as well as men, should have the right to make an informed choice as to whether they want to work in hazardous conditions. Students who disagree with the Court's ruling may say that the state has a duty to protect the health of an unborn fetus if a parent chooses to endanger it.

★ CASE STUDY 61

Payne v. Tennessee, 1991

1. Victim impact evidence is a presentation of the emotional injury and other damaging effects a crime has on a victim's family and friends.

2. In the first phase of a capital murder trial, the jury decides whether or not a defendant is guilty. In the sentencing phase of the trial, the jury fixes or recommends a sentence.

3. Students' answers may vary. One possible answer is that since they recommended the death penalty, members of the jury evidently gave very little weight to the testimony of Payne's witnesses.

4. Students' answers will differ, but they may include these ideas: that a sentence should be based solely on evidence of the crime presented during the first phase of a trial; that since each side in the penalty phase of a trial is interested only in pressing for its advantage, the material presented at this phase is most likely skewed or biased and is therefore not worthwhile; that evidence about the victim's character has nothing to do with the blameworthiness of the defendant; and that admitting victim impact evidence may encourage a jury to recommend a punishment based on the worthiness or unworthiness of the victim or the degree of loss to a family or community.

5. Supreme Court decisions provide guidelines for Congress, state legislatures, and federal and state courts as to what is or is not constitutional. Changing these legal guidelines can cause confusion and cast doubt on the integrity of the judicial process.

★ CASE STUDY 62

Arizona v. Fulminante, 1991

1. The original trial court judged Fulminante's confessions to have been voluntary, denied his motion to suppress them as coerced, and convicted Fulminante of murder. The Arizona Supreme Court reversed Fulminante's conviction and ordered that he be retried without the use of the first confession which the Arizona Supreme Court judged to be coerced.

2. A harmless error is an error that (applying the beyond-a-reasonable-doubt standard) is deemed not to have affected the outcome of a case.

3. Fulminante claimed his confession should not be admissible as evidence against him because he said it was coerced and that admitting it as evidence against him at trial was a possible violation of his right to due process under the Fifth and Fourteenth Amendments.

4. The 1967 ruling said that a coerced confession can never be considered "harmless error" and was always grounds for overturning a conviction. The ruling in the *Fulminante* case set a new precedent: that a coerced confession introduced at trial, in itself, does not necessarily require that a conviction be reversed.

5. Students' answers will vary. Students who agree with the Court's reasoning in 1967 may point out that a confession would have such a powerful effect on the jury that it could never be considered harmless error if it was discovered to be coerced after the confession was presented at trial. Students who disagree with the Court's reasoning in 1967 may say that each case is different from every other case and should be decided on the merits of the particular case. There could be some situations in which a coerced confession does not impact the court's decision to the extent that a conviction would have to be overturned.

★ CASE STUDY 63

Shaw v. Reno, 1993

1. The boundaries for the Twelfth District were created to increase minority representation in Congress.

2. Five white citizens in the Twelfth District claimed that their right to equal protection under the law, as stated in the Fourteenth Amendment, had been violated.

3. The Court was not opposed to creating districts on the basis of race. It objected to districts that were based solely on race. Race could be taken into account as long as traditional districting principles were also followed—compactness, contiguity, and respect for political divisions.

4. Justice Stevens criticized the Court's emphasis on the shape of a district because he believed that discriminatory racial gerrymandering could occur just as easily in a regularly shaped district as in an oddly shaped district. He stated impartiality is violated when a group with power over the election process defines electoral boundaries to enhance its own political strength at the expense of minorities, but that impartiality is not violated when the majority facilitates the election of a member from the minority.

5. Students' answers will vary. Students who favor creating minority districts may say that minority representation in Congress and in state legislatures is important for justice and fairness in this country, otherwise minority voters do not have equal protection under the law, and that white voters have not been harmed. Students who oppose gerrymandering may say that the practice was reprehensible when it was used to keep African Americans out of power, and the practice is just as objectionable now even if it is used to accomplish a reverse purpose.

★ CASE STUDY 64

National Organization for Women (NOW) v. Scheidler, 1994

1. The RICO Act was originally passed to make it illegal for organized criminals to use violence or extortion to shut down businesses.

2. Students' answers may vary. Those who believe that the Court should have enforced the statute as written may argue that it is the Supreme Court's responsibility to determine the intent of the law—using a broad interpretation. Those who believe the Court should have enforced the intent of Congress may argue that Congress was specific about the intent of RICO. The law was intended to combat criminal activity such as bribery, extortion, and racketeering.

3. The Court ruled that RICO, although it was intended to punish criminals, applied to the NOW case, even if the group involved did not have any financial motive.

4. The Court's decision did not punish Scheidler and the others. It sent the case back to a district court for retrial.

Supreme Court Case Studies 147

5. Justices Souter and Kennedy urged the courts to use prudence because of the "First Amendment rights that could be at stake."

★ CASE STUDY 65

Agostini v. Felton, 1997

1. Public school teachers could provide remedial instruction to parochial school students on the premises of their parochial schools.
2. The mayor was delighted that the city would no longer have to spend money to lease vans in which to provide remedial instruction for parochial school students.
3. The Court said that it would no longer judge religion-related cases on the basis of the three presumptions that it had previously held.
4. Students' answers may vary. One possible answer is that while it is always risky to predict how the Supreme Court is likely to rule, the decision in the *Agostini* case indicates that the Court had created a more receptive climate for church-state cases.
5. Students' answers will vary. Students who agree with the decision may say that remedial instruction paid for with federal tax money should be available to all children who need it no matter what their religious beliefs or where they go to school as long as the instruction does not promote religion. Students who disagree may say that the decision encourages an entanglement between teachers paid with public money and parochial schools and thus erodes the principle of separation between church and state which is fundamental to the Constitution.

★ CASE STUDY 66

Illinois v. Wardlow, 2000

1. The Court said that a location's characteristics are relevant in helping determine whether the circumstances warrant further investigation.
2. The lower courts believed that merely fleeing from the scene was not sufficient to create reasonable suspicion.
3. Answers will vary. Students may agree with the lower courts that Wardlow's behavior was not reasonably suspicious, or they may take into consideration that flight in an area of drug trafficking is reasonably suspicious.
4. No. The evidence that was seized is not the issue in this case. The conduct of the officers in the stop and search is the constitutional issue.
5. Police officers may be less concerned with the constitutionality of stop and frisk searches.

★ CASE STUDY 67

Alexander v. Sandoval, 2001

1. The state had amended its constitution to make English the official language. This meant that such tests would have to be given in English.
2. Sandoval cited Title VI of the Civil Rights Act of 1964, which prohibits discrimination on the basis of national origin.
3. The majority believed that Title VI did not provide a "private right of action" for a citizen who felt discriminated against if the state policy was not intentionally discriminatory.
4. Justice Stevens pointed out that the Court had ruled in prior decisions that a private right of action exists. He believed the justices were not interested in applying the intent of Title VI.
5. Answers will vary. Students may support English as the official language as a policy not directed against any individual or group. Others may believe that such a policy will necessarily put some groups at a disadvantage.

★ CASE STUDY 68

Whitman v. American Trucking Associations, 2001

1. Congress has responsibility to pass laws. In this case, the issue was whether a federal agency had assumed the power of Congress.
2. The lower courts believed that Congress had delegated too much power to the EPA.
3. The Supreme Court held that the Clean Air Act provided enough guidance for the EPA to make decisions about NAAQS.
4. The Supreme Court said that these laws should specify what decision-making authority the agencies have in carrying out the laws Congress has passed.
5. This ruling provides support for federal agencies to make decisions that support the intent of congressional legislation.